The Fredericksburg Campaign

DECISION ON THE RAPPAHANNOCK

EDITED BY GARY W. GALLAGHER

THE UNIVERSITY OF NORTH CAROLINA PRESS   CHAPEL HILL & LONDON

© 1995 The University of

North Carolina Press

Manufactured in the United States of America

The paper in this book meets the guidelines for permanence and durability
of the Committee on Production Guidelines for Book Longevity of the
Council on Library Resources.

Library of Congress Cataloging-in-Publication Data
The Fredericksburg Campaign : decision on the Rappahannock / edited by
Gary W. Gallagher.

p.   cm.

Includes bibliographical references and index.

ISBN 978-0-8078-2193-0

ISBN 978-0-8078-5895-0 (pbk.: alk. paper)

1. Fredericksburg (Va.), Battle of 1862.   I. Gallagher, Gary W.

E474.85.F 86   1995

973.7'33—dc20   94-35152

CIP

99   98   97   96   95   5   4   3   2
11   10   09   08   07   5   4   3   2   1

CONTENTS

INTRODUCTION

The military events that unfolded along the Rappahannock River on a cold December 13, 1862, are well known and seemingly uncomplicated. Ordered forward by Ambrose E. Burnside, a commander usually portrayed as supremely inept, thousands of Union soldiers in the Army of the Potomac flung themselves against well-protected Confederates in a series of desperate and doomed assaults. Nightfall ended a slaughter that claimed more than 12,500 northern casualties. After flirting with the idea of resuming the attacks on the fourteenth, Burnside reluctantly pulled his battered army back across the Rappahannock. R. E. Lee and the Army of Northern Virginia could only watch the withdrawal, unable to follow up their easy defensive victory because Union artillery on Stafford Heights covered the retreating infantry. A few weeks later Burnside was gone, a new Federal commander prepared to engage Lee along the same stretch of Virginia landscape, and the fighting at Fredericksburg apparently had changed nothing.

A pair of quotations attributed to Lee and Abraham Lincoln probably sum up the essence of the battle of Fredericksburg for most students of the Civil War. On December 13, Lee saw Confederate infantry repulse a Union thrust and then pursue their enemy out of some woods and onto a plain west of the Rappahannock. According to John Esten Cooke, a member of "Jeb" Stuart's staff, the commanding general turned to James Longstreet and said in low tones, "It is well this is so terrible! we should grow too fond of it!" These two brief sentences have done much to define Lee and the Army of Northern Virginia for generations of readers: the brilliant soldier, his martial ardor aroused, quietly exulting as the men of his famous army demonstrated their prowess on yet another battlefield.[1] Across the Potomac River, unhappiness with the progress of the war among Republican leaders fed rumors of major changes in the president's cabinet even before Fredericksburg. News of the disaster on the Rappahannock deepened the crisis for Lincoln, who told a friend, "If there is a worse place than Hell, I am in it." In a dozen words the president conveyed frustration with Burnside, despair at the scale and futility of Federal losses, and awareness of the battle's likely impact on northern politics and morale.[2]

A third contemporary quotation evokes the memorable physical setting at Fredericksburg and also hints at the destruction visited on the city. Artillerist Edward Porter Alexander, who helped place the southern guns that would torment Union attackers on the thirteenth, left a vivid description of the sights on December 11 as Burnside's soldiers prepared to cross the Rappahannock: "The spectacle which was now presented from the Confederate hilltops was one of the most magnificent and impressive in the whole course of the war," wrote Alexander in his widely read memoirs.

> The city, except its steeples, was still veiled in the mist which had settled in the valleys. Above it and in it incessantly showed the round white clouds of bursting shells, and out of its midst there soon rose three or four columns of dense black smoke from houses set on fire by the explosions. The atmosphere was so perfectly calm and still that the smoke rose vertically in great pillars for several hundred feet before spreading outward in black sheets. . . . The dark blue masses of over 100,000 infantry in compact columns, and numberless parks of white-topped wagons and ambulances massed in orderly ranks, all awaited the completion of the bridges. The earth shook with the thunder of the guns, and, high above all, a thousand feet in the air, hung two immense balloons. The scene gave impressive ideas of the disciplined power of a great army, and of the vast resources of the nation which had sent it forth.[3]

These and other familiar passages from the literature on Fredericksburg admittedly capture much of the battle's meaning and drama, but the topic offers ample possibilities for further exploration. Many questions of interest to a new generation of historians have not been asked about Fredericksburg; others await investigators who will exploit hitherto neglected unpublished sources as well as the large body of printed material on the battle. The contributors to this volume, who as a group consulted both readily available and obscure materials in preparing their essays, hope to persuade readers to reconsider some comfortable assumptions about the campaign, to think about aspects of the battle and its aftermath that have received little if any previous attention, and to place the military action in a larger social and political context.

Civil War scholarship reaches an almost perfect consensus about Ambrose E. Burnside's competence to command an army. Excoriated as a man of scant vision who refused to modify his plans in the face of changing circumstances, Burnside lumbers through innumerable accounts as a well-meaning but pitifully inept officer whose lack of strategic or tactical skill wasted thousands of Union lives. William Marvel confronts this portrait head-on, arguing that Burnside, for all his faults, had reason to believe he might achieve tactical success on December 13. Poor performances by key subordinates contributed to the Federal debacle at Fredericksburg, insists Marvel, and self-serving postwar accounts by Burnside's enemies helped shape the general's enduring negative image. Readers at ease with the dominant interpretation of Burnside might not be won over, but they will find much to challenge their thinking.

Alan T. Nolan's assessment of Lee's generalship at Fredericksburg also should inspire a strong reaction. Firmly convinced that Lee displayed too much aggressiveness on many occasions, Nolan applauds his handling of the campaign against Burnside. Unlike the Confederate raids across the Potomac in the fall of 1862 and summer of 1863, occasions when Nolan believes Lee unnecessarily precipitated costly battles, the Union's direct strategic challenge to Richmond and the Army of Northern Virginia in November 1862 required a response. Lee controlled his usual desire to seize the offensive and fought a sound tactical battle that blunted Burnside's move and conserved precious Confederate manpower. Although the campaign showed Lee at his best, stresses Nolan, its outcome in no way modified the general's predilection for the strategic and tactical offensive. The Gettysburg campaign left no doubt that Fredericksburg was an aberration in Lee's career during 1862 and 1863.

George C. Rable's essay examines the process by which northerners and southerners struggled to come to terms with the cost of Fredericksburg. The North had an especially difficult time coping with what appeared to be pointless carnage, but Fredericksburg sent shock waves through both societies. The reports of prolific slaughter, of civilians driven from their homes by artillery fire and rampaging soldiers, and of barbarities inflicted on the wounded prompted troubling questions about civilized norms of behavior and fueled a search for scapegoats. Soldiers reconsidered their notions of courage, while many inside and outside the army looked anew at their religious assumptions. Overall, Rable provides a powerful case study of the myriad ways in which battles cast shadows that linger well beyond the close of fighting.

Union soldiers left the field at Fredericksburg with gruesome memories of their comrades lying in profusion at the base of Marye's Heights. Seven months later, Federal veterans shouted "Fredericksburg! Fredericksburg!" as they drove back the men of George E. Pickett and James Johnston Pettigrew from the Angle at Gettysburg. Carol Reardon brings into focus the experiences of one group of northern soldiers who assaulted Marye's Heights—the untried Pennsylvanians of Andrew A. Humphreys's division. She discusses their Pennsylvania origins, their severe trials on December 13, the immediate aftermath of the battle, and later squabbles among Union soldiers about which units had performed most admirably in the attacks. Her essay puts a human face on the image of northern infantrymen advancing to their ruin on the Union right at Fredericksburg.

The fifth essay turns the spotlight on the reaction to Fredericksburg within Lee's army and throughout the Confederacy. Many writers have ignored this aspect of the campaign altogether—probably because they assumed a positive southern response to such a clear-cut Union defeat. Those who have addressed the topic generally emphasize a South buoyed by a victory that ended Burnside's threat to Richmond and caused consternation in the North. Some historians have followed Lee's lead in seeing the battle as an empty triumph that left no lasting scars on the Army of the Potomac. But evidence from the time betrays a more complex set of responses that raise questions about Confederate civilian expectations, the relative merits of offensive and defensive victories, and how events on the battlefield affected people behind the lines.

No group suffered more as a result of Fredericksburg than the citizens of the town and surrounding countryside. William A. Blair's essay reminds readers that Fredericksburg already had endured one long occupation before the Army of the Potomac arrived in November 1862, thereby correcting any misconception about when the war first appeared in earnest along the Rappahannock. Blair reviews changing Union attitudes about how Confederate civilians should be treated, discusses the considerable impact news about the sack of Fredericksburg had on Virginia and other parts of the Confederacy, and highlights the centrality of emancipation to the lives of black and white residents of the area. His conclusions, which he concedes are tentative, suggest that the Union occupation and its attendant depredations might have strengthened rather than weakened Confederate resolve to continue the struggle for independence.

A. Wilson Greene's essay also explores connections between the civilian and military spheres, focusing on political maneuvering within the Army of the Potomac and the state of morale among Burnside's soldiers following Fredericksburg. Leaving no doubt that Burnside's failures during January 1863 owed much to attempts by various subordinates to undermine their leader, Greene also shows how the general's own actions and personality hastened his demise. The Army of the Potomac, which ranked as the most political of all Union forces, never saw politics intrude more sharply in the arena of military command. Within the ranks, Greene detects far less gloomy resignation than others have portrayed. The defeat at Fredericksburg caused no long-term failure of spirit among Burnside's soldiers, he maintains; indeed, the army might have recrossed the Rappahannock successfully in January but for problems of command and a period of extremely foul weather.

These essays indicate some fruitful ways to approach military campaigns of the Civil War. Far from exhausted topics open only to increasingly minute dissection of tactical movements, the activities of Union and Confederate armies invite serious scrutiny by historians interested in a range of issues. If defined to include their antecedents and subsequent impact, battles and the larger operations of which they formed a part offer abundant opportunities to revise older interpretations, raise new questions, and enhance our understanding of the conflict as a whole.

Any work of collective scholarship depends on the goodwill and cooperation of many individuals. Bill Blair, Will Greene, Bill Marvel, Alan Nolan, George Rable, and Carol Reardon displayed genuine enthusiasm for this project. The fact that several of them also possess sharp wits proved a distinct boon on more than one occasion. George Skoch rendered excellent cartographic support, demonstrating again that he can convert rough sketches into clear maps. Kate Torrey and Ron Maner of the University of North Carolina Press provided their usual encouragement and expert advice, and Stephanie Wenzel improved the manuscript with her copyeditor's pencil. Finally, I wish to thank the Research and Graduate Studies Office of the College of the Liberal Arts at Penn State, which provided support for the preparation of maps, illustrations, and the index.

INTRODUCTION

Notes

1. John Esten Cooke, *A Life of Gen. Robert E. Lee* (New York: D. Appleton, 1871), 184. In *R. E. Lee: A Biography*, 4 vols. (New York: Charles Scribner's Sons, 1934–35), 2:462, Douglas Southall Freeman cited Cooke's biography but changed the quotation to "It is well that war is so terrible—we should grow too fond of it!" Freeman's more dramatic form of Cooke's quotation is cited far more frequently than the original and has become one of the most famous of Lee's utterances. In *Military Memoirs of a Confederate: A Critical Narrative* (New York: Charles Scribner's Sons, 1907), 302, Edward Porter Alexander remarked that "it is told that, on one of the Federal repulses from Marye's Hill, Lee put his hand upon Longstreet's arm and said, 'It is well that war is so terrible, or we would grow too fond of it.' " Freeman considered Alexander's book the most valuable account of the operations of Lee's army and may have taken his wording, which differs only in the deletion of *or* and the substitution of *should* for *would*, from Alexander while citing Cooke's work because it first established the basic quotation. Freeman did not follow Alexander in portraying Lee's comments as a reaction to fighting below Marye's Heights. It is worth noting that James Longstreet's postwar writings made no mention of Lee's saying anything like this to him on December 13, 1862.

2. William H. Wadsworth to Samuel L. M. Barlow, December 16, 1862, quoted in James M. McPherson, *Battle Cry of Freedom: The Civil War Era* (New York: Oxford University Press, 1988), 574.

3. Alexander, *Military Memoirs*, 291.

The Making of a Myth

AMBROSE E. BURNSIDE AND THE UNION
HIGH COMMAND AT FREDERICKSBURG

WILLIAM MARVEL

It is good to begin where the Fredericksburg campaign began, as George B. McClellan turned over the Army of the Potomac to Ambrose E. Burnside in that tent near Rectortown. It is a commonplace today that the appointment of Burnside as commander of the Army of the Potomac was met with universal dismay, at least in the army. Thirty years ago Warren W. Hassler wrote that Burnside was "probably the most incompetent of all the generals then serving with the Army of the Potomac," and he went on to say that William B. Franklin would most likely have been the popular choice. "Major General Henry W. Slocum insists," stated Hassler, "that Franklin was really Lincoln's choice, except that there was strong political opposition to him. Even Halleck himself—who could play politics when necessary—exclaimed to a friend at the time of Burnside's appointment, 'Oh, the curse of political expediency! It has almost ruined the army, and if carried out will soon ruin the country.'"[1]

This passage of Hassler's says a lot about the development of Burnside's modern reputation. Slocum's words come not from Slocum, as Hassler suggests, but from the secondhand gossip of William Franklin's own brother, which was published in 1898—two years after Slocum passed beyond any hope of contradicting the statement. A defense attorney would call it hearsay, and it is biased hearsay at that. Halleck's comment is even more suspect, for while Hassler says it came "at the time of Burnside's appointment" and implies that it was made in horrified reaction to that appointment, it is actually extracted from a letter to John Schofield of September 20, 1862, and has nothing to do with Burnside. If anything, it seems to refer more to the reappointment of McClellan and the subsequent failure at Antietam.

Despite the distorted recollections of some participants and the occasion-

1

*Maj. Gen. Ambrose
Everett Burnside.
Editor's collection*

ally bizarre interpretations of subsequent students, Burnside's ascension to command did not cast an immediate pall over the entire army. "We are well pleased with Burnside," said a captain in the Iron Brigade a fortnight after the change of command. "Thank God for the prospect ahead now, our soldiers will fight as well under B. as McC." The railroad general Herman Haupt told his wife, "I like Burnside very well. I think he will go ahead. He talks right at any rate and I feel more encouraged than I have for a long time." Many did harbor reservations about Burnside, however—particularly those close to McClellan, who may have heard his preliminary excuses about Antietam—and although Burnside aggravated any latent suspicions about his competence with his own private expressions of humility, the estimates of initial discouragement succumbed to gradual exaggeration as the years went by. Even those who believed in Burnside at the outset tended to forget they had done so: one Massachusetts captain who was quite happy with Old Burn when he took over, and still thought him as good as any general in the army four weeks after Fredericksburg, remembered forty-five years later that "the army as a whole was greatly dissatisfied with the change."[2]

Burnside's first act catapulted the chiefs of three corps to the level of "grand division" commanders. The first of these, Edwin V. Sumner, head of the Right Grand Division, would serve Burnside as he had all other generals, with unquestioning obedience and, when it was requested or when Sumner thought it was imperative, with candid advice. Like many officers in this army, he was known for persistence rather than brilliance, so much so that he had earned the nickname "Old Bull." Also like many of his contemporaries, he had risen beyond the station for which his experience and capacity had fitted him.

To head the Center Grand Division, Burnside chose Joseph Hooker, whose chief quality was overweening ambition and whose principal friend and advocate was Joseph Hooker. Hooker's insubordination had already confounded Burnside at South Mountain. Burnside suspected that he had been stripped of his own wing command at Antietam because of Hooker's conniving, and indeed Hooker's intrigues commenced again almost as soon as he assumed his new office, which Burnside appeared to give him in deference to seniority alone. Some thought Burnside was just keeping the chair at headquarters warm for Hooker.[3]

The third wing, the Left Grand Division, went to William B. Franklin. The youngest of the three, Franklin was still a shade older than Burnside, and he had preceded him at West Point by four years, graduating at the top of his class. He had remained in the army ever since, mostly as a capable engineer, but in his eighteen months of field commands he had earned no great reputation—the future allegations of his little brother notwithstanding. He did not distinguish himself either way at First Bull Run, while his performance in the Peninsula and Antietam campaigns can best be characterized as conspicuously cautious. His slow march to John Pope's aid at Second Bull Run left Pope dissatisfied and suspicious (though it was more George McClellan's fault than Franklin's), and Pope had asked for a court of inquiry in the matter, blaming McClellan and his friends Franklin and Fitz John Porter for that disaster. The inquiry came to nothing in Franklin's case; but McClellan had been relieved, and a general court martial convened to try Porter just eighteen days before the battle of Fredericksburg. One of Porter's staff officers supposed the script called for Porter to be "crushed" and that "Franklin will soon follow." Franklin himself could not have been insensitive to that possibility.[4]

Of his three top subordinates, therefore, Burnside could best trust only the unimaginative Sumner. He probably recognized Hooker as a finagler who might undo him merely to grab command of the army, but he may not have fully understood how fine a line Franklin believed he trod. Thus hampered, Burnside started for Fredericksburg with the largest army any American had ever wielded on the tactical offensive.

In order to shorten his line of communications, Burnside opted to shift to the Fredericksburg route from the Orange & Alexandria Railroad, hoping to cross into that city before the Confederates could defend it. He moved with commendable speed, arriving well ahead of the enemy, but, thanks primarily to the omissions of General in Chief Henry W. Halleck (despite Halleck's contrived excuse), the materials for a pontoon bridge did not arrive in time. Burnside decided—wisely, it would appear—not to risk a detachment across the river. After the retreat from the Peninsula, the disaster at Second Bull Run, and the lost opportunity at Antietam, he may have doubted whether the army or the country could stand another failure; enough soldiers were writing pessimistically about the war's prospects that he was probably right on that point, which rather forced him to move against Lee's army right where it sat.

He faced three options. First, he could cross at the upstream fords and try to sweep behind Lee's left, as Joe Hooker suggested on November 19, while Fredericksburg was still lightly defended. Hooker wanted to abandon his supply line and cross at United States Ford, after which he proposed to march on Bowling Green and draw provisions from Port Royal. It sounded like a good enough idea, and he lobbied the secretary of war about it behind Burnside's back as well as offering the plan to Burnside, but it had at least two flaws. For one thing, Hooker never actually said whether United States Ford was passable, and he made the request in the middle of a two-day downpour that ought to have closed any ford. He also neglected to note that James Longstreet's Confederate corps was marching toward Fredericksburg at that

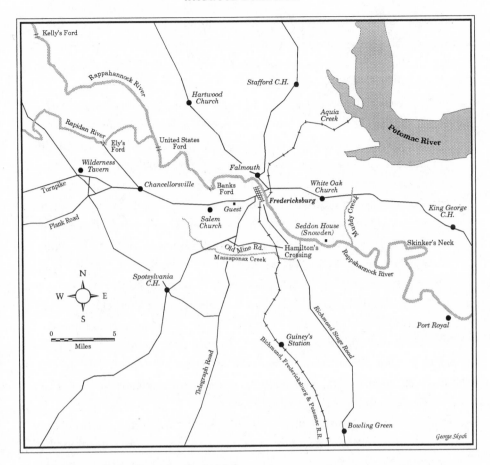

Rappahannock riverfront near Fredericksburg

very moment and might prevent the speedy passage that Hooker would have to manage to avoid disaster.

Burnside would take no such risk, for he still expected the pontoons at any moment. They did not arrive for a few more days, however, so Burnside planned for a crossing several miles downstream at Skinker's Neck, within range of Port Royal and the protection of Union gunboats. After a week or so the Confederates began to prepare an intimidating greeting there; with the added disadvantage of the dozen miles of bad road that intervened between Skinker's Neck and his nearest supply base, Burnside gave up that idea, too.

The only remaining alternative to a demoralizing withdrawal (or going into winter quarters, which seemed just as bad) was to bridge the river in the immediate vicinity of the city, and that is what Burnside proposed to do. If he could dash across and catch Lee by surprise, he might be able to throw his teeming army between Longstreet's corps and Stonewall Jackson's, which he supposed held the Skinker's Neck defenses.

Burnside called a council of his generals at noon on December 9 and told them what he had decided to do. Sumner and Hooker would burst right into the city while Franklin would sweep across the plain below town. That night General Sumner briefed the officers of his two corps on the plan of attack. If the Second Corps commander, Darius N. Couch, did not misrepresent the tone of that meeting, "there were not two opinions among the subordinate officers as to the rashness of the undertaking." Getting wind of that poor opinion, Burnside called Sumner's generals together the next night to quiz them about their objections, and Couch recalled that Burnside chastised the officers for offering such discouragement, rebuking Winfield Hancock in particular. Hancock, Couch, and the rest agreed to give their chief all their support, Couch said, though he believed that even Sumner doubted the chances of success. Either Couch guessed wrong or Sumner lied, though, for just nine days after this conference Sumner told a congressional committee that he considered it the right thing to do and that he thought the Confederate works could be carried.[5]

Certainly there was opposition to Burnside's plan among the officers, for both Couch and Oliver Otis Howard remembered it years later; but the degree and nature of the original opposition is difficult to measure. Immediately after the devastating repulse, officers seemed to convince themselves that they had seen it coming all along, and as soon as Burnside was safely dead, some came forward to claim that they had told him so. In the 1880s William F. "Baldy" Smith gave the Century Company's *Battles and Leaders* series an article in which he said Burnside revealed his intention to storm the heights as the two of them rode down the riverbank below Fredericksburg. According to Smith he warned Burnside of the desperate effort it would take to carry those hills, whereupon Burnside supposedly swore him to secrecy. Smith repeated the tale in a private memoir meant for the eyes of his daughter alone, but while he recalled the wording of his augury well enough he got the location wrong, putting it this time in Burnside's headquarters at the Phillips house.[6]

Col. Rush Hawkins also waited until everyone who could say otherwise was dead before claiming that Burnside approached him for his opinion at the final council of Sumner's officers, although he misremembered both the date and the site of that meeting. It is unlikely enough that Burnside asked Hawkins about it, for he did not think much of the self-important colonel, but Hawkins alleged that he told Burnside the attack would produce "the greatest slaughter of the war." Hawkins also recollected that a staff officer, Joseph Taylor, backed him with the pronouncement that "your plan will be murder, not warfare." Hawkins, who was one of the few brigade commanders Burnside had never recommended for a star, denied that the belated publication of his prophecy was grounded in any "spirit of pride," but the disavowal itself bears the flavor of protesting too much.[7]

Warren Hassler and Edward J. Stackpole accepted these dubious stories as gospel, and as the centennial of the battle of Fredericksburg approached, their work reinforced the image of an officer corps on the verge of despair over Burnside's intentions. That impression may have led to further distortions as well. When Stackpole's *Civil War Times Illustrated* published the letters of Sumner's chief commissary and son-in-law, William Teall, the edited version included the announcement that "your father has determined to cross immediately in rear of his advance guard, and his staff all feel that they are to march into the jaws of death itself." The editor took considerable liberties with these letters, and in this instance he arbitrarily changed Teall's tense from the past perfect to the present perfect, which suggested that the officers considered the entire operation ominous. In the original Teall actually said that Sumner *had* determined to follow his spearhead, which made the staff feel they *were* to march into the jaws of death. The fear came from the combined belief that they were to ride much farther forward than the staff usually did and that Longstreet would smash them at the bridgeheads. That interpretation appears to be confirmed in Sumner's unpublished letter to Burnside of two weeks before, in which he advised against a crossing before the city because it "must be attended with great loss, not only from their artillery, but every house within musket range would be filled with infantry pouring a stream of fire upon the bridges." Once the crossings were secure and Sumner had been ordered to remain on the left bank, his staff's air of despondency evaporated, but by cutting out a passage that revealed Teall's sense of deliverance from death on December 11, the editor maintained a pessimistic atmosphere consistent with the most recent treatments of the topic.[8]

Burnside hoped to start his vanguard into the city and onto the plain with the dawn, but fire from William Barksdale's Mississippians and a few Floridians along the riverbank delayed construction of the bridges in front of the city. Downstream, the first of Franklin's bridges was finished by nine o'clock, and the second a couple of hours later. Before the city, though, flurries of musketry and salvos of artillery failed to flush the defenders out of their holes, and Burnside grew restless. He might have marched a brigade or two across Franklin's finished bridges and sent them up the riverbank to clean out the troublesome skirmishers, but they would have been vulnerable to flank fire as they moved upstream and might have invited an attack from the main body. His other option was to pulverize the waterfront with every gun that bore on it, and he tried that first, turning 147 muzzles on the historic city for two solid hours. Even that did little good, and in desperation he sent pontoonloads of riflemen across to fight it out door-to-door with the pesky sharpshooters. Not until evening was he free to cross the preponderance of his forces.

Burnside has been criticized for bullheadedness, but it would have been better for him at this point had he suffered more from that trait. All that day he had planned to throw Franklin against the southern limit of the heights beyond Fredericksburg and to have Sumner simultaneously assault Marye's Heights; had Burnside spent the night of December 11 pushing most of his army across those new bridges, and had both wings rushed for those two points at dawn on December 12, Franklin would probably have met far less resistance than he finally did, and a breakthrough on his front would have forced Lee to retire. Instead, Burnside ordered Sumner and Franklin to keep only a few brigades on the right bank that night, to guard the bridgeheads.

Burnside never explained why he did that, perhaps because it did not seem important at the time. For those of us who enjoy the availability of Confederate records, it is apparent that Lee had not yet determined whether Burnside intended to attack downstream as well as before the city, and that Lee had therefore withheld Stonewall Jackson's divisions as far away as Skinker's Neck and Port Royal. Burnside owned no such information, and he appears to have begun to suppose that the element of surprise was already lost, which might require him to shift his forces. Perhaps he wished to keep Lee off balance, or possibly he feared crowding the far shore in the darkness and risking a disastrous night attack. Whatever the reason, modern students with their clear vision can believe that the battle was lost by that delay.

Maj. Gen.
Edwin Vose Sumner.
Francis Trevelyan
Miller, ed., The
Photographic History
of the Civil War, *10 vols.*
(New York: Review of
Reviews, 1911), 10:179

Crossing and placing the troops consumed most of the daylight hours of December 12, and Burnside began revising his original plan to accommodate the inevitable increases in Confederate strength. Initially he had planned to rely upon sheer numbers to carry the battle, intending Sumner and Franklin to march independently forward, with Hooker helping whichever one needed the weight. Unlike his predecessor, Ambrose Burnside credited a fairly accurate estimate of Lee's strength. He might well have expected his 100,000 to bull their way through if Longstreet's 40,000 had been all that held the adjacent hills, but with most or all of Jackson's troops in place, Burnside would have to act more imaginatively.

In his letter to Burnside shortly after they arrived at Falmouth, Edwin Sumner had suggested that the army cross about where Franklin eventually did, and build a work of some thirty guns to cover the bridges. After that he proposed to "form our whole force in line of battle, and then by a determined march, turn their right flank." Sumner wondered "if it is not probable that we should force them from the field, and after this was done, we could occupy Fredericksburg and reestablish our lines of communications, making that city a depot."

It was a variation of this plan that Burnside now pursued. He did not build the fieldwork Sumner had proposed, but he decorated Stafford Heights with scores of rifled guns to bear on the plain while Romeyn B. Ayres lined up a *tête-de-pont* of thirty-six guns. Burnside's plan, which Stackpole called "fuzzy" and John Codman Ropes called "wild and absurd," actually seems pretty clear in light of Sumner's earlier proposal. Obviously Old Bull meant that the army should shake off its line of communications and sweep around Lee's flank, else he would not have referred to reestablishing those communications, and that is what Burnside evidently expected Franklin to do—break free of the bridges, leaving them to the care of the artillery and a couple of Hooker's divisions, and swing around the southern end of the heights to envelop Lee's right flank. As Sumner had supposed, that should have required Lee to retreat. Rather than simply force Lee into a withdrawal, however, Burnside wished to complicate the retreat with a sudden attack on Marye's Heights, with the hope of doing the Confederates some real harm.

Stackpole's and Ropes's confusion probably originated with Burnside's reference to Franklin proceeding down the "old Richmond road" with the bulk of his command while "a division at least" was supposed to take the southern end of the heights at Hamilton's Crossing on the railroad. The Richmond Stage Road ran parallel to the tracks there, and if that had been the route Burnside meant for him to take, Franklin would be sending the assaulting division in one direction and the rest of his troops in another. Burnside did not refer to the Richmond Stage Road, however, but to something he called the "old Richmond road." David Birney's maps of the battlefield incorrectly label the road to Hamilton's Crossing the "Bowling Green road," and Bowling Green was the next town on the way to Richmond. Franklin's subsequent testimony to the Committee on the Conduct of the War indicates that he, too, believed that to be the Bowling Green Road. John F. Reynolds, chief of the First Corps, also referred to it as "the main road" that he was supposed to attack, and had that universal misunderstanding been clear to Stackpole, he might have softened some of his more sarcastic remarks.[9]

Burnside rode over to Franklin's front that afternoon and conferred with him, Reynolds, and Baldy Smith. When he left these subordinates, they appear to have been convinced that he was going to send over a couple of Hooker's divisions, which would protect the bridges while Franklin went at the enemy's flank with everything he had. Months later, after Franklin found that he was to be blamed for the failure, he began complaining that Burnside had promised to send him written orders very soon, but that the orders did not come and Franklin therefore did not prepare for the anticipated movement. Franklin also said he sent an aide to the telegraph office sometime after midnight to inquire about the orders, and that the aide came back with news that the orders "were then being prepared." Yet, for all the documentation both Franklin and Burnside later supplied to support their conflicting interpretations, Franklin's inquiry did not surface in headquarters correspondence, and he never offered either a copy of that reply or a statement by the aide he allegedly sent—or, for that matter, even the name of the aide.[10]

Burnside confirmed that he meant to follow the Friday afternoon script when he directed Hooker to send two Third Corps divisions to the foot of Franklin's bridges with instructions to cross over them if it became necessary to defend them. Not until the next morning did Burnside send Franklin his orders, which were dated at 5:55 A.M. He chose Brig. Gen. James A. Hardie as his liaison, and in his impatience to get Franklin moving he gave Hardie the pencil copy of the order, which the clerks were still transcribing. He showed Hardie the original of Sumner's orders, which had not been copied, so he could put Franklin's role in perspective with the whole production. Burnside then hurried Hardie off with a promise to send Franklin a copy of the order by an orderly, and he instructed the brigadier to remain with Franklin for the entire day and telegraph frequently of the progress of the left wing. There is no indication that he elaborated on the orders themselves, nor would he have been likely to do so if he believed they conformed with his conversation with Franklin the previous afternoon.

Edward Stackpole repeated a rumor that Hardie stopped for "a hearty breakfast" before beginning his jaunt to Franklin's headquarters, taking an hour and fifty minutes for what Stackpole believed should have been a fifteen-minute gallop. Hardie himself heard that rumor three months after the battle and disputed it. He explained that he started immediately for Franklin's headquarters, but the mud was so slick and the sky so dark that he had to walk his horse most of the way, covering the distance in an hour and ten or fifteen minutes. Assuming that he left as early as 6:00, which is probable, he handed the order to Franklin at about 7:15. Franklin himself once commented that he received it "about 7 o'clock," but he quickly revised that to 7:30, and finally he extended that to 7:45, all of which makes very little difference except to illustrate how Franklin stretched it out to improve his case—and to demonstrate how Hassler and Stackpole readily accepted the evidence that was most damaging to Burnside, for both of them accepted the 7:45 version.[11]

Unless Hardie's watch was much slower than Franklin's, it is not possible that he delivered the order as late as 7:45, for by 7:40 he had telegraphed to Burnside that Franklin was complying with the first part of the order. If Hardie showed up as late as 7:30, though, that weakens Franklin's contention that the order differed substantially from what he and Burnside had discussed the evening before: he later testified that this discrepancy generated an extended discussion between him and his subordinates, yet that debate could not have lasted as long as ten minutes. Burnside's order to Franklin read as follows:

General Hardie will carry this dispatch to you and remain with you during the day. The general commanding directs that you keep your whole command in position for a rapid movement down the old Richmond road, and you will send out at once a division at least to pass below Smithfield to seize, if possible, the height near Captain Hamilton's, on this side of the Massaponax, taking care to keep it well supported and its line of retreat open. He has ordered another column of a division or more to be moved from General Sumner's command up the Plank road to its intersection with the Telegraph road, where they will divide, with a view to seizing the heights on both of these roads. Holding these two heights, with the heights near Captain Hamilton's, will, he hopes, compel the enemy to evacuate the whole ridge between these points. He makes these moves by columns distant from each other, with a view of avoiding the possibility of a collision of our own forces, which might occur in a general movement during a fog. Two of General Hooker's divisions are in your rear, at the bridges,

*Maj. Gen.
William Buel Franklin.
Francis Trevelyan
Miller, ed.,* The
Photographic History
of the Civil War, *10 vols.
(New York: Review of
Reviews, 1911), 10:179*

and will remain there as supports. Copies of instructions given to Generals Sumner and Hooker will be forwarded to you by an orderly very soon. You will keep your whole command in readiness to move at once, as soon as the fog lifts. The watchword, which, if possible, should be given to every company, will be "Scott."

After Franklin found himself in hot water for a limp effort, he testified that these orders flew in the face of his last council with Burnside, for he said they seemed to require something much less bold than a footloose rush around Lee's flank. He said he "was strengthened in this opinion" by Hardie. Ultimately, according to Franklin, he came to the conclusion that he was expected to execute nothing more than a reconnaissance-in-force.[12]

Burnside's syntax and word choice were indeed regrettable. On its face the order contains a number of questionable points, and it is understandable that Franklin might have been confused by it. That makes it all the more difficult to understand why he did not ask Burnside for a clarification, for neither did it convey what Franklin tried to make it say. It is perhaps only in the context of a prearranged course of action like the December 12 discussion of a full-force movement toward Hamilton's Crossing, breaking connection with the river, that the order makes good sense, yet no query ever drifted from the left wing to the Phillips house. Listening to the progress of Fitz John Porter's trial in Washington, the naturally cautious Franklin seems to have grown more cautious still, and he appears to have grabbed at an interpretation that might keep him out of trouble.

Franklin directed John Reynolds to lead off his attack with the minimum unit Burnside had required: George G. Meade's division of Pennsylvania Reserves. John Gibbon's smaller division went along on Meade's right, lagging behind in nominal support. Three hours passed between Burnside handing Franklin's orders to Hardie and Meade signaling that he was ready, and the fog under which Burnside had hoped to take Hamilton's Crossing had already begun to dissipate. That allowed John Pelham to unloose a brace of guns against Meade's left and rear, stopping his progress for well more than an hour, during which time Reynolds deployed Abner Doubleday's division perpendicularly to Meade's. Franklin could thus truthfully say that he attacked with three divisions rather than one, but Doubleday did little more than spar with the enemy's artillery while Gibbon's men lay down to avoid the shells.[13]

Franklin later gave testimony indicating he, too, believed that the road to Hamilton's Crossing was the Richmond road, noting that "those heights would have been in the [Richmond] road." Had Meade been ready to move immediately, or had the orders arrived earlier, that extremity of Lee's line would have been weaker by a couple of divisions, for Jubal A. Early's and D. H. Hill's troops only arrived that morning, most of them exhausted after their march from downriver. Meade stopped short of that road, however, turning instead onto a farm lane perhaps half a mile north of the desired route. That threw him headlong toward Stonewall Jackson's now-almost-solid front, but Franklin appears to have known too little about what lay before him to recognize the mistake.[14]

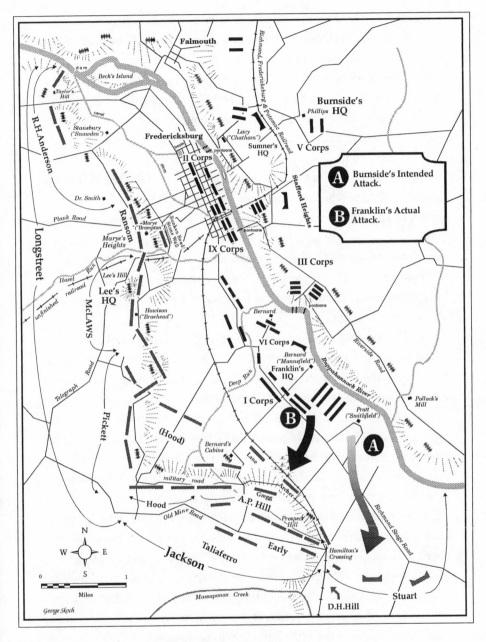

Battlefield at Fredericksburg, December 13, 1862

Franklin withheld the three divisions of Baldy Smith's Sixth Corps, which was stronger than Reynolds's First Corps by one-third. Although the Third Corps divisions of David Bell Birney and Daniel E. Sickles remained at the bridges to defend them, and William W. Burns's Ninth Corps division completed the link to Sumner's right wing, Franklin kept Smith's three big divisions waiting while Meade moved virtually alone against the southern line; Franklin defended that injudicious deployment by harking back to Burnside's written orders.

Franklin told the Joint Committee on the Conduct of the War that he left Smith idle "because the order under which I acted directed the line of retreat should be kept open," evidently meaning that the precaution applied to his entire force during the length of the operation. Such an interpretation required him to ignore English grammar, however. If his orders are clear on any point, it is that he was to keep a line of retreat open only for the spearhead that was to venture out into the fog to take Hamilton's Crossing and the artillery that sat upon it.

Franklin also excused himself from fighting Smith's corps by pointing out that Burnside had ordered him to "keep my whole command in position to move along the old Richmond road." That was true enough, but Franklin neglected to add the key words of that sentence—that he was to move down the road "at once, as soon as the fog lifts." The most obvious intent of that phrase is that Franklin would receive no further orders, but should take his *whole command* down the road as soon as the fog lifted, which it had long ago done. Again Franklin found a more tortuous interpretation, suggesting that he dawdled because he was waiting for another order to move.

These strained excuses came only after Franklin realized that he was going to earn the greatest blame for the defeat, and they smell dreadfully of contrivance even if he did eventually convince himself that it was all true. He appears to have highlighted the real problem on the left wing in his first interview with the committee, six days after the battle. When he was asked about the extent of his effort, he said, "I fought the whole strength of my command as far as I could, and at the same time keep my connexion [*sic*] with the river open." Burnside did not want Franklin to keep his connection with the river open; he wanted him to cut loose with his "whole command" once the fog lifted, and to leave the bridges to Birney and Sickles. The orders truly did reflect Franklin's understanding from the December 12 council with Burnside, that he was to make a significant attack on the left: if he did not see that in the bland words of Burnside's dispatch, it may have been because he sought language strong enough to protect himself from congressmen and courts martial in the event of disaster.[15]

By late morning Burnside grew nervous about his left, which he had expected would now be turning Lee's flank. At 10:30 he sent an aide, Capt. Philip Lydig, to find out what was going on. While that aide was on his way, Burnside received a telegram from Hardie that said Meade had advanced half a mile. Reynolds had had "to develop his whole line," Hardie said, and the enemy seemed to be preparing a strong attack on Franklin's left. Cavalry pickets reported that the enemy had been moving troops down the river late the previous night, Hardie added. All of that (including Hardie's mistake about Confederate troops moving downriver instead of upriver) appears to have persuaded Burnside that this was the moment for which he had been waiting: Franklin was making sufficient headway that Lee was shifting his weight from his own left to his right. Without waiting for the aide to return, Burnside ordered Sumner forward.[16]

Although Burnside issued Sumner his orders shortly after 11:00, they did not carry across to the foremost brigades and take effect until about noon. The troops found themselves open to artillery fire for several hundred yards before they encountered a canal ditch that could be crossed at only two points. On the other side of the ditch they realigned under cover of a bluff, then surged up over it into a storm of case shot and canister. The blue lines continued forward until suddenly, from behind the stone retaining wall of the sunken Telegraph Road, close-packed southern infantry ripped their ranks with a blaze of musketry. First one Yankee brigade took cover a hundred yards before the stone wall, then a second and a third. When one division had been used up another was flung at this impromptu fieldwork, and then another. The ditch funneled everyone toward the wall, preventing all attempts to flank it.

An opinionated veteran of the Second Corps who faced that wall later charged that General Couch tried to warn Burnside about the ditch and that Burnside snapped that he knew what he was doing, having served in Fredericksburg briefly the previous summer. Like most of the more damaging testimony against Burnside, this came long after he was dead, but even if it is true, Burnside was not alone in forgetting about the disadvantages of the slope. He had been consulting closely with his provost marshal, Marsena R. Patrick, whose brigade had spent weeks in the town less than four months before, and neither Patrick's memory nor that of any of his former officers appears to have included the sunken road or other serious impediments. The tremendous volleys from the protected Confederate riflemen were a complete surprise.[17]

For all the drawbacks of attacking the Confederate position on the Telegraph Road, it probably posed the most logical location for an assault on this half of the southern defenses. Everywhere else concave sectors dimpled Lee's line, yielding endless potential crossfires, but here lay a salient that stretched far toward the Federals' own position, shortening the distance any assault would have to cover and diminishing the defenders' effective firepower as much as possible.

The first charge on the stone wall was barely under way when Burnside read a disappointing telegram from Hardie. Only then was Meade "advancing in the direction you prescribed this morning." That sounded quite different from the implications of Hardie's last wire, and Burnside dispatched another aide, Capt. James Cutts, with instructions for Franklin to push his right (Smith) and his front (Reynolds) ahead. As Lydig left Franklin's headquarters, he passed Captain Cutts, and when Lydig reached the Phillips house at 12:30, he apprised Burnside that the Sixth Corps was not engaged. The captain observed that Burnside seemed surprised, and he said the general expressed annoyance with Franklin for having committed only his smaller corps.

Dense smoke and high winds prevented any glimpse of Franklin's progress by either telescope or observation balloon, so Burnside was as good as blind while he tried to coordinate the two attacks, for there was no sense in calling off Sumner now. Over the next hour Hardie sent three more telegrams, each describing heavy fighting, but the last mentioned that "Reynolds will push Gibbon in, if necessary." That alerted Burnside that Franklin had not even begun to wield his considerable firepower, and if he needed any confirmation of that he got it from Captain Cutts, who had just reined up to report that Franklin had not advanced and had said he would not be able to do so.

"But he must advance," Burnside reportedly replied, and he sent a third aide with a direct order to "make a vigorous attack with his whole force" because "our right is hard pressed." Franklin's version of the order included the comment that "your instructions of this morning, are so far modified as to require an advance upon the heights immediately in your front." Captain Robert Goddard galloped off with that order at about 1:30.

Even in the daylight and with the mud softened a little it took Captain Goddard nearly an hour to reach Franklin. Hardie acknowledged receipt of the order at 2:25, and later Franklin would insist that this was the first communication he had received from Burnside since the initial order of 5:55 A.M.; that recollection was immediately contradicted, however, by the statements of Lydig and Cutts.[18]

Hardie relayed Franklin's promise to "do his best," adding that new troops had gone in. Meade's division had long ago come streaming out of the woods on the heights, though, and Gibbon's division had been soundly repulsed. The new troops Franklin threw in were from the Third Corps bridge guards, for he continued to retain Smith's 24,000 men as little more than a reserve.

On Sumner's front the Second Corps had spent itself in assaults on the stone wall, and Sturgis's division of the Ninth Corps had followed suit. At the same moment that Burnside sent Franklin his last assault order he directed Hooker to march the Fifth Corps across the river to storm the wall. Hooker found General Couch, who felt the day could be won if all Hooker's men were thrown in on the right, but Hooker examined the field with Winfield Hancock and came away convinced that his task was impossible. Sometime after 2:00 P.M. he sent Burnside word to that effect, but Burnside insisted on the advance: Burnside had, after all, just received not only Franklin's promise to "do his best," but a signal-station message from Couch that one good division would probably turn Lee's left flank behind the city. Another dispatch had come from Orlando B. Willcox, also by signal flags, that Sturgis was within eighty paces of the crest and calling desperately for another division. Yet Hooker felt so certain of failure (or so he said) that he rode to headquarters personally to discourage the commanding general from sending in any more troops. Fighting Joe claimed this took no time at all, but by now it was well after 3:00.[19]

Franklin had sent one strange dispatch in which he exaggerated the damage done to his left and said he could not move forward, and one copy of that message asked whether the Eleventh or Twelfth Corps might not be sent across the river—when those corps were nowhere near the battlefield. That communication arrived at about the same time as a later telegram from

Hardie, who said things looked somewhat better. A few minutes later, however, Orlando Willcox signaled that Couch had carried Marye's Heights; this message is headed "4.25 P.M.," but internal evidence clearly puts it at about 3:25.[20]

Burnside had attacked Lee in the first place because he believed the morale of both the army and the public required it. Now he had committed himself and had already suffered heavy casualties. He naturally did not wish to waste the day's effort and risk further demoralization with victory in sight, and he had some reason to believe that a simultaneous push on both flanks would crumble the Confederate line. Given such heartening information from Willcox, whom Burnside correctly judged to be devoted to him, Burnside rejected the opinion of Hooker, whom he mistrusted.

At a dinner party in New York two months later, perhaps after a glass of wine had loosened his lips, Burnside revealed that he was still confident of victory that December afternoon when someone told him that "one of our generals . . . *was doing all he could to make the attack a failure.*" Burnside admitted to his civilian audience that the news so enraged him that he barely suppressed an urge to ride over and shoot the miscreant. The guest who recorded this conversation supposed that Burnside spoke of Franklin, and to date historians have assumed that to be true, but the diarist said the offending general was "on the right, I think," which would have ruled Franklin out. That additional comment, along with Burnside's threat to hang Hooker a few weeks later, suggests that it was the commander of the Center Grand Division whom he had wished to shoot. If so, it is small wonder that he discounted Hooker's opinion. With the winter day so near its end he had no time for a personal observation, and he gave Hooker the same peremptory orders that he had sent Franklin. Hooker, at least, complied.[21]

It was the division of Andrew A. Humphreys that Hooker chose to send in. Humphreys, a brigadier who had attended West Point with Robert E. Lee, commanded two brigades composed mostly of nine-month Pennsylvania militia. He led the first of his two brigades against the right of the stone wall sometime after 4:00 P.M. Artillery on the Confederate left all but enfiladed his line, and when the reinforced infantry in the sunken road opened on his narrow front, it stopped the Pennsylvanians cold. While Willcox ordered a brigade in on the left to offer him support, Humphreys rode back to his second brigade of rookies and told them not to fire a shot, but to run right over the prone survivors of earlier attacks and dash over the wall with their bayonets fixed. This brigade, too, suffered the flank fire and the pointblank musketry, as well as the interference of their discouraged comrades on the front line, and Humphreys failed again.

While Humphreys made his first effort, Burnside received a 3:40 wire from Hardie that included another promise to prepare for a frontal attack "as soon as the left is safe," and that telegram ended with the postscript, "Engaged now heavily in front," which implied that the attack was being made. By the time of Humphreys's second repulse, though, Hardie had indicated that it was too late for Franklin to do anything, so Burnside called an end to the day's fighting.[22]

The senior grand division commander at Fredericksburg, Sumner, performed as he had through more than four decades of service: he obeyed orders enthusiastically but without much hint of imagination. His subordinates employed their troops in the way too many of their generation did, a brigade at a time, although they, at least, had some excuse in the restricted field on which they operated.

Joseph Hooker had little opportunity to exercise his military talents at Fredericksburg. He has earned some credit for his foresight in trying to dissuade his chief from further assaults, but one wonders whether his objections were based in firm belief, in his well-known propensity for insubordinate carping, or in a wish to see Burnside fail miserably so Joe Hooker might shine. Whatever his motives, Hooker's hesitation removed even the slight chance that relentless pressure and concerted effort might break Longstreet's front.

William Franklin demonstrated not only the tactical timidity that plagued him always, but an acute political caution that left him nearly paralyzed. Though he had less reason to do so, he appears to have suffered from something that had troubled Burnside at Antietam: the sense that he was being groomed as a scapegoat in case of disaster. Franklin, too, allowed his forces to fight piecemeal, never daring to swing Smith's powerful corps into action. Like his friend McClellan, Franklin seemed afraid to win; it was enough for him not to be beaten. He doubtless did not harbor the treasonous intent some have attributed to him, and one might almost forgive him the misunderstanding of Burnside's orders were it not that his subsequent excuses seem so fabricated as to raise the question of whether he did not lie about that, too.

He should have comprehended the orders in light of his conference with Burnside the night before, for all the elements of the strong flank attack they discussed on December 12 are contained in those orders.

The blame for Fredericksburg has been piled, with a venom that increases with each decade, at the feet of Ambrose Burnside. Initially many blamed the president or Henry Halleck for driving him to make the attack, and despite Halleck's sins in that regard it was Burnside himself who put an end to that complaint. By assuming the responsibility he meant to relieve the administration, and like Robert E. Lee he was willing to say that the battlefield failure had been all his fault; but culprits and scholars alike have gone too far in using that magnanimity to excuse other failures.

Edward Stackpole threw all the fault on Burnside. For his summation of that general, he quoted Martin Schenck's 1956 *Civil War History* article, "Burnside's Bridge," which suggests an explanation for "the almost wanton recklessness at Fredericksburg" in "the field of psychology—or perhaps psychiatry." That article is a telling choice, for it was based on the most superficial research and mistaken facts, and Schenck's speculation has little merit. The selection of that passage seems typical, however, of the discretion exercised by Stackpole, whose book and magazine article on Fredericksburg are more responsible than anything else for my generation's dismal view of Burnside.

Vorin Whan, who was more careful than Stackpole and certainly less biased, recognized many factors that others ignored, including those that forced Burnside to attack when and where he did. Still, he found Burnside accountable for nearly everything that went wrong. He might have modified his assessment further, however, had he made a closer study of the correspondence that passed between the army commander and his subordinates.

Burnside did, of course, share in the responsibility for the disaster of December 13. His greatest lapse was probably the decision not to continue crossing the river on the night of the eleventh and attack on the morning of the twelfth, although that mistake is much more evident now than it was at the time. He also erred in not familiarizing Hardie with his desire for a full-fledged assault, and for not endowing Hardie with the authority to make Franklin respond. To whatever degree the passive tone of his orders to Franklin hobbled that general, he is also at fault, although that tone was stylistically typical of not only Burnside but Lee. Burnside did not write with great clarity anyway, and if his instructions were phrased more awkwardly than usual, it may have been because he was stretching himself too thin, sleeping barely three hours a night after December 10. That, perhaps, was his next greatest mistake: despite the efficient organization he had created, he kept too close a watch on the management of his unwieldy army, and that was probably a direct result of his reservations about his capacity to command so great a force. The resulting exhaustion doubtless contributed to some of his less judicious decisions during the battle, just as similar fatigue appears to have impaired Stonewall Jackson during the Seven Days, when he, too, took missteps that militated against Confederate success on several occasions. Burnside performed about as well as anyone else might have with hesitant subordinates, but it is more important to note that he did not act from stupidity, insanity, or whim, as his critics have insinuated, but rather from information that those critics have overlooked—however mistaken that information may have proven to be.

When Robert E. Lee spends more than five hours hammering the Federal position at Gaines's Mill, assaulting uphill on a constricted front against a strong, entrenched enemy who is well supported by artillery, losing nearly 8,000 men in the process, he is called bold and ferocious. When Ambrose Burnside spends nearly five hours hammering Marye's Heights, assaulting uphill on a constricted front against a strong, entrenched enemy who is well supported with artillery, losing nearly 8,000 men in the process, he is called stubborn and stupid. In each case, the army commander operated in anticipation of a left-flank movement that never came. The only real difference is that when John Bell Hood told his Texans to rush at the enemy without firing and get in among them with the bayonet, they succeeded, whereas when Andrew Humphreys gave the same instructions to his division of untried militiamen, they failed.

We forget that the strength of entrenchments and the declining effectiveness of the bayonet were concepts not yet understood by even the best generals of 1862, and that numerous foreign observers counted Fredericksburg the battle that taught that lesson. Thanks to Burnside's disdain for controversy, and also to the sarcasm of his critics, we have become accustomed to thinking of him in pathetic terms. From self-serving primary sources like the recollections of George McClellan, William Franklin, and Baldy Smith through the more distorted secondary works of our own day, we have been conditioned to think of Burnside as a benevolent bungler, and although we still seem to like him, we do not appear to like him well enough to consider, for once, his side of the story.

Notes

1. Warren W. Hassler, Jr., *Commanders of the Army of the Potomac* (Baton Rouge: Louisiana State University Press, 1962), 100–101.

2. Henry C. Marsh to his father, November 25, 1862, Indiana State Library, Indianapolis, Ind.; Henry Haupt to Mrs. Haupt, November 15, 1862, Louis M. Haupt Family Papers, and William F. Draper to "My Dear Father," January 9, 1863, William Franklin Draper Papers, Library of Congress, Washington, D.C.; William F. Draper, *Recollections of a Varied Career* (Boston: Little, Brown, 1908), 94.

3. Stephen M. Weld, *War Diary and Letters of Stephen M. Weld* (Boston: Massachusetts Historical Society, 1979), 150.

4. Ibid.

5. William W. Teall to Mrs. Teall, December 7, 10, 1862, William W. Teall Letters, Tennessee State Library and Archives, Nashville, Tenn. (repository hereafter cited as TSLA); Darius N. Couch, "Sumner's 'Right Grand Division,' " in *Battles and Leaders of the Civil War*, ed. Robert Underwood Johnson and Clarence Clough Buel, 4 vols. (New York: Century, 1887–88), 3:108 (hereafter cited as *B&L*); U.S. Congress, *Report of the Joint Committee on the Conduct of the War in Three Parts* (Washington, D.C.: GPO, 1863), pt. 1, p. 658 (hereafter cited as *JCCW*; all references are to part 1).

6. William Farrar Smith, "Franklin's 'Left Grand Division,' " in *B&L*, 3:130; William F. Smith, *Autobiography of Major General William F. Smith, 1861–1864*, ed. Herbert M. Schiller (Dayton, Ohio: Morningside, 1990), 60.

7. Rush C. Hawkins, "Why Burnside Did Not Renew the Attack at Fredericksburg," in *B&L*, 3:126.

8. Hassler, *Commanders*, 109; Edward J. Stackpole, *Drama on the Rappahannock: The Fredericksburg Campaign* (Harrisburg, Pa.: Military Service Publishing, 1957), 127–28; William W. Teall, "Ringside Seat at Fredericksburg," *Civil War Times Illustrated* 4 (May 1965): 26; William W. Teall to Mrs. Teall, December 10, 11, 1862, Teall Letters, TSLA; Edwin V. Sumner to Ambrose E. Burnside, November 23, 1862, box 3, Ambrose E. Burnside Papers, Generals' Reports and Books, RG 94, National Archives, Washington, D.C. (repository hereafter cited as NA).

9. U.S. War Department, *The War of the Rebellion: A Compilation of the Official Records of the Union and Confederate Armies*, 127 vols., index, and atlas (Washington, D.C.: GPO, 1880–1901), atlas, plate 30, maps 3 and 4 (hereafter cited as *OR*; all references are to series 1); *JCCW*, 700, 710.

10. *JCCW*, 707; William B. Franklin, *Reply of Maj.-Gen. William B. Franklin to the Report of the Joint Committee of Congress* (New York: D. Van Nostrand, 1863), 6.

11. Stackpole, *Drama on the Rappahannock*, 170; James A. Hardie to Ambrose E. Burnside, March 12, 1863, box 6, Ambrose E. Burnside Papers, RG 94, NA; *JCCW*, 707, 710; Franklin, *Reply to Joint Committee*, 6, and 1867 ed., 1, 2; Hassler, *Commanders*, 112.

12. *JCCW*, 709–10.

13. *JCCW*, 708, 710.

14. *JCCW*, 700, 710.

15. *JCCW*, 661, 709–10.

16. *OR* 21:91, 127–28.

17. Francis A. Walker, *History of the Second Army Corps in the Army of the Potomac* (New York: Charles Scribner's Sons, 1891), 137, 155.

18. William W. Teall to Mrs. Teall, December 13, 1862, Teall Letters, TSLA; Franklin, *Reply to Joint Committee*, 23–24; *OR* 21:127–28.

19. *OR* 21:92, 160, 162, 356; Couch, "Sumner's 'Right Grand Division,'" 114–15.

20. *OR* 21:92, 118–19.

21. George Templeton Strong, *The Diary of George Templeton Strong*, ed. Allan Nevins and Milton Halsey Thomas, 4 vols. (New York: Macmillan, 1952), 3:297; Henry W. Raymond, ed., "Extracts from the Journal of Henry J. Raymond," *Scribner's Monthly*, March 1880, 704.

22. *OR* 21:92.

Confederate Leadership at Fredericksburg

ALAN T. NOLAN

In terms of Confederate leadership, Fredericksburg may be summed up by the old saying, "shooting fish in a barrel." That is what happened at Fredericksburg. Two official communications in the *Official Records* provide an excellent summary of the battle. On November 14, 1862, General in Chief Henry W. Halleck notified Ambrose E. Burnside as follows regarding Burnside's proposed Fredericksburg movement: "The President has just assented to your plan. He thinks it will succeed if you move rapidly; otherwise not." Lee's report of Fredericksburg, dated April 10, 1863, says this about Burnside's assault on December 13, 1862: "The attack on the 13th had been so easily repulsed, and by so small a part of our army, that it was not supposed the enemy would limit his efforts to an attempt, which, in view of the magnitude of his preparations and the extent of his force, seemed comparatively insignificant."[1]

In the late fall of 1862, on the eve of Fredericksburg, the fortunes of the war had tilted dramatically against the Confederacy, even in the Virginia theater. The Confederate movements into Maryland and Kentucky had been frustrated at Antietam and Perryville, and Lee and Bragg, respectively, had retreated. Perhaps even more significantly, the raids into Maryland and Kentucky had dispelled the southern notion that these border states were anxious to join the Confederacy or contribute heavily to its support. In the West, the North continued to penetrate along the Mississippi River and therefore to threaten Vicksburg. The issuance of Lincoln's preliminary proclamation of emancipation had radically changed the dynamics of the war and at least suggested that the Confederacy was to be perceived less favorably in Europe.

It is plain that, as specifically related to the Army of Northern Virginia, Lee's Maryland venture had significantly damaged that army in casualties and morale. Lee had lost approximately 13,000 men (including missing), more

Gen. Robert Edward Lee.
Francis Trevelyan Miller,
ed., The Photographic
History of the Civil War,
10 vols. (New York:
Review of Reviews, 1911),
10:69

than 26 percent of his force, at Antietam, on the heels of the loss of approximately 9,000 (19 percent) at Second Bull Run and significant losses at South
Mountain.[2]

Lee candidly reported the symptoms of morale deterioration. On September 21 he addressed President Jefferson Davis about the state of the army: "Its
present efficiency is greatly paralyzed by the loss to its ranks of the numerous
stragglers. I have taken every means in my power from the beginning to
correct this evil, which has increased instead of diminished." On September
22 Lee again wrote to Davis about this subject. "In connection with . . .
straggling . . . the destruction of private property by the army has occupied
much of my attention," he stated. "A great deal of damage to citizens is done
by stragglers, who consume all they can get from the charitable and all they
can take from the defenseless, in many cases wantonly destroying stock and

other property." Three days later Lee told the president that after withdrawing from Maryland on September 18 he had intended to cross the Potomac again, "to advance upon Hagerstown and endeavor to defeat the enemy at that point," but had changed his mind, he said, because the army did not "exhibit its former temper and condition."[3]

Casualties, including those in the officer corps, required a reorganization of the Army of Northern Virginia. Douglas Southall Freeman titles a chapter in *Lee's Lieutenants* "A Crisis in Reorganization." Referring to the army's general officers of lower rank, Freeman observes that "that organization now had to be rebuilt."[4] To this process General Lee's attention was committed over a period of weeks in the late fall. The first and easiest step was the appointment of James Longstreet and Stonewall Jackson to head the now officially authorized corps commands.[5] This was followed by the formal structuring of the corps and promotions to the ranks of major general and brigadier. When the process was completed, the army included Maj. Gen. J. E. B. Stuart's cavalry division, comprising four brigades and Maj. John Pelham's horse artillery, and Brig. Gen. William Nelson Pendleton's reserve artillery, together with the artillery in the two corps. Longstreet had the First Corps, composed, in addition to corps artillery, of five divisions: Maj. Gen. Lafayette McLaws's, Maj. Gen. Richard H. Anderson's, Maj. Gen. George E. Pickett's, Maj. Gen. John Bell Hood's, and Brig. Gen. Robert Ransom, Jr.'s. Jackson's Second Corps had four divisions, commanded, respectively, by major generals D. H. Hill, A. P. Hill, and Jubal A. Early (commanding Ewell's division) and Brig. Gen. William B. Taliaferro (commanding Jackson's division).[6]

The period after Antietam also saw changes in the Army of the Potomac, the most profound involving George B. McClellan's removal and replacement. But that army had also been refitted and substantially reinforced during McClellan's long delay in Maryland, from September 17 to October 30. On the latter date the Army of the Potomac finally moved south into Virginia. Ambrose E. Burnside's appointment to replace McClellan on November 7, as well as communications between Washington and the army, made it plain that the administration expected Federal action.[7] Reacting to the administration, Burnside promptly prepared a plan of campaign.[8]

In the late fall of 1862 Lee was not in a position to mount a strategically offensive move. Confederate leadership, for the time being, was to be reactive to Federal aggressiveness. These were the circumstances that led to the battle of Fredericksburg.

As of Burnside's appointment to replace McClellan, the Army of the Potomac was encamped near Warrenton, Virginia. The Army of Northern Virginia was divided. Jackson's corps was in the Winchester area in the Valley; Longstreet was near Culpeper Court House, between the Rapidan and the Rappahannock.[9]

The interesting thing about the battle of Fredericksburg, and about Confederate leadership at the battle, involves what happened between Burnside's communication of his plan on November 9 and his launching attacks at Fredericksburg on December 13, 1862. We speak from time to time about accidental battles. In June and July of 1863 the armies were on a collision course in Pennsylvania, but Gettysburg was the place of collision by chance and circumstances. Fredericksburg surely ranks as another prominent accidental battle of the war. Neither army intended to fight there. This becomes obvious if one consults the communications of the leadership prior to the battle, during the period between November 9 and December 13.

McClellan had exhausted the Lincoln administration's patience with his inaction by November 5, the day on which the Federal change-of-command order was issued and Halleck dispatched a highly pregnant letter to Burnside: "General: Immediately on assuming command . . . you will report the position of your troops and what you purpose [sic] doing with them."[10] On November 7 (but not sent until November 9 through Chief of Staff Gen. G. W. Cullum) Burnside advised Halleck of his plan to concentrate his army near Warrenton, "impress upon the enemy a belief that we are to attack at Culpeper or Gordonsville, and . . . then to make a rapid move of the whole force to Fredericksburg, *with a view to a movement upon Richmond at that point*" (emphasis added).[11]

This statement makes it plain that Fredericksburg was to be the *base* for a Federal move on Richmond rather than the point of attack. Burnside's November 9 communication also referred to "moving by way of Fredericksburg," stated that Fredericksburg lay "on the shortest route to Richmond," and projected "a rapid movement . . . direct upon Richmond." In short, Burnside's plan was premised on his ability to cross the river at Fredericksburg promptly and with little or no opposition, and then to move toward Richmond.

Because of his plan to cross the Rappahannock, Burnside requested that pontoon trains be sent to Fredericksburg. On November 12 Halleck ordered

Brig. Gen. Daniel P. Woodbury of the engineer brigade in Washington to instruct the chief quartermaster to transport "all" pontoons and bridging materials to Aquia.[12] On November 14 Burnside's chief engineer twice telegraphed General Woodbury to inquire about the progress of the pontoons. Woodbury's response acknowledged delay but also described a plentiful supply of pontoons and stated that the first train would start for Falmouth on the sixteenth or seventeenth.[13] Burnside was reassured.

Lee intended at all times to confront any Federal move south. Initially uncertain regarding Burnside's intent, he was ultimately persuaded that Fredericksburg was to be Burnside's route. Even then Lee did not plan to fight at Fredericksburg. Instead, he contemplated meeting the Federal army at the North Anna. At Culpeper on November 19 Lee wrote to Jackson at Winchester. He was not decided on Burnside's route but possessed enough evidence to start Longstreet's corps to Fredericksburg. In spite of this he announced that "I do not now anticipate making a determined stand north of the North Anna."[14]

After the battle, in a December 16 letter to the secretary of war, Lee reiterated that fighting at the North Anna had been his intent. He was then anticipating another crossing of the Rappahannock by the defeated Burnside, perhaps at Port Royal. In announcing his own intent Lee said, "I think it more advantageous to retire to the Annas and give battle than on the banks of the Rappahannock." He then stated that that had been his intent initially, when Burnside first arrived at Fredericksburg. Lee also noted that the narrowness and winding character of the Rappahannock made it unlikely that he could prevent a Federal crossing in the vicinity of Fredericksburg. He had fought at Fredericksburg, he wrote, not because of any military advantage to that site but because he did not like to open the area south of Fredericksburg to Federal "depredation" and because he wanted to collect forage and provisions in the Rappahannock Valley.[15]

The North Anna idea had persisted. General Longstreet's article in *Battles and Leaders* says that after Jackson's arrival at Fredericksburg the commander of the Second Corps stated a preference for fighting at the North Anna because he believed that a victory there, unlike a victory at Fredericksburg, would permit pursuit of the enemy.[16]

With the Confederate army widely divided, and in pursuance of his plan of crossing at Fredericksburg and then moving south toward Richmond,

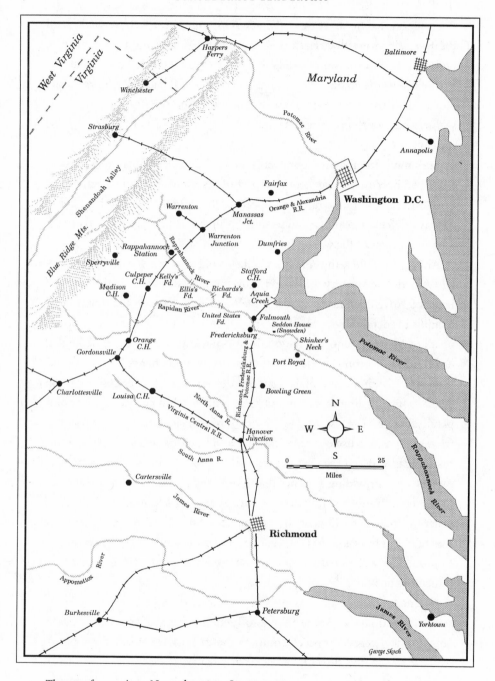

Theater of operations, November 1862–January 1863

Burnside started his army toward Fredericksburg. The march went well, and the Federals promptly arrived on the northern side of the river: Edwin V. Sumner's two corps were at Falmouth on November 17, and William B. Franklin's on the eighteenth. Joseph Hooker's corps reached Stafford Court House, six miles from Falmouth, on November 19, the day Burnside himself arrived. Pontoons were not there, and the river was not believed to be fordable.[17]

Lee's move to Fredericksburg was much less direct. His planning must be described because it is very much a part of his leadership. His communications especially demonstrate two aspects of that leadership: first, his carefulness as a defensive planner, and second, his high level of responsibility for the Virginia theater of the war.

Although a field army commander, Lee had broad responsibility for overall Confederate strategy and troop movement in the Virginia theater. In a letter of November 14 to Secretary of War George Wythe Randolph, after reciting a Federal movement out of the upper part of Fauquier County to the north of Manassas and Warrenton, the Confederate commander wrote that he "thought it probable that he [the enemy] would change his line of approach to Richmond and make a sudden descent upon Fredericksburg, from which point his line of communication with Washington would be comparatively safe." Lee also told Randolph of his consideration of ways of frustrating Burnside's use of Fredericksburg as a point of concentration, noting that he had ordered the destruction of the railroad from Fredericksburg to Aquia Creek. Providing evidence that, like Burnside, he saw the Federal move to Fredericksburg as simply the base for a move to Richmond, Lee discussed ordering the destruction of the railroad from Fredericksburg to Hanover Junction. But he was uncertain regarding Burnside's intent: "Were I certain of the route he will pursue, I should commence immediately to make it as difficult as possible."[18]

On the following day, November 15, Lee directed Brig. Gen. W. H. F. Lee to send a mixed reconnaissance force to Fredericksburg. If they found it occupied, they were to proceed south to the railroad crossing of the North Anna. Also on the fifteenth he advised Col. W. B. Ball, commanding at Fredericksburg, of the ordered reconnaissance and said that "it is probable that he [the enemy] is marching upon Fredericksburg."[19]

Lee changed his mind two days later regarding Burnside's intent. To President Davis he stated that he had apprehended a Federal shift to Fredericksburg to use it as a base, but there was no evidence of such a move. "I have heard of no preparation to build the wharves at Aquia Creek," he wrote, and there were no apparent provisions for subsisting a large army. This provoked new speculation. On the same day as his November 17 letter to President Davis, Lee wrote to the secretary of war: "I think it, therefore, probable that the movement in execution is with a view of transferring the army south of the James River, and the appointment of General Burnside to command favors this supposition." Late on the seventeenth he advised Secretary Randolph that his scouts reported three Federal brigades advancing on Fredericksburg, but he speculated that this might be a feint.[20]

On the following day, November 18, Lee reported to Adjutant and Inspector Gen. Samuel Cooper that his scouts reported Sumner's corps moving toward Fredericksburg. Two divisions of Longstreet's corps and W. H. F. Lee's cavalry brigade had been started for Fredericksburg, according to Lee. Also on November 18, from near Culpeper Court House, Lee wrote to Jackson, who was still near Winchester in the Valley. Lee told his subordinate that the cavalry reported Federals moving in force to Fredericksburg, but the Confederate plan, he said, "awaits confirmation of intelligence." Lee further stated that there was no observable preparation for a transfer to south of the James River. Finally, he told Jackson that it was advisable to put some of his divisions in motion across the mountains and "advance them at least as far as Sperryville or Madison Court-House."[21]

On the nineteenth Lee told President Davis that two divisions of Longstreet's corps had moved to Fredericksburg on the eighteenth and two more were to follow that day. Still apparently uncertain regarding Burnside's Fredericksburg destination, Lee said, "I shall wait to hear again from Stuart, and then proceed as circumstances dictate." Also on the nineteenth, writing to Jackson at Winchester, Lee noted that "Longstreet's corps is moving to Fredericksburg, opposite to which place Sumner's corps has arrived." He then expressed his preference for a North Anna battle site, as previously noted. Lee also told Jackson on the nineteenth of a November 18 message from Stuart that the entire Federal army had marched to Fredericksburg and advised Jackson that Stuart "considers the information he received as conclusive" on the issue. Lee said further that he was waiting for a report from Stuart on November 19. He would "then start for Fredericksburg, if circumstances warrant." Jackson was not told to move from Winchester.[22]

Finally, on November 22, Lee could report from Fredericksburg to General Cooper that the entire Federal army was before him on the other side of the river. On the following day he told Jackson this and asked him to move east of the Blue Ridge "and take such a position as you may find best." Jackson also learned that Lee remained uncertain of enemy plans and expressed the fear that Federals would be transferred from Fredericksburg to some other location.[23]

Lee's anxiety about Federal intent was briefly piqued on the twenty-second. Reporting to Davis on the twenty-fifth he told of Federals moving to their rear on November 22, virtually disappearing from the heights opposite Lee. It had not been a transfer of operations, Lee wrote, but for the purpose of avoiding Confederate artillery fire and for subsistence convenience. Lee stated that he now believed the Federals did propose to go south by way of Fredericksburg. He did not know where the crossing would occur but believed that Hanover Junction was an object of the movement. He intended to break up the railroad south of Fredericksburg but was reluctant to do so because of the effects of the damage on civilian morale. He tendered to Davis the issue of concentrating closer to Richmond and explained that he had waited to order Jackson to Fredericksburg because Jackson's presence on Burnside's flank was tactically valuable.[24]

Lee also wrote twice to Jackson on the twenty-fifth. His first dispatch reiterated his view that a move by Jackson to Culpeper would be advantageous and stated that Burnside apparently intended to advance on Richmond from a Fredericksburg base. He stated further that although Jackson's corps "may, therefore, be needed" in Fredericksburg, he need not hasten his march. The second dispatch of the twenty-fifth carried a 7:00 P.M. time. It recapitulated the earlier dispatch and recommended the Culpeper destination for Jackson, but suggested that Jackson's advance troops march as far as Rappahannock Station and that his cavalry cross the river. These moves, Lee said, would deter an advance by Burnside.[25]

On November 26, in another letter to Jackson, Lee adverted for the first time to the possibility that Burnside might attempt to cross the river in front of Fredericksburg. He also said that "some other point on the river" might be the place of crossing. He requested that Jackson advance "by easy marches" to Fredericksburg. In view of the possibility of Burnside's crossing, Lee believed "that the whole army should be united." On the following day, having forwarded a status report to President Davis, including word of the arrival on the Stafford Road of a Federal pontoon train, Lee wrote again to Jackson designating the area of Massaponax Creek as Jackson's appropriate destination. On the twenty-eighth Lee reiterated to Jackson the Massaponax Creek destination and added that he was busy in a personal reconnaissance of the river. He did *not* expect Burnside to cross in front of Fredericksburg and speculated that the Port Royal area might be the planned site because of the possibility of support from gunboats and ready access for the Federals to the Old Richmond Road for a movement south.[26]

As a part of his reconnaissance, under date of December 2, 1862, Lee received a very interesting report from a captain of engineers. Lee, of course, had requested the report, which reflected "an examination of the Rappahannock River with reference to positions suitable for forcing a passage from the north side." Incorporating references to "Coast Survey Charts" and detailed observation, it seems a sophisticated document.[27]

On December 6 Lee again reported to the president. He cited Burnside's inaction and set forth a comprehensive statement of Federal troops elsewhere in the theater. The communication indicates that Burnside's inaction played on Lee's fear of Federal operations elsewhere, including south of the James River.[28]

Lee did not know that there was an objective reason for Burnside's inaction. It was the Federal judgment on or about November 17–19 that the river was not fordable[29] *and* Federal command failure to deliver the pontoons on which Burnside's plan relied. On November 22 a Burnside dispatch unwittingly acknowledged that the premise of the Federal plan had already been compromised, and predicted what was to occur on December 13. Referring to his pontoon requisition in the initial statement of his plan on November 9, Burnside said:

> It is very clear that my object was to make the move to Fredericksburg very rapidly, and to throw a heavy force across the river before the enemy could concentrate a force to oppose the crossing, and supposed the pontoon train would arrive at this place nearly simultaneously with the head of the column. Had that been the case, the whole of General Sumner's column—33,000 strong—would have crossed into Fredericksburg at once over a pontoon bridge, in front of a city . . . garrisoned by a small squadron

of cavalry and a battery of artillery which General Sumner silenced within a hour after his arrival.

Had the pontoon bridge arrived even on the 19th or 20th, the army could have crossed with trifling opposition. But now the opposite side of the river is occupied by a large rebel force under General Longstreet, with batteries ready to be placed in position to operate against the working parties building the bridge and the troops in crossing.

The pontoon train has not yet arrived, and the river is too high for the troops to cross at any of the fords.[30]

Thus, Burnside's plan, and opportunity, to cross on November 18, with the pike to Richmond open and Hanover Junction vulnerable, was gone. The pontoons story goes on and on. They began to arrive on November 25, but there was still inadequate bridging material.[31] On November 26 Burnside met Lincoln and Secretary of War Edwin M. Stanton at Aquia Creek. On November 28, in Washington, Burnside again discussed the situation with the administration.[32] Despite the evaporation of the whole strategic idea, a crossing in the face of the Army of Northern Virginia was to occur.

Although neither commander was yet aware of it, they were now committed to the accidental battle *at* Fredericksburg. There was, however, one more decision that sealed this eventuality. The Federals had made preparations to cross at Skinker's Neck, fourteen miles below Fredericksburg, but Confederate demonstrations there changed Burnside's mind. In addition, Burnside came to the belief that the enemy would be most surprised by his crossing at Fredericksburg.[33]

On December 11, the day the Federal bridges were finally laid, Burnside issued orders to the Federal grand division commanders. These orders have an eerie quality because they do not advert to the radical change in circumstances between Burnside's initial planning for his campaign and December 11, that is, the arrival of the Army of Northern Virginia across the river. Sumner was told to cross at the upper bridge and to take "the heights that command the Plank road and the Telegraph road." His "first corps" was to move directly to the front, supporting it by "your other corps." Franklin was to cross, move immediately to the front, and take "the heights which command the Plank and Telegraph roads." He was to "move down the old Richmond road, in the direction of the railroad." Hooker was to cross and hold

Fredericksburg from the Federal side of the Rappahannock.
Francis Trevelyan Miller, ed., The Photographic History of the Civil War, *10 vols.*
(New York: Review of Reviews, 1911), 1:26

himself in readiness to support either Sumner or Franklin.[34] What had been intended as a change of the Federal base *to* Fredericksburg for an advance on Richmond had become the battle *of* Fredericksburg.

Burnside's forces crossed on December 11 and 12.[35] Two of Jackson's divisions were still moving up, and the other two, Early's and D. H. Hill's, were quite remote. The latter two were not ordered up until late afternoon on December 12, and both divisions had to make night marches to join Lee's defensive line. But Burnside did not attack on the twelfth.[36]

The logistics of the armies were dictated by the terrain. As Lee stated in his report, "The plain on which Fredericksburg stands is so completely commanded by the hills of Stafford (in possession of the enemy) that no effectual opposition could be offered to the construction of the bridges or the passage of the river without exposing our troops to the destructive fire of his numerous batteries. Positions were, therefore, selected to oppose his advance after crossing."[37] The heights on the Federal side of the river dictated Lee's initial defensive tactics.

General Longstreet has left us a specific impression of Lee's position:

> The hills occupied by the Confederate forces, although over-crowned by the heights of Stafford, were so distant as to be outside the range of effective fire by the Federal guns and, with the lower receding grounds between them, formed a defensive series that may be likened to natural bastions. Taylor's Hill, on our left, was unassailable; Marye's Hill was more advanced toward the town, was of a gradual ascent and of less height than the others, and we considered it the point most assailable, and guarded it accordingly. The events that followed proved the correctness of our opinion on that point. Lee's Hill, near our center, with its rugged sides retired from Marye's and rising higher than its companions, was comparatively safe.[38]

On the Confederate right a plain extended about a mile from the heights held by Jackson's soldiers to the riverbank, on which the Federals south and east of the town were to be exposed. Timber covered the ground toward the Massaponax. On the Confederate left Marye's Heights rose immediately behind the town. The Confederates had cut a military road along the crest of the high ground to facilitate communication and movement from one part of the line to another. A convenient bend in the Rappahannock three miles above Fredericksburg allowed Lee's left to rest at the river. His right touched the Massaponax where it flowed into the Rappahannock, approximately three miles below the lower Federal pontoon bridges. There existed a nine-mile theoretical front for Lee to defend, but only approximately six or seven of these miles could be readily attacked. Kenneth P. Williams, believing that Lee had approximately 60,000 infantry available, estimates that the Confederates therefore had roughly six men per yard to defend the vulnerable part of their front. In *Lee's Lieutenants* Freeman computes on the basis of 68,000 Confederates but reaches the same figure of six men per yard.[39] Stuart's cavalry and horse artillery, with infantry support, anchored Lee's right in the valley of the Massaponax, occupying ground on both sides of that stream.[40]

Although Lee had no expectation of preventing the Federal crossing, he did intend to make it costly. From McLaws's division of Longstreet's corps, William Barksdale's brigade on the eleventh took position in the town and skillfully fired on the Federal bridge builders. The Federal response included bombarding Fredericksburg in an unsuccessful effort to drive off Barksdale's Mississippians. Barksdale's activities, concluded in the late afternoon, set Burnside's timetable back the better part of a day. Ultimately the bridges were completed, but the Federals mustered on the western bank of the river only after most of Lee's troops were in position. Had Sumner's troops crossed unopposed on schedule, Franklin's force could have been across at the lower site by midday and would have faced only two of Jackson's divisions.[41]

The fighting at Fredericksburg began on the Confederate right, in the sector defended by Jackson's corps. Jackson had approximately 35,000 infantry and 50 guns, including Stuart's on his right, to defend a front of about two miles.[42] His men occupied a wooded ridge that was inland from the Richmond, Fredericksburg & Potomac Railroad. The ridge was dominated by Prospect Hill. Jackson's first line of troops were those of A. P. Hill's Light Division. The divisions of Early and Taliaferro formed a second line. D. H. Hill's division, identified as the reserve, was still farther back. Jackson's formidable line was approximately one mile deep.[43] In front of Jackson was the railroad, then the Old Richmond Road, a half-mile farther east. Another 800 yards in front of A. P. Hill's men was the Rappahannock. The ground from the railroad to the river was level and open with one significant exception. Approximately 1,300 yards to the left front of Hamilton's Crossing was a wooded ravine. The base of the woods, approximately 200 yards wide, abutted the Confederate side of the railroad tracks, and the woods then extended inland.[44] The placement of A. P. Hill's line in reference to this woods represents the only significant Confederate leadership error of the day. Instead of occupying the woods at the ravine, James H. Lane's brigade of A. P. Hill's division was placed approximately 250 yards to the left of the woods, and James J. Archer's brigade was placed at the woods' right corner, leaving approximately 500 yards of unoccupied front between Lane's right and Archer's left. Maxcy Gregg's brigade of A. P. Hill's division was placed behind the woods, that is, on the Confederate side, in A. P. Hill's line.[45]

In discussing Confederate leadership, some comment is appropriate concerning who was at fault for this gap. A. P. Hill was the immediate commander. Jackson and Lee performed a reconnaissance of the Confederate line on December 12. According to Robert L. Dabney of Jackson's staff, his commander became aware of the gap on the morning of the thirteenth and

Lt. Gen. Thomas
Jonathan Jackson.
Francis Trevelyan
Miller, ed., The
Photographic History
of the Civil War, *10 vols.*
(New York: Review of
Reviews, 1911), 1:305

predicted that the Federals would attack at that point.[46] Dabney and the other
early church fathers of the Confederacy are not very reliable witnesses. Dabney's story is intended to show us that Jackson was prescient. If the story was
true, I am convinced that Jackson would have promptly plugged the gap. I am
therefore skeptical of Jackson's awareness of the gap. Its existence would seem
to be A. P. Hill's problem. Jackson and Hill were in the midst of one of their
embarrassing conflicts, and Jackson's report is plain as to the blame for the
costly struggle at the gap. He refers to "the interval which he [Hill] had left
between Archer and Lane." In any event the Federal divisions of Meade and
Gibbon assaulted the gap, penetrated the line, and presented a significant
threat to Hill's position.[47] Jubal A. Early's division, supported on his left by
General Taliaferro's brigades, drove the Federals back and pursued them to
the plain, until checked by Federal artillery. The crisis passed perhaps by 2:30
or 3:00 P.M. Conspicuous in Early's action were the brigades of A. R. Lawton
(Col. Edmund Atkinson), Early (Col. James A. Walker), and Isaac R. Trimble
(Col. Robert F. Hoke).[48]

   Both James I. Robertson, Jr., and A. Wilson Greene assert that A. P. Hill had "disappeared" all afternoon on December 13. But Hill's report, dated January 1, 1863, speaks in the first person as if he was an observer. It further refers to an "interval" in his line between Archer and Lane.[49]

That this fighting on Jackson's front was significant is indicated by casualty data. Meade lost 1,800 of his 4,500 men. For the day, Jackson's corps lost approximately 3,400 men, two-thirds of them from A. P. Hill's division.[50]

On the Confederate left, Longstreet's front, Lafayette McLaws's division of the First Corps was posted on Marye's Heights with Richard H. Anderson's division on its left. The divisions of George E. Pickett and John Bell Hood were on McLaws's right. Robert Ransom's division, initially designated the reserve of the First Corps, was then assigned to support McLaws's left in the defense of Marye's Heights. Under Longstreet's direction, the corps batteries were placed in pits. Firing trenches and abatis were added. The famous sunken road at the foot of the heights lay behind the equally famous stone wall.[51] As is well known, the Federal bloodletting on the Confederate left was severe.

In terms of leadership, even Freeman says that Longstreet "observed everything, kept his eye on everything." Several of the general's actions suggest that that was the case. Prior to the Federal assault, Longstreet noted that Cadmus M. Wilcox's brigade, on the left of Anderson's division, seemed exposed. He communicated this to Anderson but also realized that T. R. R. Cobb's brigade of McLaws's division needed to be aware of Wilcox's situation so as not to be exposed if Wilcox moved.[52] Responding to Longstreet, Joseph B. Kershaw dramatically led two of his regiments to Cobb's line as Cobb was dying and his soldiers seemed to falter. In mid-afternoon, under Longstreet's direction, E. Porter Alexander's artillery battalion and additional guns from Virginia and Louisiana batteries replaced the Washington Artillery because the latter guns were out of ammunition.[53] In short, there was no Confederate crisis on the left.

December 13 closed on a scene of utter defeat for the Federals. Federal losses were more than 12,500 men, in excess of 11 percent of Burnside's force.[54] As I have said, it was an accidental battle, brought on in the final analysis by Burnside's insistence on crossing the river and attacking in the face of the Confederate army, which was almost ideally positioned to defend. The Federals did not resume their attacks. They recrossed the river on the night of the fifteenth, and the Confederates did not pursue.[55]

There was some criticism in the southern press about the absence of a counterattack or pursuit by the Confederates. Jackson reported that on the thirteenth he had prepared to counterattack from the Confederate right with infantry following artillery. He waited until late in the evening so that if the move were unsuccessful, his retreat would be "under the cover of night." He reported further that "the first gun had hardly moved forward from the wood 100 yards when the enemy's artillery responded, and so completely swept our front as to satisfy me that the proposed movement should be abandoned."[56] I see no reason to doubt Jackson's judgment.

In his article in *Battles and Leaders* Longstreet addressed the issue of pursuit:

> It has been asked why we did not follow up the victory. The answer is plain. It goes without saying that the battle of the First Corps, concluded after nightfall, could not have been changed into offensive operations. Our line was about three miles long, extending through woodland over hill and dale. An attempt at concentration to throw the troops against the walls of the city at that hour of the night would have been little better than madness. The Confederate field was arranged for defensive battle. Its abrupt termination could not have been anticipated, nor could any skill have marshaled our troops for offensive operations in time to meet the emergency. My line was long and over broken country,—so much so that the troops could not be promptly handled in offensive operations.

Lee also responded persuasively to the point in his report, part of which has been set forth at the beginning of this paper. He wrote:

> The attack on the 13th had been so easily repulsed, and by so small a part of our army, that it was not supposed the enemy would limit his efforts to an attempt, which, in view of the magnitude of his preparations and the extent of his force, seemed to be comparatively insignificant. Believing, therefore, that he would attack us, it was not deemed expedient to lose the advantages of our position and expose the troops to the fire of his inaccessible batteries beyond the river, by advancing against him; but we were necessarily ignorant of the extent to which he had suffered, and only became aware of it when, on the morning of the 16th, it was discovered that he had availed himself of the darkness of night, and the prevalence of a violent storm of wind and rain, to recross the river.[57]

*Lt. Gen. James
Longstreet.
Robert Underwood
Johnson and Clarence
Clough Buel, eds.,*
Battles and Leaders of
the Civil War, *4 vols.
(New York: Century,
1887–88), 3:254*

I have been critical of Lee's generalship because of his offensive grand strategic sense of the war, his aggressiveness.[58] He believed that the Confederacy could win the war by defeating the Federal armies, by militarily overpowering the North. This is what he said he believed; this was the thrust of the way he directed his army. In my view, Lee was wrong. The South simply did not have the strength to win the war militarily. Its only chance to win was to prolong the war and make it so costly to the North that the northern people would give it up. The analogy, of course, is Washington's strategy during the Revolution. It is the strategy of wearing the other side out, of winning by not losing. It would have required Lee to embrace a strategically defensive strategy, undertaking only occasional promising offensive moves, and thereby conserving his outnumbered and limited manpower. Instead of this grand strategy, Lee was typically on the strategic offensive in 1862 and 1863. He also directed Jubal Early to fight offensively in the Valley in 1864. Lee's actions, no matter how brilliantly conducted and whether his battles were won or lost, led to his heavy, disproportionate, and irreplaceable casualties that ultimately resulted in his being besieged. They destroyed the viability of his army. His leadership was therefore destructive to the Confederacy.

Having in mind the foregoing, my opinion is that Fredericksburg was Lee's most intelligent and well-fought battle during 1862 and 1863. In the first place, unlike Second Manassas and Antietam and Gettysburg, for example, it was not borrowed trouble, an inevitably costly offensive campaign. Burnside's plan posed a genuine immediate threat to Richmond and to Lee's army. Strategically, it was necessary for Lee to frustrate that plan.

Second, Lee suppressed his risky and Napoleonic bent, his costly aggressiveness. He accepted the strategic and tactical defensive and was not only highly successful but also did not suffer the massive and disproportionate casualties that frequently marked his battles. His casualties were 4,600 men, 6.4 percent of his force, as opposed to Burnside's 12,500, 11.8 percent of his force. General Pendleton commented in his report that the "loss of valuable life [was] so much less than usual."[59]

Lee also planned carefully, taking excellent advantage of the bastions that Burnside's actions had provided him. He seems to have taken personal charge of the wise placement of his army. To me, it was Lee at his best.

Ironically, the Confederate victory at Fredericksburg had very different meanings for Lee and Longstreet. Longstreet deemed the battle a success, and it was a factor in persuading Longstreet of the wisdom of the tactical defensive. Freeman identifies Longstreet as "an unqualified advocate of a tactical defensive by the Army of Northern Virginia." Lee, on the other hand, was disappointed with Fredericksburg. To his wife he wrote on December 16 that the Federals "suffered heavily as far as the battle went, but it did not go far enough to satisfy me. Our loss was comparatively slight. . . . The contest will have now to be renewed." Freeman writes at some length of Lee's and Jackson's chagrin that there had not been more to Fredericksburg, quoting Lee as having later written, "We had really accomplished nothing; we had not gained a foot of ground, and I knew the enemy could easily replace the men he had lost."[60] Fredericksburg, in short, did not mute Lee's commitment to the Armageddon theory of battle and the offensive, strategically and tactically.

The differences between Lee and Longstreet surfaced in Pennsylvania in 1863, with Longstreet referring expressly to Fredericksburg to support his objection to Lee's offensive tactics at Gettysburg. After the war, Longstreet commented that in discussing tactical options in Pennsylvania he called Lee's "attention to the Battle of Fredericksburg as an instance of defensive warfare, where we had thrown not more than five thousand troops into the fight and had beaten off two-thirds of the Federal army with great loss to them and slight loss to my own troops."[61]

Descartes wrote that "a thousand questions do not make a doubt." Longstreet learned that one question, or maybe two or three, would bar him from the pantheon of the cult of the Lost Cause.

Notes

1. U.S. War Department, *The War of the Rebellion: A Compilation of the Official Records of the Union and Confederate Armies*, 127 vols., index, and atlas (Washington, D.C.: GPO, 1880–1901), 19(2):579, 21:555 (hereafter cited as *OR*; all references are to series 1).

2. Thomas L. Livermore, *Numbers and Losses in the Civil War in America, 1861–1865* (1901; reprint, Dayton, Ohio: Morningside, 1986), 92–93, 88–89.

3. *OR* 19(1):143, (2):627.

4. Douglas Southall Freeman, *Lee's Lieutenants: A Study in Command*, 3 vols. (New York: Charles Scribner's Sons, 1942–44), 2:250.

5. *OR* 19(2):643.

6. *OR* 21:538–45, 19(2):683.

7. *OR* 21:82–83.

8. *OR* 19(2):552.

9. *OR* 21:83, 550–51.

10. *OR* 21:83.

11. *OR* 19(2):552.

12. *OR* 19(2):553, 572.

13. *OR* 21:84–85.

14. *OR* 21:1021.

15. *OR* 21:549.

16. James Longstreet, "The Battle of Fredericksburg," in *Battles and Leaders of the Civil War*, ed. Robert Underwood Johnson and Clarence Clough Buel, 4 vols. (New York: Century, 1887–88), 3:71–72 (hereafter cited as *B&L*).

17. *OR* 21:101–2.

18. *OR* 19(2):717.

19. *OR* 21:1013–14.

20. *OR* 21:1014–16.

21. *OR* 21:1017, 1019.

22. *OR* 21:1021–22.

23. *OR* 21:1026–28.

24. *OR* 21:1029.

25. *OR* 21:1031–32.

26. *OR* 21:1033–35, 1037. This road had three names at the time: the Old Richmond Road, the Bowling Green Road, and the Port Royal Road. In this essay, it is called the Old Richmond Road.

27. *OR* 21:1042–43.

28. *OR* 21:1049–50.

29. *OR* 21:85.

30. *OR* 21:103.

31. *OR* 21:85, 798.

32. Kenneth P. Williams, *Lincoln Finds a General: A Military Study of the Civil War*, 5 vols. (New York: Macmillan, 1949–59), 2:508.

33. *OR* 21:87.

34. *OR* 21:106–7.

35. *OR* 21:88–89.

36. *OR* 21:622, 630, 663, 643, 1057.

37. *OR* 21:546.

38. Longstreet, "Battle of Fredericksburg," 73.

39. Williams, *Lincoln Finds a General*, 2:527; Freeman, *Lee's Lieutenants*, 2:341 n. 17.

40. *OR* 21:547.

41. Freeman, *Lee's Lieutenants*, 2:336–38; *OR* 21:546, 552.

42. *OR* 21:1057, 636.

43. *OR* 21:630–31, 643.

44. The distances are from Freeman, *Lee's Lieutenants*, 2:341–42.

45. Ibid., 2:342–43; *OR* 21:631–32.

46. Freeman, *Lee's Lieutenants*, 2:343, 347; Douglas Southall Freeman, *R. E. Lee: A Biography*, 4 vols. (New York: Charles Scribner's Sons, 1934–35), 2:450–51.

47. *OR* 21:632, 511, 480.

48. *OR* 21:547, 554, 664.

49. *OR* 21:645–48.

50. *OR* 21:140, 635.

51. *OR* 21:568–70; Freeman, *Lee's Lieutenants*, 2:359–65.

52. Freeman, *Lee's Lieutenants*, 2:364; *OR* 21:611–13; William Miller Owen, "A Hot Day on Marye's Heights," in *B&L*, 3:97–98.

53. *OR* 21:570, 588–89, 571.

54. Livermore, *Numbers and Losses*, 96.

55. *OR* 21:95.

56. *OR* 21:634.

57. Longstreet, "Battle of Fredericksburg," 82–83; *OR* 21:555.

58. Alan T. Nolan, *Lee Considered: General Robert E. Lee and Civil War History* (Chapel Hill: University of North Carolina Press, 1991), 59–106.

59. Livermore, *Numbers and Losses*, 96; *OR* 21:567.

60. Freeman, *Lee's Lieutenants*, 3:45–46; Robert E. Lee, *The Wartime Papers of R. E. Lee*, ed. Clifford Dowdey and Louis H. Manarin (Boston: Little, Brown, 1961), 365; Freeman, *R. E. Lee*, 2:472–73.

61. Freeman, *Lee's Lieutenants*, 3:46–47; James Longstreet, "Lee's Invasion of Pennsylvania," in *B&L*, 3:247.

It Is Well That War Is So Terrible

THE CARNAGE AT FREDERICKSBURG

GEORGE C. RABLE

During the battle of Fredericksburg, Robert E. Lee remarked to James Longstreet, "It is well that war is so terrible—we should grow too fond of it!"[1] Well
might Lee have exulted over the Army of Northern Virginia's success that day.
On the right, Stonewall Jackson's forces had thrown back a Union assault that
for a time had seriously penetrated the Confederate line, while on the left,
Longstreet's artillery and infantry had repulsed a series of Federal assaults
toward Marye's Heights. Union casualties had been extremely heavy, but the
Confederates had also been bloodied, and to most soldiers it must have been
the first part of Lee's statement that told the essential truth about Fredericksburg.

All large Civil War engagements and many minor ones were "terrible" in
many respects, but the name *Fredericksburg* soon evoked extraordinary images of horror—especially for the Army of the Potomac. Fought on a day
less than two weeks before Christmas following a bitterly cold night during
which many regiments had bivouacked without fires, Fredericksburg seemed
much like mass murder, a great bloodletting with uncertain results and, if
one dared think it, no purpose at all.

As they surveyed the field and later compiled casualty reports and com-
mendations for the gallant men who had fallen, even Lee's generals must have
realized the truth of the old maxim that the next worst thing to losing a battle
is winning a battle. Like much Civil War combat, Fredericksburg proved
deadly to humble privates and general officers alike. While rallying his men
against George Gordon Meade's advancing Federals who had poured through
a gap between James J. Archer's and James H. Lane's brigades, Brig. Gen.
Maxcy Gregg was struck by a minié ball that lodged near his spine. Taken to a
nearby house, Gregg learned from a surgeon that his wound was mortal. With
a quiet nobility this ardent southern rights man accepted the grim news.

Brig. Gen. Maxcy Gregg.
Robert Underwood
Johnson and Clarence
Clough Buel, eds.,
Battles and Leaders of
the Civil War, *4 vols.*
(New York: Century,
1887–88), 3:72

Hoping to set right some minor dispute, Gregg asked that Stonewall Jackson pay him a visit. Appearing in the early morning hours of December 14, Jackson tried to ease Gregg's mind over any past differences and urged him to "turn your thoughts to God and to the world to which you go." With tear-filled eyes, Gregg quietly thanked Jackson for his kindness. In great pain, Gregg nevertheless strove to avoid crying out or showing any emotion save resignation to his fate. A chaplain from the 12th South Carolina Regiment read him the 138th Psalm containing the promise that the Lord would "stretch out thy hand against the wrath of my enemies, and thy right hand delivers me." Gregg died the following day.[2]

Writing to South Carolina governor Francis Pickens, Lee praised Gregg's "disinterested patriotism and . . . unselfish devotion" and hoped that other South Carolinians would follow his example.[3] In this brief dispatch Lee could hardly grapple with larger questions of meaning, and it was up to Gregg's eulogist, the Reverend Benjamin Morgan Palmer, to expound on the significance of the general's life and death. At the funeral service held at a Presbyterian church in Columbia, South Carolina, on December 20, 1862, this prominent spokesman for Confederate civil religion extolled Gregg's classical virtues. According to Palmer, a perfectly balanced character typified the Palmetto State's leadership class. Thus Gregg was a "true man" whose "courage, honesty, and strength were tempered with the softer graces of gentleness and love." He appeared as an exemplary Roman hero "incapable of falsehood" with a finely tuned sense of justice, a "polished and courtly gentleman" whose quiet reticence concealed the inner core of a strong personality. Indeed, this one-time nullifier, fire-eating politician, and soldier had a gentler, more contemplative side. Although his hands were "strong in the great battle of life," the mighty warrior could "love with a woman's heart at home." Preferring the scholarly repose of his study to "the low, material pleasures" of the world, Gregg "drank in the wisdom of the past" while spurning both low cunning and unseemly ambition. An unwavering commitment to state sovereignty had never been sullied by party intrigue, and he had died defending lifelong principles.

To Palmer, Gregg's death held a twofold significance. His example would convince others to sacrifice their comfort because "the privations and hardships we undergo are nothing, when weighed against the precious blood which has been shed to purchase freedom to our land." Equally important, Gregg had fallen in a holy cause. Admitting that the general had never made a formal profession of religious faith, Palmer assured his audience that Gregg had expressed interest in spiritual matters and had no doubt privately shown a devotion to his creator. Such a life should inspire his fellow soldiers and all Confederates to redouble their efforts in the Lord's war against a "bold and infidel fanaticism [that] has undertaken to impeach the morality of God's administration, and with reckless blasphemy denounces as profligate the government of the universe."[4] If Gregg's life seemed to embody more stoic than Christian virtues, and this sermon could not entirely reconcile the tensions between the two, Palmer had shown how eulogists helped define the significance of suffering and death in this war.

As Yankee and rebel alike struggled to make sense of seemingly senseless carnage, their efforts also revealed persistent sectional differences. Maj. Sidney Willard of the 35th Massachusetts had been wounded on the afternoon of December 13 while leading his regiment during the advance of Edward Ferrero's brigade toward the Confederate rifle pits to the right of the stone wall. At first refusing to take whiskey to ease his pain, this pious New Englander died on December 14.

In a memorial tribute delivered at West Church in Boston on December 21, Cyrus Augustus Bartol offered an appropriate Yankee counterpoint to Palmer's eulogy of Maxcy Gregg. As if responding directly to the southern minister's exaltation of the Confederate struggle for liberty, Bartol maintained that Willard—"a good husband . . . a good soldier, a good Christian, a good man"—fell a martyr to the cause of civil and religious freedom. A young man raised in the church, a flawless student who would leave a room in disgust whenever he heard foul language, Willard was nevertheless compassionate toward weaker colleagues who yielded to the temptations of strong drink. When the war began, he had bravely marched south to free the slaves, fully realizing that the struggle for equal rights was far from over in the North. Like the life of Maxcy Gregg, the life of Sidney Willard was meant to inspire young people to deeds of valor.[5]

Celebrations of dead heroes with all their sectional nuances helped each side clarify their political, cultural, and even spiritual identities while promoting internal unity and patriotism. Yet such ceremonies and speeches could not entirely explain and could hardly relieve the agony of civil war in general and the terrors of December 1862 in particular.

Although the ordeals experienced by the soldiers in the Fredericksburg campaign were similar to those of many other men at other times and places, its particular combination of monstrous slaughter, intense pain, raw courage, and pointless sacrifice left an indelible impression on many participants and sent shock waves into the cities, towns, and rural communities of the divided United States. Any major battle leaves its physical and psychological marks on the immediate vicinity and the local inhabitants, but the flight of refugees from Fredericksburg and the shelling of the town on December 11 seemed an especially dramatic example of how the war could suddenly disrupt the routine lives of countless people.

There had been a few stubborn souls or those who simply had no place to go who had remained in their homes as the Federals prepared their artillery barrage. A minister's wife and her three children huddled in a house hit eight times by shells but were miraculously unharmed. Confederate soldiers could see the town burning as old men, women, and children tried to flee at the last instant. This war against the innocent and helpless, claimed one Richmond editor, punctured northern pretensions about fighting for the best government on earth. In his view the destruction of Fredericksburg became the "most unprovoked and wanton exhibition of brutality that has yet disgraced the Yankee army."[6] Given common Confederate assumptions about the character of their enemies, that was quite an accomplishment.

For outraged Confederates, however, the shelling of the town was by no means the crowning infamy. The subsequent looting of homes and businesses was even more appalling. Not only did the Federals swarm about scavenging for food, but they ran through the streets carrying pieces of furniture and all manner of household goods. Taking particular relish at sacking any home that might be loosely termed a mansion, they set about their work with a grim efficiency. Smashing pianos with axes, cutting pictures from their frames, ripping open beds, shattering mirrors, and scattering private libraries outdoors, the soldiers struck at the intimate recesses of private life. After eagerly consuming any liquor they could find, the men cavorted about sporting everything from beaver hats to a necklace fashioned from custard cups. Dresses, jewelry, paintings, and even beehives became fair game. Some Federals were appalled by the frenzied looting, but halfhearted attempts to stop it had little effect.[7] The Yankee plunderers, claimed the Richmond Enquirer, had stooped to burning Bibles. With an exaggeration remarkable even by the expansive rhetorical standards of the mid-nineteenth century, another editor called the sack of Fredericksburg "the most infamous crime ever perpetrated upon this continent." Wanton destruction became not only a powerful theme in Confederate propaganda but yet further proof that the true Yankee was a "compound of cant, cunning, treachery, avarice, cruelty, and cowardice." Indeed the crushing defeat of the Federals on December 13 seemed suitable retribution for this "barbarous horde of Bedouin Arabs."[8] Vengeance—or what many Confederates would have deemed divine justice—therefore helped explain the course and results of battle.

Even the most bloodthirsty, however, could not have foreseen such a massive slaughter. Officers and soldiers alike would later strain for words to describe the fighting of December 13, and especially the repeated Federal charges against the stone wall. "We marched up a Shower of Shot and Shell, from the rebels artillery and Muskerey," a New Jersey soldier recounted, "and a horied Sight it Was to See Men moed down by the dozens." Death came suddenly. Moving forward under heavy Confederate artillery fire, the commander of the 21st Massachusetts suddenly noticed the regimental color-bearer on the ground with both arms blown away. After his right arm had been shot off, a corporal in the 20th Maine crisply saluted Lt. Col. Joseph Frazer and asked permission to head for the rear. To soldiers on both sides, the advance of Brig. Gen. Thomas F. Meagher's Irish Brigade became an unforgettable sight. As rebel artillery raked Meagher's line, a Confederate saw "red flashes in the white gloom of a pearly powder cloud." Then came the "crackle of rifles like a thousand packs of Chinese crackers, and from that ghastly gulf of flame but few of the boys in blue reappeared."[9] The combination of courage and carnage impressed Confederates, many of whom retained images of the raw bravery exhibited by the Federals. One artillerist recalled a Union color-bearer who advanced beyond the point where his comrades had given way before falling with a mortal wound. "He was, doubtless, killed in conformity with the usages of civilized warfare," stated this man. "Nevertheless we were sorry to see him fall, and the body of that dead enemy, lying beside the flag he had so bravely carried, formed an image which rose far above that of the living who had killed him."[10]

So rapidly did men fall that the survivors from regiments involved in the hottest fighting seemed less inclined to recall much less describe the deaths of individual soldiers. Whole companies, regiments, and even brigades scattered or dissolved in front of the stone wall. The killing and wounding of so many field officers in a short period not only caused these attacks to falter but also greatly hampered those units that mounted later assaults. In the late afternoon, as Andrew A. Humphreys's division made their charge, the men tried to move through the shattered ranks of several brigades lying on the ground. Badly demoralized soldiers obstructed their advance, and many shouted wildly that Humphreys's troops would all be slaughtered.[11] Somehow stock phrases in the battle reports such as "galling fire" could hardly describe the experience for thousands of Union soldiers thrown against what many termed a Confederate "sheet" of flame.

The following day, December 14—a day of supposedly light skirmishing—

stretched human endurance to the breaking point and beyond. For the Federals who had been ordered into the fighting late the previous day, a new terror awaited. Those brigades closest to the Confederate lines on the Union right had to lie on the ground or risk being picked off by Confederate sharpshooters. "Unable to eat, drink, or attend to the calls of nature," one officer reported, even wounded men and stretcher bearers were hit. Raising a head or an arm drew fire instantly. Most of the men pressed themselves to the ground behind a small rise that offered little more than half a foot of protection as minié balls and canister whizzed over their heads. According to a soldier in the 84th Pennsylvania, the men dared not turn on their side to get a piece of hardtack from their haversacks. Little wonder that several officers later praised the discipline and nerves of men forced to remain in such uncomfortable and hazardous positions for more than twenty-four hours.[12]

Those troops not pinned down by enemy fire mingled with the survivors from the previous day's fighting. Remnants of brigades and regiments searched for surviving comrades, tried to find their commanders, or helped carry the innumerable stretchers to the makeshift hospitals in town. A Rhode Island soldier whose regiment had been lightly engaged observed the shattered elements of the Irish Brigade wandering about the streets. Ambrose E. Burnside himself clasped the hand of General Meagher and wept.[13]

Aside from the defeat, there had been and would be much to weep about during the entire Fredericksburg campaign. Battle histories typically concentrate on strategy and tactics while ignoring the rigors of campaigning and neglecting the human aftermath of major engagements. Even before the battle, short rations and cold weather had made many men on both sides too sick for marching—much less fighting—as various camp diseases, especially chronic diarrhea, took a heavy toll. The worst dysentery cases had been transferred to Washington hospitals where the men often lingered for weeks, emaciated bodies waiting for death. Autopsies revealed badly inflamed intestines and ulcerated colons along with numerous adhesions and irregularities in mucous membranes—all grim reminders of how unhealthy war could be before any shots were fired. By the time of Fredericksburg many regiments were below strength, and even as men were being killed on the battlefield, others struggled against the ravages of disease. Cpl. Samuel W. George of the 12th New Hampshire had left a wife and eight-month-old twins at home in Concord. Nearly six feet tall with black hair and dark complexion, this once-vigorous thirty-six-year-old fell seriously ill in December. Forced to stay in camp during the fighting on December 13, he could do little but think of home. Several days later, in his final moments of life, he managed to raise himself in bed for one last look at the cherished pictures of his wife and children.[14]

From the camps to the battlefield, during the night of December 13 and for the following several days, death was everywhere. Although combat experience eventually inured soldiers to the sight of dead bodies, that could not be said of the men at Fredericksburg.[15] The numbers of the slain alone were depressing enough. Looking over the ground from about fifty yards in front of the stone wall to the outskirts of town, a Confederate could see "acres" of dead Federals. In several places bodies were piled three deep or higher. At the corner of one house a soldier in the 15th Massachusetts found twenty bodies lying together. One observer claimed that a person could walk in front of the stone wall from one end to the other across Union corpses without touching the ground.[16]

On closer examination the dead appeared to have suffered every conceivable wound. Some had been shot through the head with musket balls; others were mangled beyond recognition by artillery shells. Body parts lay scattered across the field; a sergeant in the 26th New Jersey found "some of the dead . . . mashed into one complete jelly, their remains stringing over a distance of five yards." Of the more than 15,000 soldiers eventually buried in the national cemetery at Fredericksburg (many of whom fell in later battles), only 2,487 were identified. Some of the bodies were badly charred, and some of the wounded had burned to death when grass had caught fire from exploding shells. A curious rebel private stumbled across a tragic coincidence: a Yankee father and son who had both been killed lying peacefully beside each other. Soldiers writing to their home folks might begin describing these scenes but then thought better of it.[17]

Although the burial of the dead was always a grim and unpleasant task that many men avoided, again Fredericksburg held its own horrors. As they picked their way across the field on the night of December 14, Joshua Lawrence Chamberlain and several members of the 20th Maine found men "torn and broken and cut to pieces in every conceivable way." Dead and not quite dead horses lay among smashed ammunition chests and overturned gun carriages. Chamberlain's patrol nervously dug shallow graves with bayonets

Federal burial parties after the battle.
Editor's collection

and shell fragments, using musket butts or small pieces of board with names and hometowns carved on them as markers. Chamberlain later remembered getting little sleep that night.[18] Few of the dead, however, received this much attention. The cold weather made burial difficult, and a Confederate major found several bodies frozen to the ground. Many of the slain were dumped unceremoniously into trenches. As these hasty interments were taking place, a ghoulish entrepreneur distributed a "Notice to Soldiers" extolling the virtues of a new process for "embalming the dead."[19]

The reports and rumors of death quickly spread beyond the battlefield. Visiting his wounded brother in the camp of the 51st New York near Falmouth more than a week after the battle, Walt Whitman watched men carrying stretchers out each morning and then burying sick or wounded soldiers

January 5, 1863, a high fever had developed along with profuse sweating and nausea. After the man died on January 14, an autopsy revealed that infection had spread throughout the body. Although some amputations were quite successful and recovery rapid, the battle against gangrene could continue for several months. In cases where more careful or cautious surgeons managed to save wounded arms and legs, they often lost the patient anyway.[26]

Many of the wounded died in the field hospitals—if they made it there; others survived for several days but were beyond help. By the time Pvt. W. J. D. Parks of the 123rd Pennsylvania, who had been hit in the right knee during a charge toward the stone wall, was sent to a Washington hospital, he was far too feeble to withstand an operation. Anemic and feverish, he died on December 28. If operations were performed, infections proved deadly. The removal of minié balls was only partially successful because the wounds had already been contaminated by lint or other foreign matter used to bind the wounds. Surgery often failed to stop internal bleeding. By this time, ether or chloroform was commonly used, though patients occasionally died from the shock of anesthesia. But even with these problems, medical treatment in the Army of the Potomac had greatly improved since the beginning of the war.[27]

Newspaper correspondent Noah Brooks watched the Fredericksburg wounded arriving in Washington by the hundreds. "Faces grimed and blackened with smoke and powder, ragged, disheveled, and dropping with fatigue and weakness," men with mangled faces, without fingers, or without arms were "creeping, shuffling, limping, and hobbling along" toward the hospitals. Stretcher bearers in a long line carried the most seriously wounded. The predominant emotion of these men was undoubtedly fear because the dread of military hospitals haunted Civil War soldiers. With little faith in doctors and susceptible to wild suspicions, they endured poor food and sometimes indifferent care. Worse, some of the men replayed the battle over and over in their minds. A New Jersey soldier, who had suffered a mild knee wound, feverishly raved, grabbed a nurse's arm, and kept trying to dodge artillery shells. According to Louisa May Alcott, the man could not lie still and would let forth an "incessant stream of defiant shouts, whispered warnings, and broken laments," all the while calling out for a wounded friend who had probably died on the way to Washington.[28]

The anguish of men who faced a lingering death seemed in many ways the most pathetic to doctors and nurses who felt medically and spiritually powerless. Patients appeared to improve but then would slowly sink as infection ravaged their bodies. Some lived through late January, or into early February, or even until April 1863. A twenty-six-year-old private in the 16th Maine had been hit by a shell fragment in the right arm and a minié ball in the left arm during the assault of John Gibbon's division against the Confederate right. On December 14 a field hospital surgeon amputated both arms. Admitted to a Washington hospital on December 23, the private had a good appetite, was in good spirits, and appeared to be healing well. After two weeks, however, he developed a "slight chill," grew restless, and at times became delirious. Stimulants, changes in diet, and the draining of abscesses had little effect. He could no longer control his bowels, and the first signs of gangrene appeared in early February. Heavy sweats began, delirium continued, and death came on February 22. Because many of these men had been in such poor health before the battle, a combination of shock, infection, and general debility gradually proved fatal. In the most heart-rending cases, mothers, wives, or sisters arrived at the hospital just in time to see their loved one's corpse being carried out.[29]

Even in a crowded hospital these soldiers sometimes appeared as solitary sufferers, confronting death alone and without religious comfort. Brave endurance and quiet appreciation for a drink of water or a kind word impressed the nurses. One young man told Louisa May Alcott and Hannah Ropes that "I think I must be marching on" and then quietly died. Such soldiers epitomized the ideal of stoic courage so greatly admired by both civilians and soldiers. Many of these men obviously longed for death, and Hannah Ropes believed that some actually made up their minds to die. Although hospital chaplains and nurses might speak of life as a sacred gift from God, prolonged suffering strained faith and made the severely wounded impatient for death.[30]

For soldiers who survived their wounds, recovery could be lengthy and incomplete, and few students of the Civil War have paid much attention to the lasting physical—not to mention psychological—consequences of battles. Suffering from a liver wound that healed slowly, Pvt. A. J. Rogers of the 27th Connecticut received treatment at several hospitals before finally being discharged from the service with half disability on June 9, 1863. Soldiers battling the effects of an amputation and infection were bedridden for months. In all too many cases their condition was permanently disabling. Abdominal wounds healed incompletely and abscesses kept developing. Paralysis was commonplace, and many veterans lost the use of hands, arms, or legs. Limbs ached or became inflamed, often necessitating additional operations years after the original injury. On three occasions between 1872 and 1874 a doctor examined an ex-private from the 7th Michigan who had received an amputation at the right ankle joint. Finding that the end of the bone sometimes became painfully exposed and that discharges from the stump persisted, he recommended an amputation at the knee.[31] Whether this hapless sufferer consented to another operation is unknown, but such long-term problems only made the carnage harder to comprehend and to justify.

The pervasiveness of death and injury deeply affected the soldiers and disrupted the rhythms of civilian life. Even so great a triumph as Fredericksburg, observed one Richmond editor, brought devastating losses to many homes and also showed that sorrow was the common lot of all humanity. Such grim, philosophical musings echoed across the land. "The peculiar feature of war," John Haley of the 17th Maine wryly remarked, "is that each person expects *someone else* to fall."[32] Both Yankees and rebels developed complex ways of coming to terms with their experiences. Unspoken assumptions evolved into elaborate explanations as each side offered various interpretations of Fredericksburg and its significance.

To ardent Confederates this victory confirmed faith in southern virtue while reinforcing images of the Yankees as a merciless, barbaric foe. "Many of the vandal horde now lie on or beneath the soil that . . . they sought to desecrate," a North Carolina soldier informed his cousin. Those men who would shell a city and make war on helpless women and children deserved to die by the thousands, but such crimes hardly plumbed the depths of northern villainy. Despite the brave charges of several divisions, one newspaper claimed that soldiers with bayonets had had to drive the cowardly Federals into battle. Yankees pretending to surrender instead treacherously fired at their captors, and some of their troops reportedly used a newly developed poisoned bullet designed to spread deadly infection.[33]

According to Brig. Gen. James H. Lane, the "Yankee wretches" had cruelly dragged off a badly wounded lieutenant from the 37th North Carolina. Although the Federals also claimed that their wounded had been abused, the Confederates linked such tales more effectively to common assumptions about enemy savagery and their conviction that such unworthy foes were bound to be defeated.[34] Reports on the behavior of northern troops during and after the battle only strengthened beliefs already firmly held. The seeming indifference of Federals to their own dead was consistent with Confederate ideas of Yankee character. What a Virginia cavalryman termed "inhuman fiends" left their friends unburied or simply dumped the bodies into hastily dug burial trenches.[35]

Besides the obvious exaggerations and fabrications, such accounts also demonstrated how the war disturbed customary notions of civilized behavior. During the late afternoon and evening of December 13 and continuing on the following day, terrified Union soldiers used the bodies of dead comrades as a sort of human breastworks. Desperate to escape the slaughter, they crouched behind and then slept among the dead; a Massachusetts soldier remarked on the "peculiar dull thud" of bullets striking "the dead flesh." Although Confederates claimed to be appalled at such barbarism, they would quickly adapt themselves to the increasing cruelty and ferocity of a war that proved to be no respecter of moral conventions.[36] Honor itself would have to be redefined.

After all, the rebels themselves stripped the Yankee dead of guns, ammunitions, food, uniforms, and even underwear. Southern soldiers admitted the plundering and justified their actions with pleas of necessity. Had not the army been on short rations for several months, not to mention suffering from a chronic shoe shortage? A rebel artilleryman pitied his fallen foes but also knew that "these dead fellows, were the *very* men, who a few days ago, burned houses and drove old men, women, and mothers with infants at the breast, and little children into a December night to die of cold and hunger."[37] For their part the Federals seethed over the pillaging of their fallen men, and a pugnacious artillery officer briefly opened fire on some scavenging Confederates. Several northern newspapers reported the stripping of the Union dead, but any resulting public outrage was drowned out by the general dismay that set in as news spread of the stunning Federal defeat and the heavy casualties.[38]

Rather than dwell on enemy atrocities, many northerners—whether soldiers or civilians—dealt with the carnage by searching for scapegoats. As commander of the Army of the Potomac, Ambrose E. Burnside naturally came in for more than his share of condemnation. Even while chatting with Confederates during a burial truce, several Federal officers sharply criticized their commander. In their often ungrammatical but articulate way the enlisted men were even blunter. "This batel Was the grates Slaughter or the Most Masterly pease of Boothchery that has hapend during the Ware and not athing accomppehsed," wrote one disgruntled soldier. A member of the famous Iron Brigade felt "perfect contempt . . . for the man or men that run us into such a place as we have just got out of." The possibility that all this killing had served no purpose created considerable anger and resentment. During a review of the Second Corps shortly after the battle, the soldiers sullenly refused to cheer for Burnside though "a few derisive cries were heard." Whatever the newspapers might claim, the more candid Federals informed their home folks that the losses had been staggering and the hospitals were overflowing. "It was simply murder," claimed a member of the 118th Pennsylvania, "and the whole army is mad about it."[39]

Demoralization in the ranks grew. "I do not know what the people at home think of the war, but I know what the soldiers think of it," Cpl. Frank Pettit of the 100th Pennsylvania wrote to his family. "They think that fighting will never stop it and the sooner it is over the better." The usual rumors circulated and the normal grumbling occurred, but morale problems ran much deeper. Officers and men alike threatened desertion. Those who most readily despaired, such as Capt. David Jones of the 88th Pennsylvania, not only blasted Burnside but warned that the stalemate in Virginia would sap civilian and military morale alike and eventually drain away the army itself. "They aughto hang some one for this either Burnside or Halock," a bitter veteran wrote to his sister. "We fought well, except in a few instances," Walter Carter added. "The fault is our *generals* and *head officials*." No one dared question the courage (or any other supposed virtue) of the rank and file, but the more sophisticated officers tried to shift the blame away from the high command. To Emory Upton it was clear that "our defeats emanate from Washington." Meanwhile in the capital itself, indignant citizens gathered about the bulletin boards and newspaper offices as the battlefield reports trickled in, and people not only murmured against Burnside but also against General in Chief Henry W. Halleck, Secretary of War Edwin M. Stanton, and even Quartermaster Gen. Montgomery C. Meigs.[40]

Besides the denunciations of high-ranking civilian and military officials, many of these reactions carried strong political overtones. Not only had the Republicans taken a beating in the recent state and congressional elections,

*Cartoon reflecting the critical reaction to Fredericksburg in the North.
Editor's collection*

but dissatisfaction with Lincoln's cabinet and continuing debate over emancipation made the Fredericksburg debacle even more serious. While some
critics of the administration naturally blamed Burnside, others claimed that
orders from Washington had led to the disaster. "The War is a failure!" an
Albany editor bluntly asserted, and Lincoln's opponents eagerly searched for
evidence of official bungling. Democrats expected Burnside or others to
reveal how Halleck and Stanton had directed (and mismanaged) the recent
campaign. According to the *New York Herald*, "thousands of the bravest had
fallen in vain." Seeking to figure out how that "finest army that ever trod
the earth" had been defeated by a "half naked, half starved, half armed
foe," editor James Gordon Bennett faulted the War Department and the
generals. What was missing in the Army of the Potomac was not courage but
leadership.[41]

These political critiques of the campaign led to calls for George B. Mc-
Clellan's return. Many editors clung to their faith in "Little Mac" because they
had never accepted the necessity for his removal. Everyone would be satisfied

with McClellan restored to command, Bennett declared, "except the rebels, the negro-worshipers, and the two imbecile California lawyers [Halleck and Stanton] who pretend to control the War Department." Democratic papers gleefully reported that Brig. Gen. George D. Bayard, after being mortally wounded, had begged a fellow officer to "tell McClellan that my last regret, as a military man, is that I did not die serving under him."[42]

Even junior officers admitted that McClellan was still popular in the Army of the Potomac, and many believed that he would never have allowed his beloved troops to be so senselessly butchered. Those who most stridently condemned Burnside, Halleck, and Stanton joined in this chorus of recrimination. McClellan's well-known hesitancy and cautiousness were preferable to "rashness and dash," claimed a chaplain in the 5th Maine who blamed an "abolition clique" for destroying McClellan. To his fervent supporters, McClellan's problems with the Lincoln administration had originated in his respect for the Constitution and opposition to the ill-conceived Emancipation Proclamation. Democrats and even some conservative Republicans tried to forge a link between antislavery politics and the Fredericksburg disaster. Because they secretly favored disunion, Radical Republicans in both the Congress and the cabinet had supposedly plotted to ensure that neither McClellan nor Burnside had enough men and supplies to defeat rebel armies. Such editorial comments apparently gained credence among the more disheartened Union soldiers and worried the administration's staunchest friends.[43]

Because the battle of Fredericksburg was fought a little more than two weeks before Lincoln was pledged to issue a final emancipation proclamation, abolitionists naturally had to interpret the carnage in a different light or even explain it away. To antislavery veterans the dead and wounded at Fredericksburg had suffered for the cause of freedom. In a eulogy for Arthur B. Fuller, brother of famous transcendentalist Margaret Fuller and chaplain of the 16th Massachusetts, who had been killed by a rebel sharpshooter, the Reverend James Freeman Clark insisted that Fuller had died so the United States could become a country in which "there is no master and no slave." Such devotion should inspire others not merely to mouth words of sorrow for the dead or sympathy for the slave but to throw their energy and will into the fight for universal liberty.[44]

For longtime abolitionists all the blood had not been shed in vain. Despite the defeat at Fredericksburg, Gerrit Smith maintained, the slaveholders' rebellion would be crushed so long as loyal men spurned weak-kneed compromises. This show of confidence, however, seemed to require a reaffirmation of faith in Burnside. Even Napoleon had experienced setbacks like Fredericksburg, a hopeful Philadelphia editor commented. Horace Greeley wrote a series of editorials that sounded increasingly bizarre and illogical. Two days after the battle, the *New York Tribune* predicted that Burnside would soon force the Confederates into the "decisive struggle of the war." Regardless of the heavy casualties, the Union forces had at last assumed the offensive and would keep pressing the rebels. By December 19 Greeley was asserting that Burnside had "outgeneraled" Lee in withdrawing his army from Fredericksburg and was claiming that the Army of the Potomac would have easily won any battle fought on equal ground. Denying any demoralization in the ranks, on Christmas Day a *Tribune* editorial declared that aside from the casualties nothing had been lost at Fredericksburg.[45] These incredible statements well illustrate how both sides attempted to rationalize casualties throughout the war.

If the carnage had to be connected to the larger issues of the war, however, it held deeper meanings for the men most directly involved. A major battle such as Fredericksburg became more than merely a contest of strategy and tactics; it became a test of individual and collective courage. To the victorious Confederates, winning the battle proved their virtue and vindicated their cause. The men of his brigade, Col. Clement A. Evans reported, fought with a "courage characteristic of Southern soldiers." Geographically narrowing the benchmark for valor, Lt. Col. Elbert Bland of the 7th South Carolina praised his men for living up to the high standards expected of Palmetto State troops. As Gerald Linderman has pointed out, early in the Civil War many soldiers believed that courage itself would guarantee success in battle, though more broadly speaking, Confederates also maintained that courage would ensure the ultimate triumph of southern armies. Longstreet rejoiced over the Yankee invader's "humiliating retreat" and promised his men that "every such disaster to his arms brings us nearer to the happy and peaceful enjoyments of our homes and families."[46]

To individual soldiers the loss of life was even more closely associated with character in general and bravery in particular. Confederate obituaries, for instance, stressed the sterling qualities of young men who had become martyrs for southern liberty. Capt. Robert Cochrane Greene of the 21st Mississippi, according to one newspaper notice, was a man who had "won the heart of every one associated with him." Devotion, duty, and integrity: the list of virtues often grew long. Using the polarities of classical rhetoric, eulogists compared the gentleness of these young men with the violence of their deaths. Rising to heights of Victorian eloquence, ministers and officers contrasted the soaring hope of youth with its sudden and premature end.[47]

Although such statements contained much sentimental mush, they held special significance for the families and friends of the fallen while reinforcing the era's strong faith in the bonds between character and gallantry. For both armies Fredericksburg had been about courage, a courage that could be measured in reckless charges, stout defenses, and flowing blood. Casualty reports praised the extraordinary bravery of individual soldiers who had been hit by several bullets or shells. Lauding the heroism and nobility of these men, their commanding officers struggled to find some comfort in or reason for such overwhelming losses. Perhaps having proven their fortitude on many battlefields, in death these exemplary soldiers could still inspire the next generation.[48]

Naturally it was far easier for the Confederates to celebrate their fallen heroes because for the Federals the link between courage and victory had been broken. Or had it? Even in defeat such conspicuous valor as the assaults against the stone wall were noteworthy. Indeed, the strength of the Confederate positions and the horrors of the battle made the bravery of so many men all the more impressive. Pride in the Union soldiers could bolster morale at a difficult time; defective tactics could not obliterate the memory of such sacrifices.[49]

To extend this reasoning one step further, the remarkable courage displayed by the Union troops at Fredericksburg could assuage the sting of defeat and even became a substitute for victory. "In the highest sense," Walt Whitman concluded, Fredericksburg "was no failure." Whatever the implausibility of such a statement, Republicans especially tried to explain away an obvious disaster. "Although you were not successful," Abraham Lincoln claimed in a message to the Army of the Potomac, "the attempt was not an error, nor the failure other than an accident." While praising the bravery of the Federal soldiers the president had also introduced a curious element of fatalism or even luck into the discussion. What followed was even more incredible, for he congratulated the army that the number of casualties had been "so comparatively small."[50]

"Compared with what[?]" exploded the chief of artillery in John F. Reynolds's corps, who had lost faith in Burnside and perhaps in the president as well. Where was the glory for men who had died in such pointless butchery? Noting with sardonic humor the attempt by one newspaper to deny that Fredericksburg was a defeat, young Oliver Wendell Holmes, Jr., dourly concluded that slavery was only becoming stronger and that the war was probably lost. For their part, Democrats were not about to let the Lincoln administration off the hook. "As well attempt to hide the reeking graves of the soldiers under a coat of whitewash as varnish over the errors of the Generals and blunders of the Cabinet," sniffed an Albany editor. Mocking attempts by Lincoln, Greeley, and the congressional Joint Committee on the Conduct of the War to play down a serious defeat, a New York Herald editorial waspishly commented, "At this Christmas time, when good fairies fill the air, we can hardly wonder at the sudden miracle which has shown us the Fredericksburg affair in its true light, and given us occasion for national joy instead of national sorrow."[51]

Aside from understandable despair tinged with partisanship and no little sarcasm, these comments revealed more profound and serious problems. Not only had the ability of the generals, the courage of the soldiers, and even the integrity of the respective causes been sorely tried, but the Fredericksburg debacle also shook up theological convictions from camp to home front. For individuals, armies, and nations, God's role in this terrible war had become more mysterious. To what extent the suffering at Fredericksburg fit into some larger, divine plan was difficult to fathom.

Federals and Confederates had long assumed that the Almighty would not only advance their cause and help them win battles but also would protect individual soldiers. Faith and piety thus became buffers against the chaos of combat. Yet even the triumphant Confederates had to acknowledge that many Christian soldiers had fallen. Randolph Fairfax, a private in the Rockbridge Artillery, had descended from a prominent Virginia family. A dutiful child and fine student who, it was claimed, had played fairly and always obeyed his mother, he had entered high school at the age of ten. Confirmed in the Episcopalian faith at fourteen, he had shown a religious devotion and a seriousness rare in one so young. In tortured fits of conscience he had wor-

Pvt. Randolph Fairfax.
Philip Slaughter, A
Sketch of the Life of
Randolph Fairfax
(Baltimore: Innes, 1878),
frontis.

ried about studying too hard for school examinations and not preparing well enough for the last judgment. A successful student at the University of Virginia, he had also read scriptures at the local poorhouse and carefully observed the sabbath. On December 12, after being under heavy fire for two hours, Fairfax was struck by a shell fragment in the corner of the left eye and was killed instantly. Described by the Reverend Philip Slaughter as a fine soldier and model Christian, Fairfax's blameless life proved that military duty and religious piety were compatible and complementary.[52] But his death also suggested that the Lord would not necessarily safeguard even his most faithful servants in battle.

However that might be, in an evangelical culture such young men represented and continued a long tradition of Christian sacrifice. Their lives became suitable subjects for stock biographical sketches of martyrs to the faith often found in funeral sermons or pamphlets. Virginian Lewis Minor Coleman was hit in the leg on December 13 while serving with a battery on the Confederate right. His painful wound soon became infected, his body grew emaciated, and his mind wandered under the influence of opiates. Hoping to die in a way befitting a Christian soldier, after ninety-eight days of agony, on March 21, 1863, he received his wish. Like Randolph Fairfax, Coleman had been an excellent student with an "unspotted moral reputation." Yet a powerful streak of Calvinist guilt had caused him to worry about being a terrible sinner. Finally deciding that God had called him to be a teacher, in 1859 he had taken a professorship in Latin and literature at his alma mater, the University of Virginia. There he had enjoyed "chaste humor" and had become a spiritual mentor for students. Although exempted from conscription by age and occupation, he had joined an artillery company early in the war and had diligently promoted piety among the troops.[53] His example of selfless devotion to duty would presumably live on and become part of the edifying history of the war for southern independence.

By insisting that men like Fairfax and Coleman had become Christian heroes who would be long remembered by future generations, Confederate writers, preachers, and propagandists attempted to prove that out of all the carnage, some good might flow. But the theology of the situation became complicated because a powerful sense of fatalism suffused nineteenth-century religious life. The ways of God were not the ways of man; the human mind could not grasp the Almighty's larger designs. Many Christians still believed that each wound and each death manifested God's will for that individual and in a broader sense maintained that the Lord controlled the war's course. "The advantage of moral force is all on our side," declared a Richmond editor in late November 1862, and Fredericksburg only reaffirmed this faith in providential guidance. The moral and physical degeneration of the North continued while blessings on the Confederacy multiplied. Maintaining that the great Jehovah was surely punishing the Yankees for crimes against the southern people, D. H. Hill saw the "signal interposition of God" in the victory at Fredericksburg. This helped clarify how so much had been achieved by the Army of Northern Virginia at relatively small cost in human life. Although Lee referred to "divine mercy" rather than "divine favor," even "Marse Robert's" assessment of the battle contained a spiritual certitude if not spiritual hubris.[54]

In the aftermath of Fredericksburg, Federal assessments of God's relationship to the course of the war became both more painful and more complicated. After witnessing the carnage, many soldiers must have wondered if the Lord any longer looked after the brave and the virtuous. Commonplace pieties now seemed almost obscene. Shortly before his resignation as a surgeon in the 5th Wisconsin, Alfred Castleman bitingly remarked on the "pleasure . . . of our Men of God, when, at their nightly prayers they in the same breath thank . . . God for the murders we have been permitted to perpetrate— the misery to inflict—and ask for peace on earth, and good will to man." Yet some survivors maintained that a higher power had spared their lives. After being in several battles (including Fredericksburg) without suffering so much as a scratch, William Ferrell of the 105th New York still affirmed that the "Almighty God can save a man through all dangers." Such statements, however, belied difficult readjustments in popular theology. Although divine grace may have shielded him from harm, William M. Sheppard of the 24th New Jersey told his wife that "there was nothing to protect the union soldiers but the protection that Christ throwed around us when he said it is finished." Somewhat inconsistently, he also believed that the Lord's "plan of redemption" would envelop him "where the bullets were flying so thickly."[55] Traditional religious formulas retained their appeal, but the heavy casualties at Fredericksburg made even the most pious uneasy and perhaps less sure of their ability to discern God's will.

Faithful Christians on both sides attempted to understand what purpose could be served by all the suffering in what appeared to be an endless war. Working in a Washington hospital as a nurse, Hannah Ropes still saw the struggle as "God's war." Despite the sickening sights of a ward filled with amputation patients, she trusted that the cause of universal liberty was bound to triumph over the forces of slavery. "How have the mighty fallen! How disastrous are the ways of man!" intoned a Massachusetts veteran as he speculated that God might somehow be chastening the northern people. A

Georgia soldier hoped that "God would intercede and give us peace once more" but nevertheless realized that it was the Lord's will—and not man's desires—that would be fulfilled.[56] Human history remained part of a larger, slowly unfolding divine plan. Yet even for the victors, confidence in national destiny (and individual protection) became less certain, and in the North a spiritual malaise seemed to engulf soldiers and civilians.

On the night of December 14 the sounds of familiar hymns swelled across the battlefield as the Federals still worked to remove the dead and wounded. To pious soldiers the Lord reigned in the midst of defeat, suffering, and sorrow. Readily acknowledging God's continuing sovereignty over the affairs of men, Chaplain John R. Adams of the 5th Maine could not help asking why the ruler of the universe should permit the Confederates to triumph. Alarmed by accounts of religious revivals in the rebel armies, Adams speculated that northerners were surely being chastised for their sins but also doubted that the Lord would show favor to a slaveholding society's rebellion.[57]

These explanations, however, could not be entirely satisfying. The horrors of Fredericksburg threatened to overwhelm the power of human beings to rationalize their experiences and to sustain a faith in themselves, in their leaders, in their cause, and in their God. Somehow, believing that the enemy deserved to suffer, or blaming incompetent generals, or trying to sanctify a bloodbath by celebrating individual courage, or even avowing that the war continued to unfold according to some sacred blueprint no longer seemed quite adequate. Union and Confederate soldiers could agree that war was indeed terrible, but Lee need not have worried that they might "grow too fond of it."

In Fredericksburg on December 14, according to a Richmond newspaper, "a magnificent aurora borealis made its appearance just at sunset, tinging the heavens blood red."[58] What could such a dramatic but ominous symbol portend? Did the red—as this newspaper report speculated—signify the "blood of those martyrs who had offered their lives as a sacrifice to their native land," or did it commemorate the loss of so many noble men to the cause of the Union? As soldiers in both armies marveled at the natural splendor of the northern lights, and perhaps tried to discern its meaning, there could still be seen the silhouettes of the unburied dead and the now fading cries of the wounded could still be heard.

Acknowledgments

The author thanks Robert K. Krick, chief historian, Fredericksburg and Spotsylvania National Military Park, for his great assistance in locating manuscript sources for this essay.

Notes

1. Douglas Southall Freeman, *R. E. Lee: A Biography*, 4 vols. (New York: Charles Scribner's Sons, 1934–35), 2:462.

2. Douglas Southall Freeman, *Lee's Lieutenants: A Study in Command*, 3 vols. (New York: Charles Scribner's Sons, 1942–44), 2:374–76; James Power Smith, "With Stonewall Jackson in the Army of Northern Virginia," in *Southern Historical Society Papers*, ed. J. William Jones and others, 52 vols. and 2-vol. index (1877–1959; reprint, Wilmington, N.C.: Broadfoot, 1990–92), 43:34 (hereafter cited as *SHSP*); J. Monroe Anderson to "Dear Misses Gregg," January 9, 1863, Maxcy Gregg Papers, South Caroliniana Library, University of South Carolina, Columbia, S.C. (repository hereafter cited as SCL). For a thorough treatment of Gregg's background and military career, see Robert K. Krick, "Maxcy Gregg: Political Extremist and Confederate General," *Civil War History* 19 (December 1973): 293–313.

3. U.S. War Department, *The War of the Rebellion: A Compilation of the Official Records of the Union and Confederate Armies*, 127 vols., index, and atlas (Washington, D.C.: GPO, 1880–1901), 21:1067 (hereafter cited as *OR*; all references are to series 1).

4. Benjamin Morgan Palmer, *Address Delivered at the Funeral of General Maxcy Gregg in the Presbyterian Church, Columbia, S.C., December 20, 1862* (Columbia, S.C.: Southern Guardian Steam-Power Press, 1863), 3–11.

5. Cyrus Augustus Bartol, *The Nation's Hour, A Tribute to Major Sidney Willard, Delivered in the West Church, December 21* (Boston: Walker, Wise, 1862), 3–25, 46, 53, 55, 58.

6. Asa W. Bartlett, *History of the Twelfth Regiment New Hampshire Volunteers in the War of the Rebellion* (Concord, N.H.: Ira C. Evans, 1897), 405; Henry Robinson Berkeley, *Four Years in the Confederate Artillery: The Diary of Private Henry Robinson Berkeley*, ed. William H. Runge (Chapel Hill: University of North Carolina Press [for the Virginia Historical Society], 1961), 35–36; Richmond *Daily Dispatch*, December 13, 16, 1862.

7. Henry C. Mason to his father, December 17, 1862, copy, Fredericksburg and Spotsylvania National Military Park Library, Fredericksburg, Va. (repository hereafter cited as FSNMP); Charles Carleton Coffin, *Four Years of Fighting: A Volume of Personal Observations with the Army and Navy* (Boston: Ticknor and Fields, 1866), 149; Richard Tylden Auchmuty, *Letters of Richard Tylden Auchmuty, Fifth Corps, Army of the Potomac* (n.p.: Privately printed, 189[?]), 83–84; John Quinn Imholte, *The First*

Volunteers: History of the First Minnesota Regiment, 1861–1865 (Minneapolis: Ross and Haines, 1963), 108; Thomas M. Aldrich, *History of Battery A, First Regiment Rhode Island Light Artillery in the War to Preserve the Union, 1861–1865* (Providence, R.I.: Snow Farnham, 1904), 160; George H. Allen, *Forty-Six Months with the Fourth Rhode Island Volunteers* (Providence, R.I.: J. A. and R. A. Reid, 1887), 173–74; William H. Peacock to Sarah F. Monto, December 30, 1862, copy, FSNMP; Marsena Rudolph Patrick, *Inside Lincoln's Army: The Diary of Marsena Rudolph Patrick, Provost Marshal General, Army of the Potomac*, ed. David S. Sparks (New York: Thomas Yoseloff, 1964), 188–89; Catherine S. Crary, *Dear Belle: Letters from a Cadet and Officer to his Sweetheart, 1858–1865* (Middletown, Conn.: Wesleyan University Press, 1965), 175; Nancy Niblack Baxter, *Gallant Fourteenth: The Story of an Indiana Civil War Regiment* (Traverse City, Ind.: Pioneer Study Center Press, 1980), 114–15; Richmond *Daily Dispatch*, December 18, 1862; Richmond *Daily Enquirer*, December 18, 1862.

8. Richmond *Daily Enquirer*, December 22, 1862; Richmond *Daily Dispatch*, December 23, 1862.

9. Isaac Hillyer to "Deer Hariet," December 20, 1862, copy, FSNMP; *OR* 21:327; Joseph Frazer Journal, December 13, 1862, Joshua Lawrence Chamberlain Papers, Library of Congress, Washington, D.C.; "Sacrifice of the Federals at Fredericksburg," *Confederate Veteran* 1 (December 1893): 370.

10. *New York Herald*, December 17, 1862; R. Prosper Landry, "The Donaldsonville Artillery at the Battle of Fredericksburg," in *SHSP*, 23:199–202.

11. William Child, *A History of the Fifth Regiment New Hampshire Volunteers, in the American Civil War, 1861–1865* (1893; reprint, Gaithersburg, Md.: Ron R. Van Sickle Military Books, 1988), 160–61; *OR* 21:432, 436–38.

12. *OR* 21:425–27; Walt Whitman, *Walt Whitman's Civil War*, ed. Walter Lowenfels (New York: Knopf, 1961), 34; Captain Eugene Arus Nash, *A History of the Forty-Fourth Regiment New York Volunteer Infantry in the Civil War, 1861–1865* (1911; reprint, Dayton, Ohio: Morningside, 1988), 116; Auchmuty, *Letters of Auchmuty*, 83–84; Thomas Gouldsbery to his brother, December 25, 1862, copy, FSNMP. After being pinned down all day, Mathew Marvin of the 1st Minnesota wrote, "I lost a chunk of my Patriotism as large as my foot. I would do almost anything to get Shut of this most unjust & unGodly uncalled for war" (Richard Moe, *The Last Full Measure: The Life and Death of the First Minnesota Volunteers* [New York: Henry Holt, 1993], 215).

13. Allen, *Fourth Rhode Island*, 170–71.

14. *Medical and Surgical History of the War of the Rebellion*, 6 vols. (Washington, D.C.: GPO, 1875–88), vol. 1, pt. 2, pp. 117–19, 124; Bartlett, *Twelfth New Hampshire*, 704.

15. These points are most usefully discussed in Gerald F. Linderman, *Embattled Courage: The Experience of Combat in the American Civil War* (New York: Free Press, 1987), 124–28, and Joseph Allan Frank and George A. Reaves, *"Seeing the Elephant": Raw Recruits at the Battle of Shiloh* (New York: Greenwood Press, 1989), 105–8.

16. R. K. Charles, "Events in Battle of Fredericksburg," *Confederate Veteran* 14

(February 1906): 68; Allen, *Fourth Rhode Island*, 172; *OR* 21:628; James Longstreet, "The Battle of Fredericksburg," in *Battles and Leaders of the Civil War*, ed. Robert Underwood Johnson and Clarence Clough Buel, 4 vols. (New York: Century, 1887–88), 3:82 (hereafter cited as *B&L*); Heros Von Borcke, *Memoirs of the Confederate War for Independence*, 2 vols. (1866; reprint, New York: Peter Smith, 1938), 2:144–48; Walter A. Eames to his wife, December 20, 1862, Eames Papers, U.S. Army Military History Institute, Carlisle Barracks, Pa. (repository hereafter cited as USAMHI); "Battle of Fredericksburg: Recollections of It and Bombardment of the City," in *SHSP*, 19:263.

17. *New York Herald*, December 21, 1862; Francis Marion Coker to his wife, December 18, 1862, Hodgson Heidler Collection, University of Georgia, Athens, Ga.; William A. Fletcher, *Rebel Private: Front and Rear*, ed. Bell I. Wiley (Austin: University of Texas Press, 1954), 50; Robert Goldthwaite Carter, *Four Brothers in Blue; or, Sunshine and Shadows of the War of the Rebellion, A Story of the Great Civil War from Bull Run to Appomattox* (1913; reprint, Austin: University of Texas Press, 1978), 200; Alan A. Siegel, *For the Glory of the Union: Myth, Reality, and the Media in Civil War New Jersey* (Rutherford, N.J.: Fairleigh Dickinson University Press, 1984), 115; Linderman, *Embattled Courage*, 248; Annette Tapert, ed., *The Brothers' War: Civil War Letters to Their Loved Ones from the Blue and Gray* (New York: Random House, 1988), 122; Regis de Trobriand, *Four Years with the Army of the Potomac* (1889; reprint, Gaithersburg, Md.: Ron R. Van Sickle Military Books, 1988), 371–72; Harvey Hudson Hightower, "Letters from Harvey Hudson Hightower, a Confederate Soldier, 1862–1864," ed. Dewey W. Grantham, Jr., *Georgia Historical Quarterly* 40 (June 1956): 180.

18. Joshua Lawrence Chamberlain, "My Story of Fredericksburg," *Cosmopolitan* 54 (December 1912): 156; John J. Pullen, *The Twentieth Maine: A Volunteer Regiment in the Civil War* (1957; reprint, Dayton, Ohio.: Morningside, 1984), 55–56.

19. W. Roy Mason, "Notes of a Confederate Staff Officer," in *B&L*, 3:101; C. C. Cummings, "Battle of Fredericksburg, December 13, 1862," *Confederate Veteran* 23 (August 1915): 358; John Worthington Ames, "Under Fire," *Overland Monthly* 3 (1869): 439–40.

20. Whitman, *Whitman's Civil War*, 35–36; "Sacrifice of Federals at Fredericksburg," 370; *New York Tribune*, December 16, 1862; *New York Herald*, December 16, 1862; Joseph E. Grant, *The Flying Regiment: Journal of the Campaign of the 12th Regt. Rhode Island Volunteers* (Providence, R.I.: Sidney S. Rider and Brothers, 1865), 46.

21. Cornelia Peake McDonald, *A Woman's Civil War: A Diary, with Reminiscences of the War, from March 1862*, ed. Minrose C. Gwin (Madison: University of Wisconsin Press, 1992), 100; Kate Stone, *Brockenburn: The Journal of Kate Stone, 1861–1878*, ed. John Q. Anderson (Baton Rouge: Louisiana State University Press, 1955), 164–65.

22. Darius N. Couch, "Sumner's 'Right Grand Division,'" in *B&L*, 3:116; D. Watson Howe, "On the Field of Fredericksburg," in *The Annals of the War, Written by Leading Participants North and South*, ed. A. K. McClure (Philadelphia: Times Publishing, 1879), 264; Edwin B. Houghton, *The Campaigns of the Seventeenth Maine* (Portland,

Maine: Short and Loring, 1866), 33; David V. Lovell to "Sister Kattie," December 19, 1862, Lovell Letters, Coco Collection, USAMHI; Chamberlain, "My Story of Fredericksburg," 154; "Porter Farley's Reminiscences," in *Rochester in the Civil War*, ed. Blake McKelvey (Rochester, N.Y.: Rochester Historical Society Publications, No. 22, 1944), 204; Abraham Welch to his sister, December 27, 1862, Welch Letter, Southern Historical Collection, Wilson Library, University of North Carolina, Chapel Hill, N.C. (repository hereafter cited as SHC); *New York Tribune*, December 27, 1862; Thomas H. Evans, " 'The Cries of the Wounded Were Piercing and Horrible,' " *Civil War Times Illustrated* 7 (July 1968): 32–33.

23. Howe, "On the Field of Fredericksburg," 261; Aldrich, *History of Battery A*, 162–63.

24. Whitman, *Whitman's Civil War*, 236–37; Allen, *Fourth Rhode Island*, 173; de Trobriand, *Four Years*, 378–79.

25. Gordon W. Jones, "The Medical History of the Fredericksburg Campaign: Course and Significance," *Journal of the History of Medicine* 18 (July 1963): 251; Sam R. Burroughs, "Reminiscences of Fredericksburg," *Confederate Veteran* 16 (December 1908): 637; Whitman, *Whitman's Civil War*, 29; Allen, *Fourth Rhode Island*, 172–73; Alfred Lewis Castleman, *The Army of the Potomac. Behind the Scenes. A Diary of Unwritten History, from the Organization of the Army by General George McClellan, to the Close of the Campaign in Virginia, during the First Day of January, 1863* (Milwaukee: Strickland, 1863), 262.

26. *Medical and Surgical History*, vol. 2, pt. 2, pp. 748, 753, 843, pt. 3, pp. 839–41; Autopsy of George S. Rollins, 3rd Maine, n.d., copy, FSNMP.

27. James Wren, *Captain James Wren's Civil War Diary: From New Bern to Fredericksburg*, ed. John Michael Priest (Shippensburg, Pa.: White Mane, 1990), 121, 124; *Medical and Surgical History*, vol. 2, pt. 2, p. 260, pt. 3, pp. 85, 382, 716, 767, 892; Jones, "Medical History of Fredericksburg Campaign," 241–56.

28. Noah Brooks, *Mr. Lincoln's Washington: Selections from the Writings of Noah Brooks, Civil War Correspondent*, ed. P. J. Staudenraus (South Brunswick, N.J.: Thomas Yoseloff, 1967), 45–46; Linderman, *Embattled Courage*, 130–33; Louisa May Alcott, *Hospital Sketches* (Chester, Conn.: Applewood, n.d.), 45. For a provocative analysis that gives some attention to the relationship between wartime experience and religion for Confederate soldiers, see Drew Gilpin Faust, "Christian Soldiers: The Meaning of Revivalism in the Confederate Army," *Journal of Southern History* 53 (February 1987): 63–90.

29. *Medical and Surgical History*, vol. 2, pt. 2, pp. 24, 243, 293, 717, pt. 3, pp. 380, 400, 443; Philadelphia *Evening Bulletin*, January 6, 1863.

30. Alcott, *Hospital Sketches*, 35–36, 49–59, 80–83; Linderman, *Embattled Courage*, 27–28; Hannah Ropes, *Civil War Nurse: The Diary and Letters of Hannah Ropes*, ed. John R. Brumgardt (Knoxville: University of Tennessee Press, 1980), 104–5, 117–18.

31. Bartlett, *Twelfth New Hampshire*, 480; *Medical and Surgical History*, vol. 2, pt. 2, pp. 12, 146, 309, 455, 457, 847, 883, 997, pt. 3, pp. 429, 603, 625, 733–34.

32. Richmond *Daily Enquirer*, December 16, 1862; John Haley, *The Rebel Yell and the Yankee Hurrah: The Civil War Journal of a Maine Volunteer*, ed. Ruth L. Silliker (Camden, Maine: Down East Books, 1985), 60.

33. John Andrew Ramsey to "Cousin Julius," December 17, 1862, Ramsey Papers, SHC; Richmond *Daily Dispatch*, December 20, 1862; *OR* 21:670; Richmond *Daily Enquirer*, December 22, 1862.

34. *OR* 21:419, 655; Richmond *Daily Enquirer*, December 16, 1862.

35. Philip H. Powers to his wife, December 17, 1862, Powers Papers, L. Leigh Collection, USAMHI; Richmond *Daily Enquirer*, December 22, 1862; Von Borcke, *Memoirs*, 2:148–49.

36. J. L. Smith to "Dear Mother," December 26, 1862, Smith Letters, FSNMP; Carter, *Four Brothers*, 201; Richmond *Daily Enquirer*, December 18, 1862; *Richmond Daily Dispatch*, December 20, 1862; James R. Hagood, "Memoirs of the First S.C. Regiment of Volunteer Infantry," p. 98, SCL.

37. Cummings, "Battle of Fredericksburg," 358; Fletcher, *Rebel Private*, 51; Berkeley, *Four Years in the Confederate Artillery*, 38–39.

38. *OR* 21:205, 261–62; Howe, "On the Field of Fredericksburg," 265; *New York Herald*, December 19, 1862; *New York Tribune*, December 18, 1862; Baltimore *American and Commercial Advertiser*, December 23, 1862.

39. Von Borcke, *Memoirs*, 2:141; Isaac Hillyer to "Deer Hariet," December 20, 1862, copy, FSNMP; Alan T. Nolan, *The Iron Brigade: A Military History* (New York: Macmillan, 1961), 187; Henry Van Aernum to "My dearest Lis," December 17, 1862, copy, Van Aernum Papers, FSNMP; Carter, *Four Brothers*, 202; Francis A. Walker, *History of the Second Army Corps in the Army of the Potomac* (New York: Charles Scribner's Sons, 1891), 198; J. L. Smith to "Dear Mother," December 15, 1862, copy, Smith Letters, FSNMP. "Nothing but murder," agreed Maj. Henry L. Abbott of the 20th Massachusetts (Henry Livermore Abbott, *Fallen Leaves: The Civil War Letters of Major Henry Livermore Abbott*, ed. Robert Garth Scott [Kent, Ohio: Kent State University Press, 1991], 154).

40. Frederick Pettit, *Infantryman Pettit: The Civil War Letters of Corporal Frederick Pettit, Late of Company C, 100th Pennsylvania Volunteer Infantry Regiment "The Roundheads," 1862- 1864* (Shippensburg, Pa.: White Mane, 1990), 42; Davis Jones to John Jordan, Jr., December 16, 1862, copy, FSNMP; Johnny [?] to his sister, December 22, 1862, copy, FSNMP; Carter, *Four Brothers*, 210; George Washington Beidelman, *The Civil War Letters of George Washington Beidelman*, ed. Catherine H. Vanderslice (New York: Vantage, 1978), 171; Emory Upton to his sister Louisa, December 23, 1862, Harrisburg Civil War Round Table Collection, USAMHI; Brooks, *Lincoln's Washington*, 41–44. Burnside himself assumed full responsibility for the defeat, and in a letter to Halleck that was soon published, admitted that his plan for the campaign had not had enthusiastic support from Halleck, Stanton, or Lincoln (*OR* 21:67).

41. Albany *Atlas and Argus*, December 18, 1862; Siegel, *For the Glory of the Union*,

113; Baltimore *American and Commercial Advertiser*, December 25, 1862; *New York Herald*, December 16, 1862.

42. *New York Herald*, December 19, 1862, January 10, 1863; Albany *Atlas and Argus*, December 25, 31, 1862; Baltimore *American and Commercial Advertiser*, December 19, 1862; Samuel John Bayard, *The Life of George Dashell Bayard* (New York: G. P. Putnam's Sons, 1874), 320–21. A *New York Tribune* reporter, however, claimed that Bayard "died in full Anti-Slavery faith, converted on his many fields of battle" (*New York Tribune*, December 15, 1862).

43. *New York Herald*, December 17, 18, 21, 1862; Abbott, *Fallen Leaves*, 149–58; John Ripley Adams, *Memorial and Letters of Rev. John R. Adams, Chaplain of the Fifth Maine and One Hundred and Twenty-First New York Regiments during the War of the Rebellion* (n.p.: Privately printed, 1890), 88–89; Alexander Way to his wife, December 17, 1862, copy, FSNMP; *New York Tribune*, January 23, 1863.

44. Coffin, *Four Years of Fighting*, 150–52; Baltimore *American and Commercial Advertiser*, December 16, 1862. Funeral sermons for men with abolitionist antecedents commonly employed the antithesis between words and actions that Lincoln used so effectively in the Gettysburg address (Gary Wills, *Lincoln at Gettysburg: The Words That Remade America* [New York: Simon and Schuster, 1992], 55–62).

45. *New York Tribune*, December 15–17, 19, 23–25, 27, 1862.

46. Linderman, *Embattled Courage*, 61–62; G. R. Bedinger to his mother, December 23, 1862, Bedinger-Dandridge Papers, William R. Perkins Library, Duke University, Durham, N.C.; *OR* 21:597, 671, 51(2):663.

47. Richmond *Daily Whig*, December 24, 1862; Richmond *Daily Dispatch*, December 1, 16, 25, 1862, January 1, 1863.

48. Richmond *Daily Whig*, December 18, 1862; *OR* 21:187, 594, 624; *New York Tribune*, December 17, 1862.

49. Linderman, *Embattled Courage*, 11–15, 32–33; *OR* 21:224, 288; Edward King Wightman, *From Antietam to Fort Fisher: The Civil War Letters of Edward King Wightman, 1862–1864*, ed. Edward G. Longacre (Rutherford, N.J.: Fairleigh Dickinson University Press, 1985), 93; Baltimore *American and Commercial Advertiser*, January 2, 1863.

50. Linderman, *Embattled Courage*, 62–64; Whitman, *Whitman's Civil War*, 38–39; *New York Tribune*, December 24, 1862; Abraham Lincoln, *The Collected Works of Abraham Lincoln*, ed. Roy P. Basler, 8 vols. and index (New Brunswick, N.J.: Rutgers University Press, 1953–55), 6:13.

51. Charles S. Wainwright, *A Diary of Battle: The Personal Journals of Colonel Charles S. Wainwright, 1861–1865*, ed. Allan Nevins (New York: Harcourt, Brace & World, 1962), 149–50; Nolan, *Iron Brigade*, 187; Oliver Wendell Holmes, Jr., *Touched with Fire: Civil War Letters and Diary of Oliver Wendell Holmes, Jr., 1861–1864*, ed. Mark de Wolfe Howe (Cambridge, Mass.: Harvard University Press, 1946), 79; Albany *Atlas and Argus*, December 25, 1862; *New York Herald*, December 25, 1862.

52. Linderman, *Embattled Courage*, 8–10, 64–65; Philip Slaughter, *A Sketch of the*

Life of Randolph Fairfax, A Private in . . . Rockbridge Artillery, Attached to the "Stone-wall Brigade" (Richmond: Tyler, Allegre, and McDaniel, 1864), 5–16, 34–47.

53. John Lansing Burrows, *The Christian Scholar and Soldier. Memoirs of Lewis Minor Coleman . . . Lieut. Col. First Regiment Virginia Artillery* (Richmond: Smith, Bailey, 1864), 3–44. For a similar eulogy of an Alabama soldier, see John J. D. Renfroe, *A Model Confederate Soldier, being a Brief Sketch of the Rev. Nathaniel D. Renfroe, Lieutenant of A Company in the Fifth Alabama Battalion, of General A. Hill's Division, Who Fell in the Battle of Fredericksburg, December 13th 1862* (Richmond: n.p., 1863), 4–16.

54. Richmond *Daily Dispatch*, November 12, 1862, January 9, 1863; Richmond *Daily Whig*, November 25, December 16, 1862; Nicholas A. Davis, *The Camps from Texas to Maryland* (Richmond: Office of the Presbyterian Committee of Publication of the Confederate States, 1863), 104; *OR* 21:550, 567, 644.

55. Castleman, *Army of the Potomac*, 265–66; William Fermoil to his wife and daughter, December 24, 1862, Fermoil Letter, copy, FSNMP; William M. Sheppard to his wife, December 17, 1862, copy, FSNMP.

56. Ropes, *Civil War Nurse*, 113, 116–17; letter of unknown Georgia soldier to "Dear Molly," December 14, 1862, United Daughters of the Confederacy Collection, Georgia Department of Archives and History, Atlanta, Ga.

57. Mason Whiting Tyler, *Recollections of the Civil War with Many Original Diary Entries and Letters* (New York: G. P. Putnam's Sons, 1912), 66; Adams, *Memorial and Letters*, 79, 93, 95.

58. Richmond *Daily Dispatch*, December 22, 1862.

The Forlorn Hope

BRIG. GEN. ANDREW A. HUMPHREYS'S
PENNSYLVANIA DIVISION AT FREDERICKSBURG

CAROL REARDON

"We went out in buoyant spirits, with the mighty array that was to invest the rebel stronghold beyond the Rappahannock. We returned tired, forsaken and dispirited—our bands mournfully filling the air with requiems for the dead." So read the Christmas eve letter of one soldier in the 155th Pennsylvania who survived the charge of Brig. Gen. Andrew A. Humphreys's division against the famous stone wall at the base of Marye's Heights at Fredericksburg. His was not the first attack on the strong Confederate position, nor was it the last. He and his comrades may or may not have gotten closest to the wall. For what he and about 4,000 fellow Pennsylvanians did on December 13, 1862, however, *Harper's Weekly* would immortalize them as the "forlorn hope" of the Union army, men who demonstrated "that the bravest of troops in the world could not stem the torrent" of Confederate fire.[1] Over the years the historical record has not stinted on praise, but it has lost much of the fine detail about the complexity of what seems to be merely a valiant but doomed frontal assault. The actions of Humphreys's division compel attention even more, however, because for nearly all these men, Fredericksburg was their baptism of fire.

Who were these men, the forlorn hope of the Union army? Most, but not all, were short-term volunteers who had enlisted for only nine months of military service. They had joined in the late summer of 1862, part of Pennsylvania's quota to fill Abraham Lincoln's call for "300,000 more." The army preferred three-year regiments, but political expediency and constituent needs put pressure on state governors to consider shorter service options as well. For Pennsylvania governor Andrew Gregg Curtin, providing short-term service proved to be a wise move. Aware of the bloody toll already exacted on the battlefield and with talk of conscription in the air, Pennsylvanians still managed to exceed in short order the state's quota of twenty-one regiments, but they did so by filling the units numbered 122 through 137 with nine-month volunteers.[2] But whether three-year enlistees or nine-month men—and there were other short-term regiments from New Jersey, Vermont, and other states as well—they swelled the ranks of the Army of the Potomac in the fall of 1862.

Very quickly the nine-month Pennsylvanians showed they would fight. Some veteran soldiers had questioned their patriotism for signing up for such a brief time, but many of the new recruits of 1862 actually considered themselves more courageous than the volunteers of 1861, for, as one later wrote, we "went into the service when war was no longer an experiment but reduced to a science."[3] Within a few weeks of enlisting, the 124th, 125th, and 128th Pennsylvania fought with the Twelfth Corps near the East Woods and Dunker Church at Antietam, and monuments to the 130th and 132nd Pennsylvania of the Second Corps stand at the Bloody Lane on that same battlefield. The eight Pennsylvania regiments comprising the Third Division of Maj. Gen. Daniel Butterfield's Fifth Corps, the men who became the Union army's forlorn hope at Fredericksburg, still had seen no action in December.[4]

Until that time it had fallen to Brig. Gen. Andrew Atkinson Humphreys to mold them into an effective fighting force. Born in Philadelphia in 1810, Humphreys graduated from West Point in 1831 and was commissioned into the Corps of Topographical Engineers. In 1861 he joined George B. McClellan's staff as chief topographical engineer of the Army of the Potomac until assigned command of this division of green troops in September 1862. His peers considered him "eminent both as a scientist and a soldier, a man of broad and liberal views, of commanding intellect, and of the highest personal honor." His new command, however, "thought, at the beginning, he was austere, and disposed to be tyrannical." Years later they would be reminded that when "they discovered his many good qualities," their "dislike turned to admiration for in him you found one who knew how to command."[5] But even Humphreys himself did not yet know just how well he would perform when the time for battle came. Perhaps his attention to detail in the daily routine of his division resulted from his awareness that despite his long military career, this was his first combat command.

Humphreys's division contained two brigades. Brig. Gen. Erastus B. Tyler

Brig. Gen. Andrew
Atkinson Humphreys.
Francis Trevelyan
Miller, ed., The
Photographic History
of the Civil War, 10 vols.
(New York: Review of
Reviews, 1911), 10:179

commanded the first brigade. An Ohio fur merchant with no military experience before 1861, Tyler won election as colonel of the 7th Ohio over future
president James A. Garfield. After the battles of Kernstown and Port Republic
in the spring of 1862, he received promotion to brigadier and took command
of four regiments of the new Pennsylvania troops in late August, arriving
with his men at Antietam too late to see any fighting.[6]

Tyler's four regiments represented a cross-section of the Keystone State's
recruits. The men of the 126th Pennsylvania under Col. James Elder mostly
came from Franklin and Fulton counties on the Maryland border. In the
126th, as in many regiments, ties of kinship remained strong. After a month
in service Lt. George Welsh could offer a personal progress report on much of

Brig. Gen. Erastus Barnard Tyler. Francis Trevelyan Miller, ed., The Photographic History of the Civil War, *10 vols. (New York: Review of Reviews, 1911), 10:231*

Company A in a single letter home: "Uncle Thomas, Cousin George, and Uncle Tracy are well and stand the life well," while his brother "Phil stands marching as well as any man in the company."[7] What these family ties might mean on the field of battle they could not yet tell. The 129th Pennsylvania under Mexican War veteran Jacob Frick came from the coal country of Schuylkill County and from the eastern part of the state. The 134th, commanded at Fredericksburg by Lt. Col. Edward O'Brien, another Mexican War veteran, came from the rural counties along the Ohio border; the unit's colonel, recently resigned after a bout with typhoid fever, was Matthew Quay, future United States senator and Republican party boss for a generation.[8] Joining the nine-month men was the 91st Pennsylvania, a three-year regi-

Col. Peter Hollingshead Allabach.
155th Regimental Association,
Under the Maltese Cross,
Antietam to Appomattox:
The Loyal Uprising in
Western Pennsylvania, 1861–
1865; Campaigns 155th
Pennsylvania Regiment,
Narrated by the Rank and File
(Akron, Ohio: Werner, 1910),
p. 97

ment raised in Philadelphia in late 1861. As new to combat as the recently enlisted nine-month men, Col. Edgar M. Gregory's soldiers were eager for active service after a year of unexciting provost duty.[9]

Humphreys's second brigade of four Pennsylvania regiments officially served under Brig. Gen. Henry Shaw Briggs of Massachusetts. Briggs was considered a "good, moral man" who readily won the respect of his troops, but severe wounds received at Fair Oaks prevented his exerting active command.[10] At Fredericksburg, then, the brigade marched into battle under its senior colonel, Peter H. Allabach. A Mexican War veteran of the 3rd U.S. Infantry, Allabach commanded the 131st Pennsylvania, raised in the Susquehanna Valley.[11] His other regiments included the 123rd Pennsylvania from the Pittsburgh area, led by Col. John B. Clark, a Presbyterian minister who held recruiting meetings in his church basement, raised many of his troops from his own congregation, and had an irritating penchant for reminding civilians that "the day of sacrifice has not expired. Many a field must yet be redeemed with human gore. Many a gallant son must die without the comfortable surroundings of home."[12] Col. Franklin Speakman led the 133rd Pennsylvania, a unit of hardy rural men from the Allegheny Mountain counties of Somerset, Bedford, and Cambria.[13] Allabach, too, had a new three-year regiment, the 155th Pennsylvania, under Col. E. J. Allen. Raised mostly in Pittsburgh, fully half of its men were "boys between the ages of fourteen and eighteen," and the unit historian would later claim that the "mortality tables show that these youths resisted disease and exposure better than did soldiers of maturer age."[14]

In late November, after a long march in increasingly cold, wet weather, Humphreys's division encamped near Fredericksburg. Veterans of the bivouac at least, they could no longer say, as Pvt. Samuel North of the 126th Pennsylvania had in September, that "Camp life is very pleasant. . . . There is so much variety and so much company that a person can not help being cheerful. . . . We can cook as good a dinner as any man need. . . . The worst part is washing dishes." They knew now that it could be much worse. As the weather grew colder, Pvt. Phil Welsh complained that on the march they were "without fire for the last three days," and "We marched about 5 or 6 miles through mud almost knee deep." Exposure and disease exacted a high toll. In the 131st Pennsylvania Pvt. Howard Helman complained about one brutally cold November night when "I don't believe I slept 15 minutes, on account of having rheumatism, and a severe pain across the lungs."

Chaplain Andrew Jackson Hartsock of the 133rd Pennsylvania kept very busy in early December: "We buried [Sgt. J. Fetter Kerr, Company I] on the summit of a hill overlooking our camp. . . . We buried him alongside of [Pvt. Henry] Minich of Co. H. We buried him nicely and left him to sleep the unbroken sleep. We thought of his wife and child, of his aged parents, how sad." Soon after he added, "When I went to the hospital . . . I found [Pvt. John] Toland of Co. I resigned and happy. I baptized him after prayers. . . . [Pvt.] David Ream of Co B and [Pvt. Andrew] Bradicum [actually Bridegum] of Co D, are evidently sinking verry fast." Shortly thereafter he "buried David Ream today at 2 P.M. We laid him beside Sargt Kerr." Not surprisingly, perhaps, Pvt. Welsh reported that "some of the boys are very tired of it (the big Mouths). They curse the Union, the Government and every thing else."[15]

By and large, however, spirits remained high, even as the men grew increasingly nervous about their inactivity so close to the enemy at Fredericksburg. Pvt. Robert Hemphill of the 123rd Pennsylvania did some wishful thinking: "I can't understand the reason of both armies lying so close to each other so long without doing anything unless they are trying to make peace or something." As early as December 1, Pvt. North was "waiting hourly for the report of the first gun to commence the great struggle," clearly worried that "the rebels from all account are making good use of the delay in fortifying." Even Chaplain Hartsock gave in to the sense of foreboding. On December 10 he wrote in his diary: "Prayer meeting excellent. This is the last prayer meeting doubtless for some of our noble band."[16]

The wait was over on December 11. Ambrose Burnside forced a crossing of the Rappahannock, and Union troops poured over the pontoons into the city. Humphreys's Pennsylvanians were not part of this initial wave. Moved closer to the bridges and camped near Burnside's headquarters at the Phillips house, they still had a forty-eight-hour wait. Pvt. James B. Ross of the 123rd Pennsylvania thought that the pine forest in which they rested seemed like "some sketches of the Revolutionary War. . . . It is quite ancient looking." In the quiet, all through the ranks, each in his own way, the men prepared to face their first battle. Some of the sick left hospital beds to rejoin their regiments. In the 123rd Pennsylvania, Pvt. John Callender insisted on going back to the ranks despite a chronic illness that had left him hospitalized for much of his service. In the 131st, Capt. Joseph Orwig noticed that "Private George Lashells was very sick, but he refused to fall out. . . . George had been ill a few days previous and I had advised him not to march, but he could not be persuaded to remain behind." He would not take the pass to the rear that Orwig offered him.[17]

Nearly all the men wondered how they would act when the great test came, but the unusual calmness and resolution of Sgt. Maj. Roswell Parker of the 131st Pennsylvania particularly impressed his comrades. Parker had broken off his law studies and even turned down a commission to serve in the ranks. On the eve of his first battle he knew his course was right: "I have an object now; it seems as if I had not half-lived before. I have pledged my life to the cause." Not all the men brimmed with confidence. In the 133rd Pennsylvania, Capt. John M. Jones told Chaplain Hartsock that "there will not be much fighting, that the rebels will not stand here." If he really believed that, Jones was nearly alone. As the sounds of battle intensified, a captain in the 131st Pennsylvania noted that increasingly "men were taken ill and compelled to go to the rear." Their departure did not go unnoticed; a sergeant in the 123rd

Pennsylvania wrote home right after the fight that "I have no desire to get into another fight, but if called to go I will not get sick on the day of the battle, as many did."[18]

Finally, at 2:30 P.M. on December 13, the Fifth Corps received orders to cross the river. Chaplain Hartsock stood on the bank to get a look at the battlefield: "I could see no line of battle," he later wrote in his diary, "the warriors were covered by the smoke of battle, but I could see the fire belching forth from every rebel battery." He rode along his regiment's line, encouraging his men to do their duty. "I do not know what my feelings were, they were strange to me," he admitted. "I had never experienced the like before," but "I felt eager for the fray, believing that we were going to certain victory."[19]

As Allabach's men led the march to the pontoons near the Lacy house, the colonel halted them to say a few words of encouragement: "It now remains for us to cross the river, make the final charge, and carry the position. I wish every man to do his duty."[20] Humphreys addressed them as well, saying in grave tones (and with some exaggeration), "Your comrades are before the enemy. They have driven him, and now hold the lines. You are the reserve of the army and we go in to win the day."[21] Even Burnside left his headquarters to mingle among the troops, who pressed around him. "You need not crowd, boys, there is plenty to do over there," he said. Pvt. Henry Stees of the 131st Pennsylvania looked up and assured him, "We are ready for the work, General."[22]

As the men approached the bridge, they came under Confederate artillery fire. With wonderful understatement, Pvt. Christian Rhein of the 123rd Pennsylvania found his situation "interesting," recalling later that "the Johnnies got a good range . . . and were sending shells shrieking towards us with more success than pleased us." The noise of the projectiles impressed the soldiers nearly as much as their capacity for destruction. Chaplain Hartsock found that the "sound of a shell is terrifying, it shocks the nervous system and causes one to fear." Cpl. Nathaniel Brown of the 133rd Pennsylvania agreed: "I confess I dislike the sound of a shell—it will make a man duck his head, dispite any effort of the will to prevent it." Most drummers and other noncombatants took cover in a large hole near the riverbank, but men of the 131st Pennsylvania recalled that despite the danger, "now and then a waiting band would strike up a tune and cheer the boys with 'Bully for You' or 'Dixie.'" They learned later that the music was a cover "so that the roar of battle, the explosion of shells" would not "make the occasion . . . too sombre."[23]

Awaiting further orders while lined up in Fredericksburg, at least some on Princess Anne Street, Humphreys's men soon discovered that constant Confederate shelling wore on their nerves. Chaplain Hartsock "remembered the speech I had made the Reg., how I urged them to be brave and now I was dodging [shellfire]. . . . I braced myself in the stirrups and determined that I would not dodge if it took my life, but soon another [shell] came near me and I instinctively dodged. It is natural to dodge the shells. . . . We all dodged."[24]

The guns felled large tree branches and showered bricks on the men of the 131st and 133rd Pennsylvania. Captain Orwig of the 131st found a close friend, Adj. James C. Noon of the 133rd, flat on the ground. Orwig had earlier seen Noon among the falling bricks and tree limbs, but when he checked on his friend, Noon "quickly and bravely recovered and told me he was not struck, but he was all unnerved. He then related to me how he felt that he would be killed, and he could not help being all unstrung." But Noon refused to fall out. Orwig was not the only one concerned about him. Chaplain Hartsock recalled that Noon "often said that he would fall in the first battle. Before we entered the field he gave me a farewell letter" to send to his family. "When he dismounted at the pontoon bridge he said 'Farewell horse.' "[25]

The most dangerous parts of Fredericksburg itself were the intersections where the relatively safe streets paralleling the Rappahannock crossed roads that ran from the heights to the river. "The Rebs were raking the streets that led to the Pontoons," Chaplain Hartsock wrote, but he knew that "our course and duty lay up one of these" roads.[26]

Finally, at about 4:00 P.M., Humphreys received orders to go to the support of the Second Corps on "the left of the Telegraph road," an extension of Hanover Street that led toward the Confederate position. Allabach's brigade moved first, advancing about 400 yards west out Hanover Street, crossing a bridge over an ice-encrusted canal, and then filing off to the left of the road into a ravine to deploy into line of battle. Tyler's men, falling a bit behind while storing their knapsacks in buildings in town, followed Allabach out Hanover Street and, for the present, moved off to the right of the Telegraph Road into a swampy meadow near a tannery. As the troops filed into line, their surgeons looked for hospital sites, rejecting most of the remaining unoccupied buildings in town as "unsafe for wounded men." Indeed, Chaplain Hartsock deemed most of the sites as "unsafe for any man."[27]

Allabach's men would see the elephant first, and they would go it alone.

They lined up two regiments abreast. The 155th Pennsylvania took the left, and the 133rd Pennsylvania the right of the first line. The 123rd Pennsylvania lined up behind the 155th, while the 131st Pennsylvania deployed behind the 133rd. These men unslung their knapsacks in the ravine, and some removed their overcoats as well, keeping with them only their arms and ammunition. Colonel Allen of the 155th left six of his youngest and frailest soldiers to guard the regiment's belongings, but Humphreys—with great profanity—ordered them back into line; the order cost two of them their lives. The 123rd Pennsylvania, apparently avoiding Humphreys's detection, left their belongings "in charge of a simpleton who we thot wasn't worth taking into the fight."[28]

While his men steeled themselves for their severest test of nerve, Humphreys completed his own preparations. He had two chief concerns. First, he ordered his two division batteries to go into line wherever they could to add their fire to that of the Second Corps guns already in place. More critical, he admitted, "I had not as yet seen any part of the ground occupied by the enemy or our own troops." Moving forward from the ravine where his men deployed, Humphreys saw "some 200 yards in advance . . . the troops I was to support, slightly sheltered by a small rise in the ground. One hundred and fifty yards in advance of them was a heavy stone wall, a mile in length, which was strengthened by a trench. This wall was at the foot of the heights in rear of Fredericksburg, the crest of which . . . was crowned with batteries. The stone wall was heavily lined with the enemy's infantry."[29]

Now understanding a bit better what would be required of his untested soldiers, Humphreys decided that personal leadership was essential on all levels of command. He ordered all officers "twelve paces to the front."[30] A surprised Allabach watched as Humphreys and his entire staff also moved out front. Lt. A. F. Cavada of the general's staff recalled how he learned his commander's intention: "General Humphreys—always a very *polite* man—turned round to [us], and in his blandest manner remarked, 'Young gentlemen, I intend to lead this assault, and shall be happy to have the pleasure of your company.' Of course, the invitation was too polite to be declined."[31]

Many years later Pvt. S. W. Hill of the 155th Pennsylvania described what happened next: "The command was given, 'Forward—guide center—march,' and [we] moved at a walk—arms at right shoulder—up and out of the depression to the level meadow. The alignment of the brigade was maintained at a walk with as beautiful a line as ever witnessed on any drill." Time may have blurred Hill's memory. Immediately after the fight, Corporal Brown of the 133rd Pennsylvania described a much less orderly advance: "With a yell we rushed up the hill and were making our way across toward the enemies work, when whiz-z-z, whist, came shot, shell and bullets—creating such a din as I never wish to hear again. . . . The dead tumbled around me and the groans of the wounded made me heartsick."[32]

Soon Allabach's line reached the Second Corps troops lying on the ground. As Humphreys observed, "This example Colonel Allabach's brigade immediately followed, in spite of an effort to prevent it, and [they] commenced a fire upon the enemy." Corporal Brown remembered no such attempt to keep moving: "The firing being too hot, we were ordered to lie down. Instantly every man was flat upon the ground."[33] Allabach later blamed the conduct of his troops on their greenness: "My troops, not having before been under fire, seemed to think that they were not to go beyond." Colonel Speakman of the 133rd Pennsylvania similarly noted that his "men, not knowing that they should pass over this line, covered themselves as well as they could in rear" of it. Allabach "found a [Second Corps] officer; asked him to withdraw his men, which I could not get him to do," and Humphreys could do no better. It was all they could manage just to get their own men to cease fire.[34]

Humphreys then made an important decision. "As soon as I ascertained the nature of the enemy's position," he explained, "I was satisfied that our fire could have but little effect upon him, and that the only mode of attacking him successfully was with the bayonet. This I resolved to do, although my command was composed of troops that entered the service in August." He also ordered Tyler to shift his brigade from the right to the left of the Telegraph Road into the ravine where Allabach's men initially had deployed and "to prepare it to support or take the place of Allabach's brigade, as the event might require."[35]

On command, Allabach's men rose up from among the Second Corps men and advanced on the stone wall. For Private Helman of the 131st Pennsylvania, "Now came the time to try our 'pluck.'" Private Hill recalled that "our line broke into a double quick with a cheer. In going thru [Second Corps] men some of our men lay down, and I presume some were shot. One of the men lying down, with '5 N.H.' (brass letters) on his cap, pulled my overcoat skirt violently and motioned me to lie down; a Captain lying there motioned me to go forward. Our colors were still going forward [so] I went."[36]

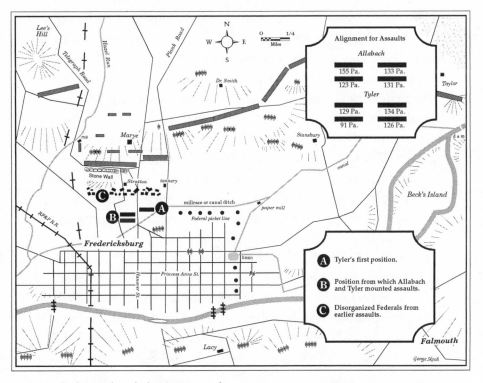

Attack of Humphreys's division, December 13, 1862

Allabach's charge did not fit the romantic image of unbroken lines of soldiers marching shoulder to shoulder so often seen in contemporary woodcuts. Confusion quickly set in. Pvt. Emmanuel Noll of the 123rd Pennsylvania observed that "all order, all formation—in fact, all discipline—had disappeared amidst the smoke and fire of battle; every man was for the moment his own commander." "There was very little for any officer to do," agreed Captain Orwig. "The men did everything. Orders were indeed given, but all the officers, everywhere, conformed with alacrity to the necessities of the occasion, which was all they could do, and these were alike mandatory to officers and privates, who advanced and fell, and rose like billows on the sea."[37]

Terrain irregularities and fence lines also broke up the advancing formations. The 131st Pennsylvania split in two during the assault: "The right . . . advanced parallel to the telegraph road, and near to it, possibly deflecting somewhat to the right. The centre and left deflected more to the left, towards the brick house." "In recounting some of the details of our charge," the regimental historian later observed with unusual honesty, "I of course, write from my point of view only. . . . Further to our left I lost much of what was done by the breaks in our line, occasioned by intervening fences, or with obstructions, and by the merciless fury of the hidden enemy behind the stone wall."[38]

Humphreys would have understood his men's desire to explain what they had done. "Of all the sublime sights within the view and comprehension of man," he once wrote, "the grandest, the most sublime, is a great battle. Its sights and sounds arouse a feeling of exaltation, compared to which, tame indeed is the sense of the sublime excited by all other great works, either of God or man." "That which makes the thrilling interest of a battle is the personal incident," he added. "A battle so lifts a man out of himself that he scarcely recognizes his identity when peace returns."[39]

For many of Allabach's men it was indeed the personal memories that made the most lasting impressions. Private Hill most vividly remembered how the corpses near him "seemed to be kept constantly in motion from the kick of the rebel bullets striking them; some of them must have been cut to tatters." In the 155th Pennsylvania one soldier described the shells falling around them as "wrath's flaming archangels." Color Sgt. Thomas Wiseman died "amid the malignant, deadly storm of leaden hail that penetrated the flesh and splintered the bones of the men" of the 155th. In turn four color corporals took up Wiseman's fallen flag, only to fall, one by one, dead or mortally wounded. In the 133rd Pennsylvania, Lt. George Ashcom received a bullet in the chest but refused help, saying, "Never mind me. I guess it is all up with me at any rate." Four of his men insisted on carrying him back to a hospital, but he agreed only after they stopped—still under fire—to help a cannon crew remount a barrel on a gun carriage. Ashcom survived. Not so fortunate was Captain Jones, the officer who had told his chaplain he thought the Confederates would not fight at Fredericksburg. Hit twice, he waved off soldiers who came to his aid, crying, "I shall never leave while my boys are here." He summoned the strength to say, "Be true as steel, my boys," before a third bullet struck him in the head. Also instantly killed by a shot through the temple was Adjutant Noon, who had rightly predicted his own death.[40]

As the charge reached its farthest point and "began to melt away," Allabach's men had had enough. The colonel remembered that his "line pressed forward to within 12 paces of the stone wall, under a galling fire of musketry and of grape and canister."[41] But they could go no farther. The retreat was no more orderly than the advance had been. Many of the men fell back to the Second Corps line and mingled with survivors of earlier charges. Some men ran all the way back into Fredericksburg itself.

A brave few did not fall back very far at all. The commander of the 131st Pennsylvania, for one, "deemed it prudent to order the regiment down upon the ground" in front of the Second Corps line. Here and there other men from Allabach's scattered command also remained in forward positions and tried gamely to keep up a sustained fire. Corporal Brown lay in six inches of mud, looking for "any sign of the rebels, the smoke was so thick." He "loaded deliberately, and took aim and fired as deliberately" for a while, but he and his comrades could not stay there indefinitely. Caught between the stone wall and the main Union line, some fell victim to "friendly fire" as soldiers behind them tried to fire over their heads at the Confederates. Orders ran up and down Allabach's ragged forward line to cease firing. They would attempt a second bayonet charge on the wall. But they were too few and too uncoordinated to do much. As Private Hill recalled, "It may be we got quite as far forward as the first time, but possibly not. Any way, it seemed impossible to pass that fated dead line. The result was the same as the first time—more men were left on that dead line, more wounded went streaming to the rear, and the rest dropped in position in front of Hancock's men and resumed firing."[42] "Twice the regiment attempted to charge their lines and carry them with the bayonet," stated Allabach in curt summary, "but owing to the heavy fire in front, and an excess of enthusiasm in the rear [his comment on the problem of friendly fire], were compelled to fall back."[43]

Humphreys understood that Allabach's men could do no more. He headed down the slope for Tyler's fresh brigade. But even as he left the front lines, stalwart bands of Allabach's men remained out in the very front, at least one recalling as his most fervent desire "hoping to live till dark." It was no wonder that their brigade commander would insist with pride until his dying day that "the old boys got nearer the gates of hell than any other regiments engaged in that battle."[44]

As Humphreys returned from the front lines, he received three separate orders from Fifth Corps commander Butterfield, Center Grand Division commander Joseph Hooker, and Burnside himself demanding that the crest should be taken before night. Mounting his orderly's horse—his own animal was dead—the general rode for Tyler's brigade. Daylight was fading fast, but

Humphreys found he could not launch the immediate attack he desired. Tyler's men, originally "crowded up as close to each other" as possible in the swampy meadow and tanyard on the right of the Telegraph Road, were just now completing their shift to the left of that avenue, and they could not deploy in Allabach's original position until Humphreys silenced several nearby batteries whose fire blocked their way.[45]

When they could do so safely, Tyler's regiments moved with alacrity, partly because they wanted to get into the fight, and partly because they wanted to get away from the meadow and tanyard. There they had been protected from most of the batteries on Marye's Heights, but they still took fire, and predictably, the first casualties made a strong impression on the green troops. As Colonel Gregory of the 91st Pennsylvania recalled it, "The enemy moved a gun from one of the earthworks on our right, and placed it in position to enfilade our lines." He quickly lost six men killed or mortally wounded, including Maj. George Todd, victim of a shell that took off a leg at the knee. Pvt. Phil Welsh in the 126th Pennsylvania watched as a second shot "struck in our company killing 3 and wounding 2. Poor Dave Washabaugh (Emma Washabaugh's brother) had his head torn off. . . . I shall never forget that time if I live one hundred years." The left of the road proved no more comfortable than the right. Because they were so close to the Union artillery, the men felt "only tolerably secure, as every now and then a shell [aimed at the cannons] would burst in among us that would almost dispel any attempt at cool, calm reflection. Horses were killed, and pieces of shell and flesh scattered in all directions."[46]

Tyler's men deployed in the same formation that Allabach's men had used. Two regiments were in the front line, the 129th Pennsylvania on the left and the 134th Pennsylvania on the right. The 91st Pennsylvania took the left of the second line, with the 126th Pennsylvania on their right. They fixed bayonets. When dispositions were complete, Humphreys warned Tyler and his regimental commanders about the Second Corps troops in their front and "directed them to disregard these men entirely, and to pass over them." Again Humphreys ordered the officers out front. As the men fixed bayonets, Tyler took one more step: "I ordered . . . the command not to fire a gun until ordered to do so by me."[47]

With bugles blaring and both Tyler and Humphreys leading the troops, this second brigade of green Pennsylvanians gave a loud hurrah and "moved

General Humphreys leads his division against Marye's Heights.
Library of Congress

forward in as good order as the muddy condition of the ground . . . would admit." Indeed, the mud "was over shoe deep" by then. Soon, as Humphreys had warned, Tyler's men came upon masses of prone Union troops whose "officers commanded halt, flourishing their swords as they lay, while a number of their men endeavored to intimidate our troops by crying out that we would be slaughtered. . . . An effort was made to get them out of the way, but failed, and we marched over them." But again, as Lt. Col. David Rowe of the 126th Pennsylvania noted, "the difficulty of passing over these men, created some confusion in the ranks."[48]

Still, Tyler's men continued on. For a while, fire from the stone wall seemed to subside a bit. Flat on the ground in front of the Second Corps line where he had decided to await events, Private Noll of Allabach's 131st Pennsylvania recalled that "not a shot was fired until the advance was within three or four rods of us, Tyler leading and waving his sword, encouraging his men by voice and example. Suddenly a wall of flaming fire, shot and shell, struck Tyler's brigade, a volume of smoke rolled down like a mountain mist, and when it lifted Tyler's brigade had vanished as completely as if they had been swallowed." Marching exposed up the slope, however, Lieutenant Welsh remembered no such great outburst of fire; to him, enemy fire was "heavy and almost incessant" all day, but when they charged, it "commenced increasing until the shots ran into each other like the roll of a drum almost—a perfect shower of lead whistling, whizzing into and over our ranks." To Humphreys, the fire, "as furious as it was before, now became still hotter. The stone wall was a sheet of flame, that enveloped the head and flanks of the column."[49]

Tyler's men tried briefly to fight. "Orders for the moment were forgotten and a fire from our whole line was immediately returned." Pvt. Phil Welsh of the 126th Pennsylvania expressed what many of his comrades likely felt in the midst of the chaos. "First the man on my right fell and then the man on my left," he wrote. "I could see them falling all around—every place I looked I saw poor fellows lying around dead and wounded. Before we made the charge we had orders not to fire until order[ed] to do so, but some of the fellows commenced to fire—I did not know what in the world to do." He could only acknowledge the intensity of the Confederate volleys: "The Minie balls whistled by with their fitful hiss, and the great guns of the enemy belched forth their thunder and scattered death and destruction all around." Welsh averred that "I do honestly believe some of the bullets was not more than one inch off of my face. I was expecting to fall every minute."[50]

Again the fight broke down into a montage of individual efforts. Capt. John H. Walker of the 126th Pennsylvania, "though wounded by a ball in his right shoulder . . . rallied his company, and declared that one arm was enough to lead his men to another charge." Capt. Herbert Thomas of the 129th Pennsylvania, Humphreys's acting inspector general, deserted his chief to lead his own company into the charge, only to fall seriously wounded. When the color-bearer of the 134th Pennsylvania was killed, Cpl. George Jones of the 126th somehow carried the fallen banner off the field and saw it was returned to its rightful owners.[51] The colors of the 129th fell five times before Col. Jacob Frick "seized them . . . on horseback, and led on the charge." In the end, wrote one correspondent with the 129th, "valor was useless against that tempest of shot and shell."[52]

They gave it their best. According to Lieutenant Welsh, writing with notable candor, "I know we were pretty near the enemy's works, how near I can't say—some say 30 yds., others 100. It was dusk and we could only tell their position by the flash of their musketry." But no matter how close they had gotten, victory had eluded them. The first Confederate volleys had staggered Tyler's front line. "The 134th Reg't in front of us faltered and then turned and fell behind us running through our ranks," Welsh wrote his mother. "We crouched down and poured in our fire—but the confusion was so great that I have no doubt that some of our men were injured by those in the rear." In a day full of mistakes, losses by friendly fire loom large in the lasting memory of Humphreys's men. Tyler, too, complained that "the trial was a terrific one for troops of many years experience and still more terrifying to men just from their farms and work-shops. That galling fire of musketry and artillery in front and the careless firing from the rear, no human courage could withstand."[53]

Tyler's men wavered. Their greenness told. "The fire in the front, the fire in the rear, every flash visible in the twilight, astounded the soldiers," conceded a chronicler of the 126th. "Bewildered, they stood for a moment irresolute; then in their excitement began to fire at the rebel line. This was fatal. The charge was over." As Humphreys wrote, the fire of Tyler's men "lasted but a minute, when in spite of all our efforts, the column turned and began to retire slowly. I attempted to rally the brigade. . . . But the united efforts of General Tyler, myself, our staffs, and the other officers could not arrest the retiring mass." Their forward progress halted and their momentum lost, many of Tyler's men fell back all the way to the ravine where they had first deployed for the charge. Lieutenant Welsh searched among them for his brother Phil and was relieved to find him unhurt. He saw that all of the 126th Pennsylvania were not so fortunate as he and his brother: "We had to get back and I assure we were not long in doing so. . . . We were not in the charge more than 15 minutes and the loss in our reg't was 100 killed, wounded & missing." Among the wounded was Welsh's Uncle Thomas.[54]

The army's forlorn hope had been dashed. In the twilight, while Tyler's men retired to the ravine, Humphreys returned to the front lines to bring back the remnants of Allabach's brigade that remained in advance of the Second Corps line. Still game, parts of the 123rd and 155th Pennsylvania retired "slowly and in good order, singing and hurrahing," actions that even impressed the Confederates who watched them leave.[55] Even now, however, the day's work was not done. Going one by one into Fredericksburg for more ammunition, Humphreys's eight regiments returned to the field and reinforced the picket line all night.

It was a night few ever forgot. Humphreys sent out details to bring in the wounded and dead. Requisitions for stretchers had gone unfilled, and the soldiers used shutters from Fredericksburg's buildings to carry their comrades. They worked quickly. Humphreys reported that the wounded "were nearly all brought in before daylight" on December 14. Chaplain Hartsock's official duties took him directly to the front lines. "After dark I went to the picket line for wounded," he explained. "Such a scene beggars description. The wounded had been carried here by their comrades, others crawled here. I supposed there are hundreds along this line. . . . When I call[ed] for wounded of the 133 P.V. I found some of ours, and [heard] the cry from every quarter, 'take me. . . . Oh take me.' "[56]

The field was alive with men helping the wounded or seeking the missing. Three officers of the 155th Pennsylvania "crowned their day's bravery by a night's work of humanity," carrying out as many as 120 wounded, "though many to whom they were but a solace passed away to brighter worlds ere the morning dawned." Captain Orwig of the 131st went out to find two men he had left on the field wounded, perhaps dead. He found them "lying near together, helpless . . . in sight of the stone wall." Carefully striking a match, he recognized a wounded and unconscious Pvt. George Stees, who earlier that day had assured Burnside that the Pennsylvanians would do their entire duty. As Orwig tended to Stees, the other wounded man called out for water. The captain also found George Lashells, the sick man he had urged to stay in camp. He helped both men to a hospital, but neither survived the night.[57]

Whether or not they joined in the search for wounded or dead comrades, soldiers could not describe the night of December 13 with detachment. Private North of the 126th told his brother that "I have heard of the horror of the battlefield but the reality is terrible. In the action and excitement it is not realized, but the thoughts and impressions seem to be burned on my brain, the still pale faces of the dead, and the shrieks and groans of the wounded and dying. Oh! it is awful!" For one survivor in the 155th Pennsylvania, "night and darkness prolonged the horrors. The cries of the wounded rose up over that bloody field like the wail of lost spirits all the night; cries for water, blankets and 'to be borne off the field' in all the paroxisms that terror and suffering can excite, went up from the sad victims of the day's havoc and filled the very air with pain."[58]

"It did not require revillee this morning to waken us from our dreams of death and horrid murder," wrote Chaplain Hartsock as December 14 dawned. Rumors flew through the ranks about a renewal of the assaults. All day the men lay quiet, hoping to stay out of sight of Confederate snipers. Colonel Clark of the 123rd Pennsylvania felt sorry for his men, who were "compelled to lie low all the day on mud mingled with the ruins of knapsacks, with here and there a dead man lying unburied." Sgt. Robert Bard thought his colonel understated matters, estimating "that there were fifteen men shot within a circle of twenty feet from where I lay." Indeed, stated Bard, "To raise one's head or to put up a cap on a ramrod would instantly draw a shot." Sometimes a shot found its mark. Just after sharing hardtack with some of his men, Captain Orwig heard a soldier call, "One of your men was just now hit." He turned to find Pvt. Emmanuel Snyder "already quite dead, having been shot through the heart. His brother, William . . . by his side." Late that evening Humphreys withdrew his men to Fredericksburg and relative safety, with members of the 126th noticing with irony that they had been posted to a local graveyard.[59]

Until they recrossed the Rappahannock in a pouring rain on December 16, Humphreys's men officially served on picket. But there were other duties as well. Providing a decent burial for fallen comrades stood high on their list. It seemed especially important to do so for some, because it could not be done for all. The new veterans were shattered to learn that their division burial parties found it "extremely difficult to distinguish our [dead], and utterly impossible . . . to bring off all who were lying there." Colonel Clark regretted that "of the several killed [in the 123rd Pennsylvania], we only got one buried before we retired across the river. The body of Alexander Dallas, of company E, was buried near where we fought. . . . The body of Lieutenant [James] Coulter was left in the hospital unburied, as was also that of Sergeant [Daniel] Kipp, of company F. The comrades of Kipp attempted his burial, but were not allowed even that sad pleasure, by the rebel sharpshooters." Chaplain Hartsock saw to the remains of his friend Captain Jones, which he "nicely washed and dressed as well as I could. Went to an undertaker's shop and *took* a finely finished coffin for him." Hartsock wanted to take the bodies of Jones and two other officers across the river, but "Col Speakman came to me and said to bury them. . . . We carried them to the Campbellite Church and buried them in their grave yard. We sang no song, but the shells from rebel batteries sang a constant requiem." Captain Orwig went to the hospital to claim the bodies of the two men he had helped to rescue the night before. He assisted in arranging for Lashells's body to be sent home, but he never did find Stees. With resignation, years later, he finally admitted that the young soldier was probably one of the many who helped "fill up the great lines of 'unknown' graves, sacredly and tenderly preserved by the grateful government for the preservation of which they gave their young lives."[60]

Many of Humphreys's men took away especially vivid memories of the hospitals. As one sergeant turned a corner near the pontoons, he confronted "a hospital tent, and saw eight dead bodies in front of it and at least twenty amputated arms and legs." After the surgeons came to treat the arm wound of Pvt. John Williams of the 133rd Pennsylvania, the chaplain decided that "John has the strongest nerve of any man I ever saw. . . . The surgeons wanted to amputate the arm but he would not permit it. They urged him to take chloroform but he remarked to me 'If I do, when I awake I will find my arm off,' and he did not take it." Williams lived, but the great hordes of casualties overwhelmed the surgeons. Colonel Clark complained that "Capt. R. D. Humes, of company I, as good and brave a man as ever drew a sword, was very severely wounded on Saturday and at noon on Wednesday, he informed me that nothing had been done with his wound. I confess it made me mad." Humes, too, survived.[61]

Not all of Humphreys's soldiers spent their time in humanitarian pursuits. Like so many other Federals, partly from need—most men who removed their knapsacks on the battlefield lost everything—and partly from anger and frustration, they gave in to the impulse to loot homes and public buildings in the already devastated city. Private North of the 126th Pennsylvania noted without casting aspersions that "Haze Boyd got Miltons complete works lying in the streets." Pvt. James Finnegan of the 155th bragged of newfound riches, blissfully unaware that the bundles of papers he carried were worthless receipts and canceled checks; he was "under the impression that it was a bank instead of an express company he was burglarizing." Despite many individual acts of assistance to townspeople, Humphreys's men felt little sympathy for them. As Private North observed, "There was abundance of flour, fish, port and in short everything but salt. The story of the South starving is all a hoax, they had things just as plenty as we have."[62]

On December 16 Humphreys's men recrossed the Rappahannock. Capt. John Lentz and a detachment from the 91st Pennsylvania were among the very last to leave, inadvertently forgotten when other pickets withdrew. Lentz returned safely, but the misadventure cost him eleven more men missing in action. Humphreys's soldiers were now veterans, but at what cost? Of the 4,000 who crossed the pontoons on the afternoon of December 13, only 2,950 marched back on December 16. Slightly more than 25 percent of the division's pre-battle strength swelled the count of northern dead, wounded, and missing at Fredericksburg.[63]

For the newly blooded Pennsylvanians, Fredericksburg ended their misconceptions about war. They did not try to sugarcoat what happened to them. They admitted defeat, and some feared for the future of their cause. Corporal Brown of the 133rd complained to his cousin that "we have been aiding the ambitious predelections of *individuals*, and not the *supremacy of the laws*," concluding that "we are nothing (us poor soldiers) but food for sharks." Still, even in defeat, few deemed their sacrifice worthless. "What the next move will be I know not; but after all this army has suffered and lost, it is to be hoped they will not yield until successful, whatever be the cost," wrote one soldier. "Too many men have fallen to fall in vain. Too much has been endured to go unrewarded." James Clark, the preacher-colonel, reminded his Pittsburgh congregation that "to know the fact that your friends fought bravely and shed their life's blood to perpetuate liberty in the land, is an honor that will never perish."[64] Colonel Frick of the 129th offered similar sentiments: "The gallantry displayed on that fatal field by our brave volunteers, under circumstances which did not admit of hope of success, is but another proof of their unconquerable determination to suppress the Rebellion and maintain the integrity of our Union at every sacrifice."[65]

Even while acknowledging defeat the new veterans exhibited distinct pride in their performance. As green troops, they had had something to prove—to themselves, to the rest of the army, and to the people back home. Many soldiers now could echo the honest self-assessment of a sergeant in the 123rd Pennsylvania who wrote home with unpretentious candor, "No one can say I acted the coward." Unit pride swelled as well. Just two days after the battle, Lt. Benjamin F. Jennings wrote to his father that "the 155th has won a name for itself already. Not a man was known to flinch." General Tyler took special pains to write about his brigade's accomplishments in a detailed letter to Governor Curtin. "Pennsylvania has good reason to be proud of her noble Soldiery in these Regiments," he insisted. "They have earned for themselves and their State a name worthy of the 'Keystone' of the Union."[66]

In the end Humphreys's men did not have to work hard to preserve or spread their story. The army's senior commanders praised them profusely in the official reports. Their sacrifices became part of the evidence presented to the Joint Committee on the Conduct of the War that investigated Burnside's performance at Fredericksburg. They were the subject of woodcuts in popular newspapers, and no reader was permitted to forget, as *Harper's Weekly* reported in the weeks after the fight, "the division was fighting its maiden battle. Older soldiers than they quailed before the murderous volleys," but they had pressed on valiantly despite the "great gaps in their ranks."[67]

Humphreys's men ultimately put what they had done behind them and simply looked forward to completing their service. There were other sad times ahead, to be sure. The cost of their hour in combat would increase almost daily for weeks and months to come. In the 123rd Pennsylvania the chronically ill Pvt. John Callender, who had insisted on joining his regiment before the battle, died in late December. He fell to disease rather than a bullet, but the death of this "good man and . . . brave soldier" was no less mourned by his comrades.[68] Survivors of the 131st were stunned to hear of the death of Sgt. Maj. Roswell Parker, the soldier who had "pledged his life to the cause." Hit in the fleshy part of the leg below the knee, a wound the doctors considered minor, Parker developed fever and lockjaw; he redeemed his pledge in mid-January.[69] Lt. George Welsh and his brother Phil waited for word on the fate of their Uncle Thomas. The lieutenant reassured folks at home that their kinsman's injuries "are painful but not dangerous and he will not lose the use of either hand or his leg." But he was wrong. Cpl. Thomas G. Pilkington died of his wounds in a Washington hospital on January 15, 1863.[70]

The healing process for the regiments was slow. For months Chaplain Hartsock could not walk through the camp of the 133rd Pennsylvania without "thinking of the comrades and friends who left camp with us, who now lie either in their shallow graves on the battlefield or on beds of suffering in the various hospitals. . . . How small our number seems." Willing to finish out his service but mindful of the cost that service already had exacted and might yet require, Pvt. Robert Hemphill of the 123rd Pennsylvania hit a common chord when he wrote home in late December: "I like soldiering first rate. . . . I am glad I come the time I did however, for perhaps I might have been foolish enough to have enlisted for three years if I had waited. But I have only a little of 3 months to stay & I am glad of it." Hemphill concluded that he "would not have missed seeing what I have since I came out for a good deal."[71]

By May, Humphreys's division of Fredericksburg fame ceased to exist. Humphreys took command of a division in the Third Corps, became Gen. George G. Meade's chief of staff after Gettysburg, and ended the war at the head of the Second Corps. He retired from the army in 1879 after thirteen years as its chief engineer. General Tyler became commander of the defenses of Baltimore and saw no more combat. The 91st and 155th Pennsylvania regiments fought in the battles of the Fifth Corps until Appomattox, but Colonel Allabach and the great majority of Humphreys's new veterans returned to civilian life, secure in the conviction that they had done their duty well.

Humphreys's division had not fought its last battle, however. At least three skirmishes lay ahead in the postwar years, clashes that would determine how their efforts would be remembered by future generations.

Humphreys wrote in his official report of the battle that "one of the greatest obstacles to my success was the mass of troops lying on our front line." Because "they disordered my lines and . . . impeded its progress," his troops had become "a massive column too large to be managed properly," and their repulse soon followed.[72] The offending soldiers were members of the Second Corps, and for years they and their friends chafed at Humphreys's criticism. In his history of the Second Corps published in 1886, Francis A. Walker praised Humphreys's "superb leadership," but he would not tolerate the "censure which is implied" in Humphreys's account of the fight. Walker admitted that Second Corps troops did constitute a "certain obstacle to the progress of a fresh column," but he deemed it unreasonable to expect veteran soldiers to yield ground they had gained at the cost of so many lives. In the end it was not really much of a controversy; the Second Corps men *were* an obstacle. Still, as the men of the 106th Pennsylvania of the Second Corps asserted most pointedly, they stayed in place in obedience to specific "orders 'to hold that position,' as *soldiers* and not skulkers."[73]

Equally disconcerting to partisans of the Second Corps, Humphreys had noted in his report that the prone men of that command "called to our men not to go forward, and some attempted to prevent by force their doing so." The *Harper's Weekly* piece also had described the "prostrate men" who "cried out 'don't go there, 'tis certain death' " and had impeded the Pennsylvanians with "protestations of every nature." Francis Walker could not refute the charges, so he tried to play down their severity: "It is likely true that among those thousands, a few may have called out to Allabach's and Tyler's men that it was useless to go forward; but their own situation on that plain swept by fire is proof enough that such men were very few." If Walker had just let it go, the ill feelings might have died. But when he suggested that the accusations actually stemmed from the embellished "tale of some colonel or captain [in Humphreys's division] to excuse the breaking of his own command," personal affidavits flowed in from Pennsylvanians. Nine enlisted men from the 131st Pennsylvania alone swore that Second Corps troops yelled out, "Don't go forward, it is useless, you will be killed," and asserted that they "put forth their hands, catching hold of our men by the trousers, blouses, canteens, and haversacks."[74] Volleys back and forth continued for years.

The third and best-known postwar skirmish concerned honors for the nearest approach to the stone wall. In 1862 Humphreys had said nothing specific about it. Likewise, his regimental commanders, when they commented at all, usually had used vague phrases: the 126th Pennsylvania advanced "quite near the stone wall"; the 131st Pennsylvania came up "to within a short distance of the stone wall"; the 133rd Pennsylvania approached "to within about 50 yards of the stone wall." Indeed, in 1862 only Lieutenant Colonel O'Brien of the 134th Pennsylvania had claimed that "my regiment reached a point nearer the enemy's works than any other, as our dead, lying close by, fully show." In later years, however, any number of Humphreys's men asserted that they "as a unit, went nearer to that stone wall (on that day) than any other troops."[75]

Partisans of the Second Corps responded vigorously. Walker pointed out that Humphreys had not seen the assaults of the Second Corps and could not know how far they had gotten, "while a hundred officers who witnessed both the earlier and the later assaults can testify that no troops went so near the stone wall that bloody day as the men of [Brig. Gen. Nathan] Kimball, [Brig. Gen. Samuel K.] Zook, [Brig. Gen. Thomas] Meagher, and [Brig. Gen. John C.] Caldwell" of the Second Corps. He chastised Humphreys's staff officers for making claims they could not prove, advising them that if "there were then no troops further to the front at the point where you personally were," it was, "however, no evidence that there may not have been troops [there] two hours or more [earlier] . . . or that other troops may not have advanced nearer to the stone wall at some other point of the Confederate line." Walker also offered as evidence the report of Col. John R. Brooke, the burial detail commander near the stone wall, who swore that the bodies closest to it belonged to men of the 5th New Hampshire, 69th New York, and 53rd Pennsylvania, all Second Corps regiments. As he saw it, "Evidence like this is beyond dispute."[76]

But Humphreys's men did dispute it. Signed affidavits from enlisted men again provided ammunition. One Pennsylvanian insisted that "I was so close to the stone wall that there was not a dead body on the field in front of me." Private Hill of the 155th Pennsylvania averred not only that Allabach's men got closest to the stone wall but also that some "men of Hancock's [Second Corps] division, who witnessed it" had given him "their opinion that we went a little farther."[77] Humphreys's staff widely republished a letter from Confederate artilleryman Robert J. Fleming, who "went out with the flag of truce between the lines to see about burying the dead. . . . I must in justice say that the dead bodies that I saw close to our works belonged to General Humphreys' Division."[78]

The Fifth Corps veterans especially rejected the accuracy of the findings of Colonel Brooke's burial party. When some old soldiers around Indianapolis described how the corpses of men of the 14th Indiana were found closest to the wall (right after the battle, a member of the burial party recalled spotting a distinctive tattoo that identified the corpse of Sgt. Clay Welch of the 14th Indiana "pinned against the stone wall"),[79] Humphreys's men took great pains to discredit the claim. Former private Seth Dickey of the 126th Pennsylvania asserted that physical evidence alone would prove the Keystone State troops advanced farthest: the fences his unit "encountered after passing over the prostrate troops of [the Second Corps] were in almost perfect condition when reached, showing clearly that no attempt had been made to break them down, which of necessity, must have been done had any charging column gone beyond them, as did Humphreys' Pennsylvanians alone." The Pennsylvanians also relied heavily on the testimony of Martha Stephens, who owned the house just in front of the Confederate line. She had reported that the night after the battle "all the clothes had been stripped from the bodies of the Union soldiers," and among the only identifiable pieces of clothing left near the farthest point of advance were "three soldier caps, bearing the numbers '131 P.V.'" Remembering how they could not identify their own division's dead the day after the battle, and knowing that "the burial party did not view the remains for a week after the conflict," Humphreys's veterans failed "to see how all the [Second Corps] corpses could be recognized." Finally, the Pennsylvanians summoned an argument they believed could not be answered: it was most likely that Humphreys's men got closest to the wall precisely because "this was their maiden fight, and every one knows that old soldiers can, in conflict, see impossibilities before them which new troops cannot comprehend, and therefore the latter 'rush in where angels fear to tread.'"[80]

Humphreys's men would get to remember their moment in history exactly as they wished. The Second Corps would have many more accomplishments to brag about, and on the scale of historical controversies these were relatively unimportant except to the participants. Still, when Humphreys's men wanted to impress upon the American people the importance of what they did at Fredericksburg, they learned to compare their efforts favorably against standard measures of military gallantry. One veteran wrote in 1886 that "the European world sounds and re-sounds, echoes and re-echoes with plaudits for the Rebel grand charge on the third day of Gettysburg. Such excessive applause is unjust to the many similar exhibitions of Union determination. The assaults of French and of Hancock, but *particularly* of *Humphreys*, were much more desperately brilliant." From a regimental history we learn that "the work done by the 131st soldiers was not exceeded on any of the historic battlefields—not by the charge at Balaklava, immortalized by Tennyson, nor by that of Pickett's men at Gettysburg." A veteran of the 126th Pennsylvania wrote that "the equal of this charge was never made in America! . . . Pickett's Charge at Gettysburg . . . was the only charge of greater dimensions of importance, but it did not have a sunken road." At the dedication of their division's memorial, the keynote speaker reminded the audience that "next to Pickett's Charge," Humphreys's charge "was the most bloody and disastrous of our Civil War."[81]

That monument was unveiled in the national cemetery at Fredericksburg in November 1908 on the very heights Humphreys's men had tried to storm in December 1862. Their division commander's statue crowns a granite pedestal that lists the eight green Pennsylvania regiments that became the Union army's forlorn hope. One speaker told an appreciative audience, including a number of survivors of the battle, that "all the other Pennsylvania regiments engaged in this action . . . have or will have, monuments on other fields," so this one was for them alone, to mark the finest moment of their military lives. "Bear in mind that these troops, entered the service only a few months previously and had never been in action," another orator reminded the crowd. "Was there ever a more wonderful example of pluck and spirit than that shown by these youngsters in [their] charge across that fire-swept field against a practically impregnable position? There are many heroic charges recorded after in the Army of the Potomac, but they were those of, as a rule, disciplined and well seasoned troops," not by "soldiers fresh from their homes and without battle experience." The old soldiers agreed that the ceremonies supplied a fitting tribute to their gallantry and to their sacrifice at Fredericksburg. They most likely also appreciated that fate had smiled on them. While the rest of the Army of the Potomac went on to Gettysburg, the Wilderness, Spotsylvania, Cold Harbor, and the trenches of Petersburg, they got their fondest wish—to go home to family and friends as battle-tested veterans to "eat and tell yarns."[82]

Notes

1. Letter from "P.," Pittsburgh *Post*, December 30, 1862; *Harper's Weekly* quoted in Samuel P. Bates, *History of Pennsylvania Volunteers, 1861–5; Prepared in Compliance with Acts of the Legislature . . .* , 5 vols. (Harrisburg, Pa.: B. Singerly, 1870), 3:188.

2. See individual unit entries in Bates, *Pennsylvania Volunteers*, vols. 3 and 4.

3. John H. Kerr, Esq., *Oration Delivered at the First Reunion of the One Hundred and Fifty-Fifth Regiment, Penn'a. Veteran Volunteers, at Lafayette Hall, Pittsburgh . . . September 17, 1875* (Pittsburgh: Samuel F. Kerr, 1875), 19.

4. For a brief overview of these units at Antietam, see Stephen W. Sears, *Landscape Turned Red: The Battle of Antietam* (New York: Ticknor and Fields, 1983), 204–5, 207, 224–25, 229, 238–40, 250.

5. Henry L. Abbot, *Memoir of Andrew Atkinson Humphreys, Read before the National Academy of Science, April 24, 1885* (n.p., 1885) 1; address of Gen. A. L. Pearson in *Fifth Reunion of the 155th Pennsylvania Volunteers, Held at Normal Hall, Clarion, Penna., July 29 and 30, 1896* (Pittsburgh: Rawsthorne, 1896), 28.

6. Ezra J. Warner, *Generals in Blue: Lives of the Union Commanders* (Baton Rouge: Louisiana State University Press, 1964), 515.

7. Bates, *Pennsylvania Volunteers*, 4:127–30; "Civil War Letters from Two Brothers," *Yale Review* 18 (1928): 150. See also Ted Alexander, *The 126th Pennsylvania* (Shippensburg, Pa.: Beidel Printing House, 1984), a useful modern regimental history.

8. Bates, *Pennsylvania Volunteers*, 4:184–86, 282–83; 155th Regimental Association, *Under the Maltese Cross, Antietam to Appomattox: The Loyal Uprising in Western Pennsylvania, 1861–1865; Campaigns 155th Pennsylvania Regiment, Narrated by the Rank and File* ([Akron, Ohio: Werner], 1910), 737.

9. Bates, *Pennsylvania Volunteers*, 3:186–93.

10. "Letter from Col. Clark," (Pittsburgh) *Pennsylvania Gazette*, October 24, 1862. See also Warner, *Generals in Blue*, 44–45.

11. Bates, *Pennsylvania Volunteers*, 4:224. Joseph R. Orwig's *History of the 131st Penna. Volunteers, War of 1861–5* (Williamsport, Pa.: Sun Book and Job Printing House, 1902), is an outstanding regimental history, especially for one that commemorates the service of a nine-month unit.

12. "Letter from Col. Clark," October 24, 1862. Recruits from Allegheny County were eligible for a bounty payment of fifty dollars. See also Bates, *Pennsylvania Volunteers*, 4:71.

13. Bates, *Pennsylvania Volunteers*, 4:282–84.

14. 155th Regt. Assn., *Under the Maltese Cross*, 17; Bates, *Pennsylvania Volunteers*, 4:800–803.

15. Samuel W. North to [?], undated letter from fall 1862, Samuel W. North Papers, Civil War Miscellaneous Collection, U.S. Army Military History Institute, Carlisle Barracks, Pa. (repository hereafter cited as USAMHI); "Civil War Letters from Two Brothers," 154; Arthur W. Thurner, ed., "A Young Soldier in the Army of the Potomac: Diary of Howard Helman, 1862," *Pennsylvania Magazine of History and Biography* 87 (1963): 152; Andrew Jackson Hartsock, *Soldier of the Cross: The Civil War Diary and Correspondence of Rev. Andrew Jackson Hartsock*, ed. James C. Duram and Eleanor A. Duram (Manhattan, Kans.: American Military Institute, 1979), 36.

16. Robert W. Hemphill to "Brother George," December 1, 1862, Hemphill Civil War Letters, Henry Family Papers, USAMHI; Samuel W. North to "Brother," December 1, 1862, Samuel W. North Papers, USAMHI; Hartsock, *Soldier of the Cross*, 36.

17. James B. Ross diary, entry for December 12, 1862, James B. Ross Papers, Western Pennsylvania Historical Society, Pittsburgh, Pa.; R. W. Hemphill to "Brother George," December 25, 1862, Hemphill Letters, Henry Family Papers, USAMHI; Orwig, *History of the 131st Penna.*, 99.

18. Henry T. Lee, *Address Commemorative of the Services of the Alumni and Former Students of Lafayette College in the War for the Union . . .* (Easton, Pa.: Board of Trustees, 1866), 18; Hartsock, *Soldier of the Cross*, 37; Orwig, *History of the 131st Penna.*, 99; Letter from "L. B." [Sgt. L. Brackenridge], Pittsburgh *Post*, December 27, 1862.

19. Hartsock, *Soldier of the Cross*, 38.

20. As quoted by Cpl. Nathaniel Brown, 133rd Pennsylvania, in Brown to Arthur Given, December 23, 1862, in 133rd Pennsylvania file, Fredericksburg and Spotsylvania National Military Park Library, Fredericksburg, Va. (repository hereafter cited as FSNMP).

21. As recalled by Chaplain Hartsock in *Soldier of the Cross*, 38.

22. Orwig, *History of the 131st Penna.*, 113.

23. Christian Rhein, "The 123d Pa.," *National Tribune*, July 11, 1907; Hartsock, *Soldier of the Cross*, 38; Nathaniel Brown to Arthur Given, December 23, 1862, 133rd Pennsylvania file, FSNMP; Orwig, *History of the 131st Penna.*, 114.

24. Hartsock, *Soldier of the Cross*, 38.

25. Orwig, *History of the 131st Penna.*, 114–15; Hartsock, *Soldier of the Cross*, 39.

26. Hartsock, *Soldier of the Cross*, 39.

27. Ibid.

28. S. W. Hill, "Allabach's Brigade. It Went as Near as Any Others to the Deadly Stone Wall at Fredericksburg," *National Tribune*, April 16, 1908; 155th Regt. Assn., *Under the Maltese Cross*, 97; Rhein, "The 123d Pa."

29. U.S. War Department, *The War of the Rebellion: A Compilation of the Official Records of the Union and Confederate Armies*, 127 vols., index, and atlas (Washington, D.C.: GPO, 1880–1901), 21:430–31 (hereafter cited as *OR*; all references are to series 1).

30. [David Watson Rowe], *A Sketch of the 126th Regiment Pennsylvania Volunteers. Prepared by an Officer, and Sold for the Benefit of the Franklin County Soldiers' Monumental Association* (Chambersburg, Pa.: Cook & Hays, 1869), 16. See also "Civil War Letters from Two Brothers," 158.

31. Frank Moore, ed., *Anecdotes, Poetry, and Incidents of the War: North and South, 1860–1865* (New York: Arundel, 1882), 210.

32. Hill, "Allabach's Brigade"; Nathaniel Brown to Arthur Given, December 23, 1862, 133rd Pennsylvania file, FSNMP.

33. *OR* 21:431; Nathaniel Brown to Arthur Given, December 23, 1862, 133rd Pennsylvania file, FSNMP.

34. *OR* 21:433, 466.

35. *OR* 21:431.

36. Thurner, "A Young Soldier in the Army of the Potomac," 155; Hill, "Allabach's Brigade."

37. Emmanuel Noll, "Allabach's Brigade. It Attacked at Fredericksburg Before Tyler's Brigade, and Went Farther," *National Tribune*, October 1, 1908; Orwig, *History of the 131st Penna.*, 119.

38. Orwig, *History of the 131st Penna.*, 118.

39. Hampton L. Carson, *Andrew Atkinson Humphreys, Brigadier-General, U.S. Army, Brevet Major-General, U.S. Army, Chief of Engineers* (n.p., [ca. 1885]), 15.

40. Hill, "Allabach's Brigade"; Kerr, *Oration Delivered*, 9, 17; 155th Regt. Assn., *Under the Maltese Cross*, 101; Hartsock, *Soldier of the Cross*, 40–41, 39; Orwig, *History of the 131st Penna.*, 115.

41. *OR* 21:444, 446; Nathaniel Brown to Arthur Given, December 23, 1862, 133rd Pennsylvania file, FSNMP.

42. Hill, "Allabach's Brigade."

43. *OR* 21:448.

44. Hill, "Allabach's Brigade"; Allabach quoted in *Fifth Reunion of the 155th Pennsylvania Volunteers*, 28.

45. Alexander, *126th Pennsylvania*, 128; *OR* 21:431, 437.

46. *OR* 21:439; Alexander, *126th Pennsylvania*, 128; "From the 129th Penna. Regt.," Philadelphia *Enquirer*, December 18, 1862.

47. *OR* 21:437, 431.

48. *OR* 21:437, 440.

49. Noll, "Allabach's Brigade"; "Civil War Letters from Two Brothers," 156; *OR* 21:432.

50. "Civil War Letters from Two Brothers," 158.

51. *OR* 21:441, 443.

52. "The One Hundred and Twenty-Ninth Reg., P.V., Col. J. G. Frick," (Pottsville, Pa.) *Miners Journal*, December 20, 1862; Philadelphia *Enquirer*, December 18, 1862.

53. "Civil War Letters from Two Brothers," 156; E. B. Tyler to Governor Andrew G. Curtin, December 29, 1862, box 19, folder 3, Office of the Adjutant General, Department of Military Affairs, General Correspondence, Dec. 1862–April 1863, Record Group 19, Pennsylvania State Archives, Harrisburg, Pa. (repository hereafter cited as PA).

54. [Rowe], *Sketch of the 126th Regiment*, 18; *OR* 21:432; "Civil War Letters from Two Brothers," 156.

55. *OR* 21:432.

56. *OR* 21:433; Hartsock, *Soldier of the Cross*, 42.

57. Pittsburgh *Post*, December 28, 1862; Orwig, *History of the 131st Penna.*, 119–20.

58. Samuel W. North to his brother, December 18, 1862, Samuel W. North Papers, USAMHI; Pittsburgh *Post*, December 30, 1862.

59. Hartsock, *Soldier of the Cross*, 43; "Letter from Col. Clark," (Pittsburgh) *Pennsylvania Gazette*, December 25, 1862; "Letter from Capt. Drum's Company—Clark's Regiment in the Fight," (Pittsburgh) *Pennsylvania Gazette*, December 19, 1862; Hill, "Allabach's Brigade"; Orwig, *History of the 131st Penna.*, 126–27.

60. *OR* 21:433; "Letter from Col. Clark," October 24, 1862; Hartsock, *Soldier of the Cross*, 44; Orwig, *History of the 131st Penna.*, 120.

61. Letter from "L. B."; Hartsock, *Soldier of the Cross*, 40; "Letter from Col. Clark," October 24, 1862.

62. Samuel W. North to his brother, December 18, 1862, Samuel W. North Papers, USAMHI; 155th Regt. Assn., *Under the Maltese Cross*, 105.

63. *OR* 21:403, 434.

64. Nathaniel Brown to Arthur Given, December 23, 1862, 133rd Pennsylvania file,

FSNMP; "Army Correspondence," (Washington, Pa.) *Reporter and Tribune*, December 31, 1862; "Letter from Col. Clark," October 24, 1862.

65. OR 21:422; also printed in (Pottsville, Pa.) *Miners Journal*, December 27, 1862.

66. Pittsburgh *Post*, December 27, 1862; "Letter from Col. Allen's Regiment—List of Casualties," (Pittsburgh) *Pennsylvania Gazette*, December 19, 1862; Erastus B. Tyler to Andrew Gregg Curtin, December 29, 1862, PA.

67. Quoted in Bates, *Pennsylvania Volunteers*, 3:188.

68. "Letter from Col. Clark—Names of the Missing—Deaths in the Hospital," (Pittsburgh) *Pennsylvania Gazette*, December 29, 1862. See also R. W. Hemphill to Brother George, December 25, 1862, Hemphill Letters, Henry Family Papers, USAMHI.

69. Orwig, *History of the 131st Penna.*, 133; Lee, *Address Commemorative of the Services*, 18, 30–31.

70. Although Alexander, *126th Pennsylvania*, identifies "Uncle Thomas" as Pvt. Thomas D. French, internal evidence in other family letters written about the time of the battle of Fredericksburg suggests that French and Uncle Thomas are in fact two separate individuals. Since Uncle Thomas was sent to a Washington hospital, it seems more likely that he was Cpl. Thomas Pilkington, who, according to Bates, *Pennsylvania Volunteers*, 4:131, died in that medical facility. According to the same source, French was mustered out with his company in May 1863.

71. Hartsock, *Soldier of the Cross*, 46; R. W. Hemphill to George, December 29, 1862, Hemphill Letters, Henry Family Papers, USAMHI.

72. OR 21:433.

73. Francis A. Walker, *History of the Second Army Corps in the Army of the Potomac* (New York: Charles Scribner's Sons, 1891), 185; Joseph R. C. Ward, *History of the One Hundred and Sixth Regiment, Pennsylvania Volunteers, 2nd Brigade, 2nd Division, 2nd Corps, 1861–1865* (Philadelphia: F. McManus, Jr., 1906), 142.

74. OR 21:432; Bates, *Pennsylvania Volunteers*, 3:188, Walker, *History of the Second Corps*, 186; Henry H. Humphreys, *Major General Andrew Atkinson Humphreys, United States Volunteers, at Fredericksburg, Va., December 13th, 1862 and Farmville, Va., April 7th, 1865* (Chicago: R. R. McCabe, 1896), 12.

75. OR 21:443–44, 446; Humphreys, *Major General Andrew Atkinson Humphreys*, 12.

76. Walker, *History of the Second Corps*, 186–87.

77. Humphreys, *Major General Andrew Atkinson Humphreys*, 13; Hill, "Allabach's Brigade."

78. See William H. Powell, *The Fifth Army Corps (Army of the Potomac): A Record of Operations during the Civil War in the United States of America, 1861–1865* (New York: G. P. Putnam's Sons, 1896), 385–87.

79. See Alexander, *126th Pennsylvania*, 134, and Nancy Niblack Baxter, *Gallant Fourteenth: The Story of an Indiana Civil War Regiment* (Traverse City, Ind.: Pioneer Study Center Press, 1980), 118–20.

80. Quoted in Alexander, *126th Pennsylvania*, 134; Orwig, *History of the 131st Penna.*, 123; Powell, *Fifth Army Corps*, 384–85.

81. J. Watts DePeyster, *Andrew Atkinson Humphreys, of Pennsylvania, Brigadier General and Brevet Major General, USA, Major General, United States Volunteers . . .* (Lancaster, Pa.: Lancaster Intelligencer Printer, 1886), 13; Orwig, *History of the 131st Penna.*, 116; William H. Groninger [126th Pennsylvania], "With Gen. Burnside at Fredericksburg," *National Tribune*, April 1, 1926; oration of Alexander K. McClure, in *Dedication of the Monument Erected by Pennsylvania to Commemorate the Charge of General Humphreys' Division, Fifth Army Corps, Army of the Potomac, on Marye's Heights, Fredericksburg, Virginia, December 13th, 1862, Dedicatory Ceremonies, November 11th 1908* (n.p., 1908), 24.

82. Oration of McClure in *Dedication of Monument*, 25; oration of Robert Shaw Oliver in ibid., 23; R. W. Hemphill to George, December 29, 1862, Hemphill Letters, Henry Family Papers, USAMHI.

The Yanks Have Had a Terrible Whipping

CONFEDERATES EVALUATE THE BATTLE

OF FREDERICKSBURG

GARY W. GALLAGHER

The literature on Fredericksburg devotes minimal attention to the ways in which R. E. Lee's soldiers and Confederates elsewhere reacted to the battle. Those works that have addressed the topic, however briefly, typically stress one of two pictures. Perhaps taking their cue from R. E. Lee, some writers describe Confederates disappointed with a triumph that inflicted no lasting damage on the Army of the Potomac. The far more common view portrays joy over a victory that turned back another Union advance against Richmond, inflicted hideous casualties on the enemy, rocked northern civilian morale, and set the stage for more juggling within the northern army's high command. A sampling of newspapers, letters, diaries, and journals from the six-week period following the battle discloses significant shading between these two extremes. Although far from definitive as a canvass of Confederate responses to the fighting along the Rappahannock, this evidence reveals clear patterns. Beyond shedding light on perceptions of Fredericksburg, it also raises questions about Confederate expectations and Lee's apparent inability to look beyond the battle's immediate military consequences—topics pertinent to historians interested in what strategy best suited the South's effort to win independence and the relative significance of offensive and defensive triumphs on the battlefield.[1]

Early Confederate writers tended to question the importance of Fredericksburg. During the war, Edward A. Pollard, editor of the Richmond *Examiner* and a bitter critic of Jefferson Davis, developed a number of themes in his *Southern History of the War* that would appear in subsequent writings. "At the thrilling tidings of Fredericksburg the hopes of the South rose high that we were at last to realize some important and practical consequences from the prowess of our arms," he noted. Burnside's battered army cowered along the river, vulnerable to a counterattack that might turn a tactical success into a decisive victory. But hopes lay dashed after news arrived of the Federal withdrawal across the Rappahannock: "It was the old lesson to the South of a barren victory. The story of Fredericksburg was incomplete and unsatisfactory; and there appeared no prospect but that a war waged at awful sacrifices was yet indefinitely to linger in the trail of bloody skirmishes." Lee could claim only "the negative advantage of having checked the enemy without destroying him, and the vulgar glory of our having killed and wounded several thousand men more than we had lost."[2]

Three years later Pollard reiterated these points in his widely quoted *The Lost Cause*. He emphasized Burnside's "appalling extremity" after the repulse of his assaults on December 13, a soaring belief in Richmond that final victory was at hand, northern fears of "the same result," and cruel disappointment at "the astounding news" of Burnside's escape. "Various excuses have been made for Gen. Lee's omission to assume the offensive, and realize the proper result of his victory at Fredericksburg," stated Pollard. "These excuses have mostly originated in the generosity of friends and admirers." Lee himself admitted his error in supposing the Federals would resume their attacks on December 14–15 and thus maintaining his admirable defensive position rather than taking the offensive.[3]

Two accounts published in 1867 affirmed Pollard's assessment. In her narrative of life in wartime Richmond, Sallie Putnam employed very similar language. "Victory once more perched on the banner of the Confederates," she maintained, "and the utter rout of the army of Burnside was only prevented, perhaps, by the failure on the part of the 'rebels' to attack his forces on the next day, while they remained at Fredericksburg." Because the Federals managed to get across the Rappahannock without molestation, the Confederates "repeated the old story of a barren victory. A powerful check had been given to the enemy, but no more than a check." William P. Snow's collection of Confederate military biographies similarly stressed the absence of substantive gain. "Thus ended another terrific battle," he wrote, "wherein immense slaughter occurred, and no positive advantage was gained to either side." Although skeptical of the results, Snow displayed empathy for Lee. Observers outside the Army of Northern Virginia believed the Confederate chief had fumbled a Cannae-type opportunity to annihilate Burnside, but Snow insisted "they little knew the almost utter impossibility of such a task on either side."[4]

Near the end of the nineteenth century, Thomas C. DeLeon's analysis in *Four Years in Rebel Capitals* conformed closely to that of previous southern critics of the results at Fredericksburg. First reports of the fighting encouraged the notion that "this time *surely* the enemy would be pushed—this time he was indeed a prey! Broken and demoralized, with a deep river in his rear that he *must cross in pontoons*, the people felt that he could surely be destroyed before reaching his Stafford stronghold." But two days of grace allowed Burnside to extricate his "shattered and broken legions." "Great was the amaze, bitter the disappointment of the people," recalled DeLeon, "and the inquiry how and why this had been done, became universal." By 1890, when *Four Years in Rebel Capitals* appeared, few southern writers dared criticize Lee overtly, and DeLeon, undoubtedly aware of his critique's implications, added that Confederates "above every other feeling had now come to cherish a perfect and unquestioning faith in General Lee; and even while they wondered at a policy that invariably left a beaten army to recover, and only become stronger—still they questioned with a firm reliance that there *must* be some reason, invisible to them but good and potent still."[5]

Modern scholars have advanced equally negative conclusions about the impact of Fredericksburg. Douglas Southall Freeman accented Lee's unhappiness with the outcome. "He was deeply depressed that he had not been able to strike a decisive blow," observed the general's most famous biographer. Moreover, added Freeman, the "army and the country shared his chagrin."[6] Clifford Dowdey, Freeman's successor as the premier Virginia interpreter of the Army of Northern Virginia, conceded positive Confederate civilian reaction while averring that, from a southern perspective, the "battle had been glorious during its action but . . . nothing had been accomplished." Dowdey concluded that "militarily the battle had no effect on the war." In his history of the Confederacy, Clement Eaton bluntly stated that Lee "lost a magnificent opportunity to counterattack the Federal army with the river at its back." Northern artillery along Stafford Heights might have inflicted significant casualties, but "the Confederates could have come so close to them that the Federal guns would have been dangerous to their own troops." Eaton depended heavily on the prominent British military analyst J. F. C. Fuller, who claimed that in failing to counterattack Lee lost nothing less than "his one and only opportunity for ending the war."[7]

Although unfavorable appraisals of Confederate accomplishments at Fredericksburg have persisted for more than a century, they stand as counterpoint to the dominant interpretation of the battle as a major victory. Some works of the latter type err on the side of hyperbole: "The news from Fredericksburg was greeted with jubilation throughout the South," commented the author of a recent popular treatment of Fredericksburg. Ignoring Lee's wellknown misgivings about the battle, this narrative quoted a correspondent for the Charleston *Mercury* who mistakenly described the general as "jubilant, almost off balance, and seemingly desirous of embracing everyone who calls on him." In a more reasoned discussion Frank E. Vandiver suggested the Confederates "almost wrecked the reconstituted Army of the Potomac at Fredericksburg. . . . Costs to Lee were comparatively light and the fruits of victory were important: the Virginia front was stable once again."[8]

Several of the best general histories of the war highlight the disproportionate Union casualties and the firestorm of debate across the North after the battle, passing over Confederate reaction in silence. In *Battle Cry of Freedom*, James M. McPherson labeled Fredericksburg "one of the worst defeats of the war" for a Federal army. He then explored the impact on northern civilians repelled by the ghastly slaughter in front of Marye's Heights and on politicians bickering about why the rebels always seemed to best the Army of the Potomac. Allan Nevins dismissed the Federal "disaster" as the work of "an improvised general [who] had fought an improvised battle" before turning his attention to the "storm of sorrow and wrath which at once swept the North." James G. Randall and David Donald thought the battle, with its "series of forlorn, desperate Union charges against the withering musketry and artillery fire of the Confederates," sent civilian morale in the North plummeting toward nadir. Without a sentence on the Confederacy, they focused northward: "Sorrow caused by the death or mutilation of thousands of brave men turned into rage as the people wondered how so fine a fighting instrument as the Army of the Potomac had been used with such stupid futility." Nor did Bruce Catton pause to look at the impact of Fredericksburg on the Confederacy in his "Centennial History of the Civil War." Like McPherson, Nevins, and Randall and Donald, he proceeded from the battlefield to the crisis of politics and morale north of the Potomac.[9] This approach to Fredericksburg's aftermath probably implies no lack of interest in the Confederacy; rather, it seems likely that the authors assumed a favorable southern reaction to victory and saw no reason to dwell on it.

Literary evidence from the six weeks after Burnside's retreat across the Rappahannock illuminates a more complex pattern of Confederate responses than previously described by historians and other writers. Most newspapers adopted a positive stance. On December 16, before Burnside withdrew, the proadministration Richmond *Daily Dispatch* called Fredericksburg "the greatest battle ever fought on this continent." Lee's defeat of an imposing host of Yankees demonstrated that "no superiority of numbers or of preparation can avail them in a pitched battle with the forces of the Confederacy—a truth so patent, and so often exemplified, that we believe they are the only people on earth who venture to deny it." The *Daily Dispatch* proclaimed total victory when news of Burnside's retreat reached Richmond. The paper did allude to reports that many Confederate soldiers regretted the enemy's escape without further harm, but cited them as evidence of unflagging spirit in the ranks rather than as criticism of Lee. Throughout the rest of the month the *Daily Dispatch* mentioned political unrest in the North, Radical Republican pressure to restructure Lincoln's cabinet, rumors of Burnside's demise, and disaffection in the Army of the Potomac as positive results of the victory. By New Year's Day the editor detected so much confidence among his readers that he warned of the need for continued resolve. The Army of the Potomac surely would mount another "On to Richmond" campaign, and no one should "hope for peace until we have destroyed, dispersed, or worn out that army."[10]

Other newspapers joined in a happy chorus. The Richmond *Daily Enquirer* told readers of "an interest and enthusiasm among our citizens, not less vivid than the intensist feeling concurrent with the memorable battles around Richmond" the previous summer. Boasting about an article in the *New York Herald* portraying a glum North, the *Enquirer* predicted that whether Burnside remained in control made no difference—his retention would demoralize the Yankee army, while his replacement by an officer acceptable to the Radicals would alienate northern conservatives. "We contend against large odds," allowed the Charleston *Daily Courier* on December 16, but "Generals of unsurpassed genius and talents," gallant soldiers who had won victories on many fields, and a righteous cause would win out. Influenced by pessimistic coverage of Fredericksburg in northern newspapers and an absence of Confederate defeats elsewhere, the *Daily Courier* raised the possibility of French intervention. The Petersburg (Va.) *Daily Express* singled out Abraham Lincoln, whose "vigorous efforts to keep up appearances" rang hollow: "The battle of Fredericksburg he knows has prodigiously shattered his Grand Army, and it will be the work of months to put it in a condition to resume offensive operations, even if it be capable of being thus renovated and reinvigorated, which is exceedingly questionable."[11]

Few papers matched the enthusiasm of the Richmond *Daily Whig*, which sketched a Federal army so disheartened it refused to continue the fight after December 13. According to the *Whig*, a captured member of Burnside's staff and other prisoners had affirmed that the Union commander canceled assaults on the fourteenth and retreated because he doubted the valor of his men. Such an army posed little danger in the near term: "The campaign in Virginia, and we think in North Carolina, is ended for the winter, so far as the enemy are concerned. It has been to them a campaign of unbroken failure and disgrace. . . . Lee winds up the campaign in Virginia with a blow at Fredericksburg that makes the whole of Lincolndom real like a drunken man."[12]

Newspapers in the hinterlands relied on letters from soldiers to help tell the story of the battle. These accounts spoke of heavy enemy casualties, dispirited Federals, and striking Confederate success. In the Atlanta *Southern Confederacy* Dr. J. N. Simmons, writing from Richmond, assured readers of a "disastrous defeat" for the Yankees. Men and officers in Lee's army had wished for additional Union assaults; however, Burnside aborted a planned offensive on December 14 because Federal soldiers "refused to risk the fate of their dead comrades." A member of Joseph B. Kershaw's brigade penned an account printed in the Sumter (S.C.) *Tri-Weekly Watchman*. "I have often heard of the dead being piled in heaps," stated this witness after viewing the Union corpses below Marye's Heights, "but never before have scene [*sic*] it literally true." He pronounced the battle "a great victory" whose "moral effect will, I think, be as great if not greater than any battle we have fought." A soldier in the 38th Georgia of A. R. Lawton's brigade, who had fought at Seven Pines, Malvern Hill, and Sharpsburg, confused readers of the Sandersville (Ga.) *Central Georgian* by mixing images of George B. McClellan's retreat after Malvern Hill with those of the Union army on the Rappahannock: "Once more the 'Dixie Boys' as usual, have triumphed and driven Old Abe's horde of thieves to the shelter of their gunboats, under whose friendly protection they are to day hiding their cowardly carcasses."[13]

Another Georgian quoted in Atlanta's *Southern Banner* speculated wistfully about what might have been before closing triumphantly. The splendid Confederate position resulted in an unparalleled repulse for the enemy. Had Burnside pressed the offensive on either the fourteenth or the fifteenth, Lee's men might have ended the war by destroying the Army of the Potomac. "As it is," wrote this captain in the 9th Georgia of George T. Anderson's brigade, "I think this battle has saved Richmond for the winter." More optimistic than ever despite the enemy's escape, he added that "*this army can never be whipped* by all the power of Yankeedom combined, and I now predict that the treaty of peace when made, be it soon or late, will find it still victorious."[14]

A minority of newspapers chose more muted language for their coverage. Pollard's Richmond *Examiner* posed questions about the victory that foreshadowed opinions in his later books. Rumors of a "demoralized and unmanageable" Federal army, a North in "the flames of revolution," and rioting in New York City that had claimed 1,500 lives circulated in Richmond on December 17 (the editor vouched for the accuracy of none of these reports), while intelligence from Lee's army indicated "unlimited rejoicings" among soldiers who regarded Burnside's retreat as acknowledgment of defeat. More insightful men, wishing for another opportunity to smite the Federals, received word of the enemy's withdrawal "with unfeigned sorrow." Lee and Longstreet presented a cheerful front, but "the stubborn fact exists the enemy had put the river between himself and the rebels he had rushed from Warrenton, to 'scatter like chaff,' and those who can not rejoice over the retreat put a cheerful face upon the matter." The other leading anti-administration paper, Charleston's *Mercury*, worried that Burnside might soon advance along some other avenue. That specter aside, the paper bravely added, "General Lee knows his business and that army has yet known no such word as fail."[15]

Opinions among civilians and soldiers outside the Army of Northern Virginia corresponded to coverage in the newspapers. Jefferson Davis spent most of December away from Richmond, returning after the New Year. On January 7 he responded to a serenade outside his home with high praise for Lee and his victory: "Our glorious Lee, the valued son, emulating the virtues of the heroic Light-horse Harry, his father, has achieved a victory at Fredericksburg, and driven the enemy back from his last and greatest effort to get 'on to Richmond.'" That success, together with Union frustration at Vicksburg and the battle of Murfreesboro—then thought to be a comparable

Confederate win—opened a tantalizing vista. "Out of this victory is to come that dissatisfaction in the North West," proclaimed Davis, "which will rive the power of that section; and thus we see in the future the dawn—first separation of the North West from the Eastern States, the discord among them which will paralyze the power of both,—then for us future peace and prosperity."[16]

Fuller news from Tennessee revealed Murfreesboro to be at best a bloody standoff, leaving Davis to mull over the losses of 1862. Varina Davis recalled that the roster of defeats from Fort Donelson and Nashville through Island No. 10, Memphis, and Murfreesboro oppressed her husband. He shared none of the revived hope for European recognition evinced by many Confederates. Indeed, wrote Mrs. Davis, Lee's "victory at Fredericksburg was the one bright spot in all this dark picture."[17]

The outcome at Fredericksburg prompted some Confederates to speak about an end to the war. John B. Jones, whose diary makes him the most famous mid-level bureaucrat in the Confederacy, observed on December 19 that "many people regard the disaster of Burnside as the harbinger of peace." The impact of Lee's victory—as well as the uncertain power of events to hold the public imagination—stand out in a passage from Jones's diary four days later: "The battle of Fredericksburg is still the topic, or the wonder, and it transpired more than nine days ago. It will have its page in history, and be read by school-boys a thousand days hence." William M. Blackford of Lynchburg, who loathed slavery but sent five sons into Confederate service, thought he saw "indications of a cessation of hostilities, though many months may pass before peace is established." The cumulative effect of Lee's campaigns in 1862 especially impressed Blackford. "The defeats of the enemy in the Valley, in the Peninsular, in the Piedmont, the invasion of Maryland, the capture of Harper's Ferry and lastly the victory at Fredericksburg," he noted, "taken all together, are achievements which do not often crown one year."[18]

Ample additional testimony supports Jones's observation about Confederates taking heart at dimmed Union prospects. "The Yanks have had a terrible whipping at Fredericksburg," exulted Amanda Virginia Edmonds from near Paris, Virginia. "The whole loss supposed to be forty or fifty thousand. Oh! I hope it is true." Two weeks later Edmonds confided in her diary that the "months do not pass speedily enough for I feel it is that much nearer peace. War's alarm is that much nearer being calmed." In early January some Confederates tied Fredericksburg to good news from other theaters. "The papers are very encouraging," went a typical comment. "We are beginning to hope for peace. We have had another victory at Vicksburg and one at Murfreesboro."[19]

Coverage in the northern press imparted confidence to persons conditioned to dispute accounts in enemy newspapers. "From their papers we learn that 'the whole nation is filled with grief and shame at the disaster before Fredericksburg,[']" Cornelia Peake McDonald of Winchester recorded on January 1, 1863. "Shouts of execration against them come up from one side, wails of despair from another, cries of vengeance against treacherous Europe, and a voice above all, as of one trying to pour oil on the troubled waters—crying cheerily, 'The Union is not lost yet.'" McDonald bragged that Yankees could "say in the words of the Hero of yore—'We have met the enemy, and we are theirs.'"[20] Edmund Ruffin, the inveterate old fire-eater who commented extensively on public events in his expansive diary, happily observed that "instead of being (as usual,) boasting," comments in northern papers "are in the tone of lamentation & gloom." Dependent on northern accounts, a loyal Confederate in Fairfax, Virginia, found that initial reports spoke of Union victory. By December 20 the tenor of coverage had changed markedly: "The papers are filled with Burnside's defeat, they do not pretend to deny, or gloss it over [as] hitherto."[21]

Georgian Mary Jones combined gratitude for victory at Fredericksburg with a heartfelt tribute to Lee. Federals probably outnumbered Confederates five or six to one, she estimated, yet despite their "deadly appliances of modern warfare" failed to overwhelm the defenders. "I have not the words to express the emotions I feel for this signal success," Jones informed her son. She felt "thankful that in this great struggle the head of our army is a noble son of Virginia, and worthy of the intimate relation in which he stands connected with our immortal Washington. What confidence his wisdom, integrity, and valor and undoubted piety inspire!" Others echoed her faith in Lee, as when war clerk Jones displayed no concern that Burnside would menace Richmond from another direction. Before the Union commander could do so, "Lee would be between him and the city, and if he could beat him on the Rappahannock he can beat him anywhere."[22]

Many Confederates perceived that the political impact of the battle outweighed its purely military effect. This should not obscure the fact that nearly everyone mentioned approvingly the grim harvest of Union attackers—some dwelled on grisly details more than others—and took delight in stories about poor morale in the Army of the Potomac. Yet few Confederates believed Federal casualties posed a long-range problem to the heavily populated North, and they had seen beaten Federals rebound before. Loss of civilian morale and political chaos among the Republicans, however, did threaten the Union war effort. Edmund Ruffin, who gloried in Burnside's repulse, asserted that "the most remarkable effects, & manifest acknowledgment of this disastrous defeat have been displayed at Washington. A private meeting (or caucus) of the members of the Senate was held, which requested the President to dismiss Seward, & to reconstruct his whole cabinet."[23]

From eastern North Carolina, Catherine Ann Devereux Edmondston surveyed an apparently chaotic North in her remarkable journal. "The news of Burnside's repulse and retreat from Fredericksburg has fallen like an avalanch upon the North," she wrote on December 21. "They have found out that Lincoln's 'jests' have but little comfort in them, that their Secretary of War is a '*bungling idiot*,' say that their President knows nothing of the state of feeling throughout the country & abuse their whole Cabinet, their Government, & their Generals in the most unmeasured terms."[24] Lucy Rebecca Buck reacted similarly to rumors of Burnside's removal, William H. Seward's resignation from Lincoln's cabinet, and quarrels between Salmon P. Chase and Edwin M. Stanton. "Glorious!" she exclaimed from her home at Front Royal, Virginia. "With division in their councils—disorganization of their army and dissatisfaction among the people I think their prospects of subjugating us a very poor one."[25]

What of the widespread unhappiness with Lee's victory described by Pollard and DeLeon? Did a substantial number of Confederates see their expectations raised to giddy heights by events on December 13, only to be smashed when Lee allowed Burnside to return quietly to the northern bank of the Rappahannock? A few civilian sources seem to bear this out. One Louisiana woman conveyed a decidedly mixed impression of the battle in her diary entry of January 1, 1863. "We have repulsed the enemy twice between the Yazoo and Vicksburg," she affirmed. "Our victory at Fredericksburg was complete but barren of result, only it has depressed and surprised the North. Altogether we are getting the better of our foes." Inability to inflict greater harm on the Army of the Potomac must explain this use of "barren" regarding a battle that caused consternation in the North. At the Bureau of War, Robert Garlick Hill Kean also rendered a mixed verdict. He believed that "Burnside's official jacket was whipped off at Fredericksburg," but he questioned rumors of disruption in Lincoln's cabinet and accused Lee of reporting too few Confederate casualties. Upset earlier that Lee had permitted the enemy to cross the Rappahannock "almost without resistance," Kean likely thought the failure to attack the Federals while they remained on the southern side of the river a mistake as well.[26]

Concern about a potential lost opportunity shows up more frequently among soldiers in the Army of Northern Virginia. The diary of artillerist Henry Robinson Berkeley furnishes an excellent example of mounting disillusionment. "When darkness came," Berkeley wrote on the evening of December 13, "we had the satisfaction of knowing the Yanks had been repulsed at every point with very heavy loss." In the absence of more Federal assaults on the fourteenth, Berkeley observed, "It seems to me that we ought to go down on the plain and drive them into the river, or at least try to do it." "I don't see why our army doesn't assail the Yanks down on the plain," he repeated on the fifteenth. "I fear they will get away from us." Dawn on the sixteenth confirmed the worst: "At light this morning we saw plainly that Gen. Burnside had withdrawn his entire army to the north side of the river and had given us the slip." An officer in the 10th Virginia, a regiment in Jackson's corps that experienced virtually no combat on the thirteenth, thought a counterattack on the thirteenth "could have turned their repulse into an utter rout." Daylight ran out, however, "and in consequence of our not pursuing them they escaped with their cannon." Fredericksburg might have ended the war "could the power have been given our Generals, like Joshua of old, to have stayed the sun an hour or two in its course." Because the contest ended without further fighting, the armies would "soon again meet in battle on some other field and God grant us the victory."[27]

Some men ventured oblique criticism of Lee. "The Yanks made repeated attempts to advance but failed in every attempt being repulsed with heavy loss," a member of Joseph B. Kershaw's brigade related to his sister. Kershaw's soldiers had supported T. R. R. Cobb's infantry in the sunken road and thus witnessed the Federal assaults at their most futile. "The fight was kept up until night when it ceased," continued this man, "every person believing the next day would be the bloody day but in this everyone was deceived even our generals." Capt. Charles Minor Blackford informed his wife that after the bloody success of December 13, Confederates "expected the battle to be renewed the next day." On the night of the fifteenth "the enemy quietly withdrew." Blackford praised Burnside's skill in accomplishing this—"for as far as I can see, it was done without the knowledge of our generals, and certainly without an effort to interrupt." "I take it General Lee knows better what should have been done than I do," he added with little enthusiasm, "or than the newspapers who criticize him for not attacking." In any event Blackford thought the "war is over, at least for the winter."[28]

James T. McElvaney of the 35th Georgia informed his mother that "our victory is pronounced by Generals Lee & Jackson Complete." Part of Edward L. Thomas's brigade in A. P. Hill's division, the 35th suffered eighty-nine casualties on the thirteenth and "expected a harder fight on Sunday." Burnside's able retreat left McElvaney unconvinced that the Army of Northern Virginia's triumph was complete: "There is a great deal of speculation as to what the enemy will do or where he will turn up again," he stated. "I would be glad to see this war end but cant see where it will stop." A colonel in the Stonewall Brigade agreed that Fredericksburg augured no dramatic shift in the war. "We repulsed them all along the line with tremendous slaughter," wrote James K. Edmondson on December 17, yet the Federals safely withdrew and likely would cross the river again at Port Royal, some twenty miles below Fredericksburg. Edmondson expected "another heavy battle in a day or so." A South Carolinian in Kershaw's brigade predicted "another great battle in less than a month" because the "enemy have by no means retreated but apparently have fallen back to their former position." He passed along a rumor that Port Royal would be the next target, expressing confidence that "Gen. Lee is well prepared to meet them and states that if attacked he will defeat them with greater ease."[29]

Regret at losing the advantage of a superb defensive position probably animated at least as many men as the failure to launch counterattacks. A Georgian explained on December 18 that his comrades anticipated Union assaults on the day following the battle: "It was universally supposed that this would be *the* terrible day and every soldier in our ranks wished for the attack to begin, for never before had we had such an advantageous position." Tuesday revealed that the enemy "had skedaddled" to safety. "It was a sad disappointment to our soldiers," he confessed. "If they had to fight, they desired to

Confederate defenders behind the stone wall, as shown in a postwar engraving of Longstreet's well-protected infantry on Marye's Heights repulsing Federal attacks. Robert Underwood Johnson and Clarence Clough Buel, eds., Battles and Leaders of the Civil War, *4 vols. (New York: Century, 1887–88), 3:80*

fight here." Another Georgian seconded this view, describing disbelief among Confederates when they grasped that Burnside had recrossed the Rappahannock. "I had no idea that they were so badly whipped," he wrote. "They can still be seen across the river. I do not think they will attack us again. All the better if they do. I think we can whip a million of them! This is one of the best positions in the world." William Beverley Pettit of the Fluvanna Artillery mentioned a "general regret that the enemy withdrew without renewing the fight, for all who viewed the battleground and the superior [strength] . . . of our position felt confident that we could whip them badly, no matter in what force they may attack."[30]

More than most of their subordinates and soldiers in the ranks, members of the high command believed the Federals had escaped too lightly. R. E. Lee's response, which may have set the tone for many of his lieutenants, will be discussed at length below. Stonewall Jackson's desire to smite the enemy with some type of offensive counterstroke is well known. In his report Jackson indicated that he ordered preparations for "an advance of our troops across the plain." But Federal artillery "so completely swept our front as to satisfy me that the proposed movement should be abandoned." Artillery chief William Nelson Pendleton identified Monday as the day "we looked for the great fight of the war. But lo! when dawn appeared no Yankees remained this side of the Rappahannock, except dead and wounded." Burnside had "used the dark, rainy night" to pull back to the protection of Stafford Heights, and the Federals now lay "out of our reach." Heros Von Borcke, a Prussian officer serving on J. E. B. Stuart's staff, visited Lee's Hill shortly after the Confederates learned of Burnside's retreat. "We found a great number of the generals assembled around our Commander-in-Chief," he recalled a few months after the battle, "all extremely chagrined that the Federals should have succeeded in so cleverly making their escape."[31]

Like their civilian counterparts the bulk of Lee's soldiers placed the battle in a decidedly favorable light. Several threads run through their letters and diaries. The extent of Union casualties inspired lengthy comment—particularly the gruesome scene below Marye's Heights. The impact of the battle on morale in Burnside's army, disaffection behind the lines in the North, and improving prospects for peace also show up repeatedly in writings from the weeks after the battle. The spectacle of one huge army coming to grips with another in the amphitheatrical valley of the Rappahannock fascinated some observers. The battle seemed to many an omen of good days ahead, marred only by the sad ruin of the city of Fredericksburg and the desperate plight of its inhabitants.

Jeb Stuart touched two of these themes in a pair of brief communications. "We were victorious yesterday," he telegraphed his wife on December 14. "Repulsing enemy's attack in main force with tremendous slaughter." Four days later he related to George Washington Custis Lee that English observers with the army "who surveyed Solferino and all the battlefields of Italy say the pile of dead on the plains of Fredericksburg exceeds anything of the sort ever seen by them." The city itself lay in ruins: "It is the saddest sight I ever saw." A

South Carolinian addressed the same topics in recounting his first sight of Fredericksburg after the battle. "The number of dead bodies were considerable that I ever saw," he stated somewhat clumsily. "Apparently men who were severely wounded and carried into houses and afterwards died. I also saw numbers of feet, legs, hands, and the like which had been shot and cut off." The town "was the most complete wreck" he ever saw: "Quite a number of houses were burnt down and those that were left standing was shot to pieces." Obviously troubled by the scene, this man knew his correspondent would "perceive my nerves are very much shattered." A captain in T. R. R. Cobb's brigade termed December 13 a "glorious day" because Confederates "slaughtered them by the thousands losing very few ourselves." Federal bodies "*literally* covered" the field outside of Fredericksburg, which itself presented a "dreadful sight." The Federals presumably wrecked the town "just in mere wantoness."[32]

Evidence of demoralization in Burnside's ranks and among northern civilians buoyed the Confederates, who often linked it to hopes for final victory. During a truce on December 17, a quartermaster with the 13th Mississippi talked with Union officers who admitted they "suffered a serious defeat in the late battle and express themselves as very tired of the war."[33] Philip H. Powers wrote home on Christmas Day: "You will see from the papers how terribly whipped Burnside was and what a commotion it has produced in Yankeedom." "I think the sky brightens and our chances for peace improve," Powers continued, but "still the war may linger on another year, or even to the end of Lincoln's term." Maj. Eugene Blackford of the 5th Alabama conversed with a number of Federals during a truce on December 15. "They all seemed ashamed to look our men in the face," noted Blackford, and "without exception, men and officers, professed themselves utterly sick of the war, and declared their desire to see it end in any way." A native Vermonter serving with the 51st Georgia drew broad conclusions from the victory. "They have retired without one achievement to cheer them or one hope," he wrote with evident satisfaction. "One nation is now shaded with disappointment and one is clo[th]ed with garments of joy. . . . A proud and haughty people are humbled and brought to a stand. A reckless politician and statesman has received another intimation of speedy ruin which will come embittered by the curses of two nations."[34]

One artillerist described Confederate pickets taunting their Federal counterparts about the battle until the latter finally "acknowledged that we gave them a severe whipping." The Federals refused to admit anyone had resigned from Lincoln's cabinet, though the Confederates had it from "quite a good authority—an aid of Gen. Stewart." A trooper from the 13th Virginia Cavalry, also quoting Union pickets, pronounced the privates in the Army of the Potomac "willing to give us anything we ask" to achieve peace. With the rank and file of the enemy alienated from the northern cause, he believed that "by spring our brightest hopes will be consummated."[35] William B. Bailey of the Louisiana Guard Artillery in Richard S. Ewell's division mentioned demoralization so serious among the enemy that "deserters are coming over to us daily in squads." "It is no use for the nigger Government to try to take Richmond, 'that can't be did,' " he exulted. "Our army can't be whipped, no matter how large a force the nigger government may send against us." A North Carolinian rejoiced that the Yankees failed "to destroy our nationality and every thing else that belonged to Southron institutions." Fredericksburg marked "the first clear back down they ever have made."[36]

A Virginian in D. H. Hill's division feared Lee's victory at Fredericksburg had been too decisive. The Army of the Potomac would be so quiet during the winter that units from the Army of Northern Virginia could be sent to defend the North Carolina coast. "It is surmised that Hill's Division will be sent off," he wrote unhappily. "We hope not, for we are not anxious to fight both winter and summer." Despite this worry, he ended his letter on a positive note: "I am now beginning to entertain hope of a speedy peace." If Bragg's victory at Murfreesboro turned out to be significant, Vicksburg held, and the coasts remained safe, "peace, I trust, will come with Spring."[37]

Not all general officers shared the outlook Heros Von Borcke described among those atop Lee's Hill on December 16. James J. Archer, who commanded a brigade in A. P. Hill's Light Division, reflected on the events of December in letters to members of his family. "The prospects I think look bright for peace since [the] battle of Fredericksburg & since the democrats at the north have found their tongues," he told his brother. A victory in the West "would settle the matter." Retaining his optimism after word of Bragg's retreat reached Virginia, Archer admitted disappointment that success at Murfreesboro "was not greater," adding that Confederates had "amply shown all sober people at the North that they are engaged in a Vain attempt & I for one look for a speedy peace." Brig. Gen. Elisha Franklin Paxton of the Stonewall

Brigade also forecast victory. "I feel, perhaps, too confident," he confessed to his wife. "Our independence was secured in the last campaign when we proved our capacity to beat the finest army they could bring in the field." War weariness in the North would prevent the Federals' fielding a larger army, and Confederate victory had become nothing more than a matter of time: "The war may be protracted, there is no telling how long; but we have shown our capacity to beat them, and we are better able to do it now than ever before."[38]

Apart from its effect on the military situation and northern morale, Fredericksburg left many Confederates with visual images of triumph on a grand scale. Capt. Shepherd Green Pryor of the 12th Georgia termed it "the grandest sight I ever saw in my life. Youv seen pictures of armies, but no artist could do that sight justice. . . . It was a grand sight after the fight to see the two armies within 1000 yards of each other, dead & wounded yankeys and horses lying over the field, & those dead & wounded all Federals." Pryor concluded rather cold-bloodedly that "such sights as those are grand to those that are use[d] to seeing dead men." A staff officer who had not written to his mother in some months took time in April 1863 to recapture the drama and sweep of Fredericksburg. Certain she had read of Burnside's "ignominious defeat," he concentrated on the vista from the summit of Lee's Hill: "Never in my life do I expect to see such a magnificent sight again. From the crest of a hill where I was stationed with Lee, Longstreet, Pickett, Stuart, and others of our principal generals the whole scene of conflict was before our eyes, and at out feet, the glorious sun shining out as tho' bloodshed and slaughter were unknown on the beautiful earth; the screaming of shells and the singing of rifle bullets adding a fearful accompaniment to the continued booming of the heavy guns."[39] This same panorama inspired Lee's oft-quoted remark, "It is well that war is so terrible—we should grow too fond of it!"[40]

In contrast to the implications of Lee's famous quotation, the aftermath of the victorious spectacle on December 13 found him notably disgruntled. Bryan Grimes, a colonel in temporary command of Stephen Dodson Ramseur's North Carolina brigade, remembered the general's "deep chagrin and mortification" upon learning definitively that the Federals were gone.[41] Lee had hoped for additional assaults against his confident and well-positioned army. "The attack on the 13th had been so easily repulsed, and by so small a part of our army," he explained in his official report, "that it was not supposed the enemy would limit his efforts to an attempt, which, in view of the

*Generals Lee, Pickett, Jackson, and Longstreet watch the battle
in a popular postwar print by H. A. Ogden.
Editor's collection*

magnitude of his preparations and the extent of his force, seemed to be comparatively insignificant." Believing the enemy would try more assaults, and mindful of his own strong position and powerful Union artillery on Stafford Heights that would decimate any counterattack, Lee opted to remain in place. "We were necessarily ignorant of the extent to which he [the enemy] had suffered," his report read, "and only became aware of it when, on the morning of the 16th, it was discovered that he had availed himself of the darkness of night, and the prevalence of a violent storm of wind and rain, to recross the river."[42] This language conveys disappointment as well as a measure of contempt for a foe who would slink away from a battlefield after what the Confederate chieftain considered less than an all-out effort.

Lee's comments to Mrs. Lee three days after the battle anticipated the thrust of his report. "Yesterday evening I had my suspicions that they might retire during the night, but could not believe they would relinquish their purpose after all their boasting & preparations," he wrote Mary, "& when I say that the latter is equal to the former, you will have some idea of its magnitude." The enemy now lay safely across the Rappahannock, having gone "as they came, in the night." Lee's concluding remarks underscored his unhappiness: "They suffered heavily as far as the battle went, but it did not go far enough to satisfy me. . . . The contest will have now to be renewed, but on what field I cannot say." Robert E. Lee, Jr., probably misread his father when he met him several days after the battle. Years later Lee recollected that he found the general "as calm and composed as if nothing unusual had happened, and he never referred to his great victory, except to deplore the loss of his brave officers and soldiers or the sufferings of the sick and wounded." This passage suggests the son inferred that modesty prevented his father from boasting of a grand victory; instead, the commander may have seen no reason to celebrate what he considered a meaningless success.[43]

In July 1863 Lee shared his negative views about Fredericksburg with Secretary of War James A. Seddon's brother John. Major Seddon subsequently talked with Henry Heth about the conversation, and Heth recalled Seddon's comments in a postwar letter. "At Fredericksburg we gained a battle," Lee said to the major, "inflicting very serious loss on the enemy in men and material; our people were greatly elated—I was much depressed." In Lee's opinion the Confederates "had really accomplished nothing" at Fredericksburg: "We had not gained a foot of ground, and I knew the enemy could easily replace the men he had lost; and the loss of material was, if any thing, rather beneficial to him, as it gave an opportunity to contractors to make money."[44] Fear of misguided Confederate elation also showed up in a letter from Lee to the secretary of war in January 1863. After imploring Seddon to increase the size of the Confederate armies, the general cautioned that the "success with which our efforts have been crowned, under the blessing of God, should not betray our people into the dangerous delusion that the armies now in the field are sufficient to bring this war to a successful and speedy termination."[45]

Lee must have found positive and negative newspaper coverage of Fredericksburg equally disturbing. Editors who accentuated Yankee losses, plunging morale in Burnside's army, northern political and civilian unrest, and heightened prospects for peace ran the risk of creating a mood in which the Confederate populace might relax its determination. More critical editors such as Pollard, by questioning Lee's failure to launch counterattacks, overlooked Burnside's cannon on Stafford Heights and other factors that likely would have doomed any aggressive Confederate movement. Their distortions could lead to a drop in morale among citizens like Sallie Putnam who worried that sacrifices on the battlefield went for naught.[46]

Lee's attitude toward Fredericksburg makes sense only if he viewed the battle in strictly military terms. It is true that the Army of Northern Virginia gained no territory and that Federal losses could be replaced easily. But repercussions within the Army of the Potomac and behind the lines in the North should have heartened Lee. As an assiduous reader of northern newspapers, he certainly knew about the battle's political ramifications and impact on Union morale. Why did he place at best only marginal value on the crises in Lincoln's cabinet and in the high command of Burnside's army? Why did reports of war weariness in the North not count for more?

The answer cannot be that Lee lacked an appreciation for factors beyond the battlefield. He frequently manifested a grasp of how military events could influence politics and civilian morale in ways beneficial to the Confederate cause. In September 1862, for example, he outlined nonmilitary goals for his army as it marched northward into Maryland. A year had passed "without advancing the objects which our enemies proposed to themselves in beginning the contest," he observed to Jefferson Davis. The time had come to offer peace to the North. If Lincoln's government rejected the offer, northerners would see that "continuance of the war does not rest upon us, but that the party in power in the United States elect to prosecute it for purposes of their own." "The proposal of peace," concluded Lee, "would enable the people of the United States to determine at their coming elections whether they will support those who favor a prolongation of the war, or those who wish to bring it to a termination."[47] Although Lee did not state the obvious, the presence of the Army of Northern Virginia on Union soil during the fall of 1862 could affect the political process considerably.

Lee again alluded to the relationship between military activity and Union civilian morale in the spring of 1863. He detected growing doubt and weakening resolve among the enemy. Should the Confederates "baffle them in their various designs" during 1863, Lee thought "our success will be certain." In the fall "there will be a great change in public opinion at the North. The Republicans will be destroyed & I think the friends of peace will become so strong as that the next administration will go in on that basis."[48] Fredericksburg stood as a prime example of "baffling the enemy's designs" and causing consternation in the North; indeed, Lee's guarded optimism in April 1863 must have stemmed at least in part from his last success along the Rappahannock.

Why, then, his public and private depreciation of Fredericksburg? Perhaps the answer lies in his concern about overconfidence expressed to Secretary of War Seddon. Whatever Fredericksburg's impact on the enemy, Lee knew the war would continue. He knew as well that fellow Confederates gave great weight to his statements. Any suggestion that his latest victory might mark a significant step toward independence could lull the public into a false sense of security. In a contest with an opponent who enjoyed vastly superior resources, such a response could be fatal.

Those who emphasize the aggressive part of Lee's military personality might suggest that he refused to view any battle in which his opponent dictated the action as positively as one in which he controlled the strategic or tactical flow. It cannot be denied that Lee's wartime correspondence bristles with allusions to striking offensive blows that could crush the enemy.[49] Yet during the talk with Major Seddon in which he claimed Fredericksburg availed the Confederacy nothing, Lee dismissed Chancellorsville as even less satisfactory. In the latter case Lee seized the initiative from Joseph Hooker and used a series of assaults during three days of hard fighting to defeat the Army of the Potomac. His estimate of the campaign nonetheless remained harsh: "At Chancellorsville we gained another victory; our people were wild with delight—I, on the contrary, was more depressed than after Fredericksburg; our loss was severe, and again we had gained not an inch of ground and the enemy could not be pursued."[50]

In the end there can be no definitive explanation for Lee's attitude. He chose to categorize Fredericksburg strictly in terms of ground gained or lost, and by that yardstick it paled in comparison with the Seven Days or Second Manassas campaigns—though those two operations caused scarcely more political or civilian unrest in the North.

This canvass of opinion relating to Fredericksburg might prove useful to historians interested in broader questions. A desire for decisive offensive victories left a substantial minority of Confederates, including some soldiers who might have become casualties had Lee counterattacked, only partially satisfied with the battle. Few of these individuals indulged in serious criticism of Lee, who, after all, had demonstrated his willingness to take great risks in pursuit of overwhelming victories in every stage of the campaigning from the Seven Days through Sharpsburg. But their expectations spawned harsher estimates of lesser generals such as Joseph E. Johnston, whose retreats on the Peninsula and later in northern Georgia left many of his fellow Confederates exasperated. Anyone who maintains that Lee should have avoided the offensive wherever possible, or that the Confederate national strategy should have traded territory for time in a broad defensive effort, must reckon with the likely civilian reaction.

On the other hand a majority of Confederates seems to have welcomed the victory and its obvious impact on morale in the most famous Federal army and among northern civilians. A fair number considered it a major step toward eventual Confederate independence. Would a string of Fredericksburgs have sustained Confederates in their quest for nationhood? A more systematic, comparative examination of responses to various battles and campaigns would afford a clearer picture of this aspect of Confederate history.

The comments of many of Lee's soldiers indicate they welcomed a shift toward fighting on the defensive after five months of bloody operations. Does this suggest the army as a whole would have been content to fight a defensive war? The army repeatedly had demonstrated its élan in offensive combat, and it would do so again at Chancellorsville, Gettysburg, and during the 1864 Overland Campaign. The ease with which they repulsed Burnside's army, however, made a profound impression. As one man put it, Fredericksburg "was but a frolic for our men, being the first time that they had ever had the pleasure of being entrenched and await[ing] the enemy." John B. Jones viewed the question more analytically. "I fear the flower of our chivalry mostly perished in storming batteries," he wrote. "It is true *prestige* was gained" in such endeavors, but Fredericksburg underscored the importance of advantageous ground. Jones hoped commanders might learn the lesson that "no necessity exists for so great an expenditure of life in the prosecution of this war. The disparity of numbers should be considered by our generals."[51] Jones did not offer advice on how to guarantee a regular supply of Federal officers who would order assaults against well-situated defenders, nor does the testimony about Fredericksburg place soldier attitudes within a larger context. As with the civilian reaction, a comparative look at different campaigns would be instructive.

Students of the Civil War tend to place victories and defeats in pairs or groups for purposes of analysis. Examples of this tendency come readily to mind: The Seven Days and Second Manassas paved the way for Lee's first raid across the Potomac and brought Europe to the verge of recognizing the Confederacy; Fredericksburg and Chancellorsville set the stage for a potentially crucial swing in the momentum of the war; Sharpsburg and Gettysburg blunted the two most promising Confederate offensives of the war; and Gettysburg and Vicksburg signaled a major turning point. Although admittedly useful (not to mention irresistible), this device obscures important differences between the operations in each pairing. Examination of each campaign's impact on the respective populations would help historians construct a more sophisticated portrait of the nation at war. If Fredericksburg, a straightforward campaign logically subject to very little difference of interpretation by either side, yields a greater range of responses than expected, it seems reasonable that more complex operations might hold greater surprises.

Notes

1. This essay rests on testimony from more than 135 individuals across the Confederacy (only Arkansas and Florida lack representation), including soldiers of all ranks within the Army of Northern Virginia, soldiers in Confederate service elsewhere, politicians, civil servants, and men and women in a variety of private circumstances. The sampling does not follow any scientific model, however, and it is possible that responses drawn from a far wider group of witnesses might yield different results.

2. Edward A. Pollard, *Southern History of the War: The Second Year of the War* (1863; reprint, New York: Charles B. Richardson, 1865), 195–96.

3. Edward A. Pollard, *The Lost Cause; A New Southern History of the War of the Confederates* (New York: E. B. Treat, 1866), 345–46.

4. Sallie Putnam, *In Richmond during the Confederacy* (1867; reprint, New York: Robert M. McBride, 1961), 198; William P. Snow, *Lee and His Generals* (1867; reprint, New York: Fairfax Press, 1982), 85.

5. Thomas C. DeLeon, *Four Years in Rebel Capitals: An Inside View of Life in the Southern Confederacy, from Birth to Death* (1890; reprint, [Alexandria, Va.]: Time-Life Books, 1983), 248.

6. Douglas Southall Freeman, *R. E. Lee: A Biography*, 4 vols. (New York: Charles Scribner's Sons, 1934–35), 2:473. In *Lee's Lieutenants: A Study in Command*, 3 vols. (New York: Charles Scribner's Sons, 1942–44), 2:383–84, Freeman offered a different perspective: "Although the Confederate commanders were chagrined that the enemy had escaped with no more punishment than that of a costly repulse, the South was jubilant." Freeman quoted from several newspapers in support of this view.

7. Clifford Dowdey, *The Land They Fought For: The Story of the South as the Confederacy, 1832–1865* (Garden City, N.Y.: Doubleday, 1955), 235; Clement Eaton, *A History of the Southern Confederacy* (New York: Macmillan, 1954), 196; J. F. C. Fuller, *Grant and Lee: A Study in Personality and Generalship* (1932; reprint, Bloomington: Indiana University Press, 1957), 174.

8. William K. Goolrick and the editors of Time-Life Books, *Rebels Resurgent: Fredericksburg to Chancellorsville* (Alexandria, Va.: Time-Life Books, 1985), 92; Frank E. Vandiver, *Their Tattered Flags: The Epic of the Confederacy* (New York: Harper's, 1970), 168.

9. James M. McPherson, *Battle Cry of Freedom: The Civil War Era* (New York: Oxford University Press, 1988), 572–75 (quotation on p. 572); Allan Nevins, *The War for the Union*, 4 vols. (New York: Charles Scribner's Sons, 1959–71), 2:350; James G. Randall and David Donald, *The Civil War and Reconstruction*, 2nd ed. (Lexington, Mass.: D. C. Heath, 1969), 225; Bruce Catton, *Never Call Retreat* (Garden City, N.Y.: Doubleday, 1965), 24–26.

10. Richmond *Daily Dispatch*, December 16 (first two quotations), 17, 19, 23, 1862, January 1, 1863 (third quotation).

11. Richmond *Daily Enquirer*, December 16 (first quotation), 30, 1862; Charleston *Daily Courier*, December 16 (second and third quotations), 19, 24, 1862; Petersburg (Va.) *Daily Express*, December 29, 1862 (quoted in Beulah Gayle Green, comp., *Confederate Reporter, 1861–64* [Austin, Tex.: Burrell Printing, 1962], 112). Lincoln's depression following Fredericksburg is well known. "If there is a worse place than Hell," he remarked, "I am in it" (James M. McPherson, *Ordeal by Fire: The Civil War and Reconstruction*, 2nd ed. [New York: McGraw-Hill, 1992], 303).

12. Richmond *Daily Whig*, December 19, 20, 1862.

13. Atlanta *Southern Confederacy*, December 27, 1862 (Simmons's letter dated December 20, 1862); Sumter (S.C.) *Tri-Weekly Watchman*, January 5, 1863 (soldier's letter dated December 17, 1862); Sandersville (Ga.) *Central Georgian*, January 14, 1862 (soldier's letter dated December 15, 1862).

14. Atlanta *Southern Banner*, January 7, 1863 (soldier's letter dated December 18, 1862).

15. Richmond *Examiner,* December 18, 1862; Charleston *Mercury,* December 15, 1862.

16. Jefferson Davis, *Jefferson Davis, Constitutionalist: His Letters, Papers, and Speeches,* ed. Dunbar Rowland, 10 vols. (Jackson: Mississippi Department of Archives and History, 1923), 5:391–92.

17. Varina Davis, *Jefferson Davis: Ex-President of the Confederate States of America, a Memoir by his Wife,* 2 vols. (1890; reprint, Baltimore: Nautical & Aviation Publishing, 1990), 2:369.

18. John B. Jones, *A Rebel War Clerk's Diary at the Confederate States Capital,* 2 vols. (1866; reprint, [Alexandria, Va.]: Time-Life Books, 1982), 1:218; William M. Blackford diary, December 31, 1862, quoted in L. Minor Blackford, *Mine Eyes Have Seen the Glory* (Cambridge, Mass.: Harvard University Press, 1954), 152–53. Many northern observers also saw Fredericksburg as an indication that peace might come soon. Joseph Medill of the Chicago *Tribune*—a friend of the Lincoln administration— articulated what many others thought when he wrote to Elihu Washburne on January 14, 1863, that "an armistice is bound to come during the year '63" (Nevins, *War for the Union,* 2:351).

19. Amanda Virginia Edmonds, *Journals of Amanda Virginia Edmonds: Lass of the Mosby Confederacy, 1859–1867,* ed. Nancy Chappelear Baird (Stephens City, Va.: Commercial Press, 1984), 129–30; Lucy Breckinridge, *Lucy Breckinridge of Grove Hill: The Journal of a Virginia Girl, 1862–1864,* ed. Mary D. Robertson (Kent, Ohio: Kent State University Press, 1979), 93–94.

20. Cornelia Peake McDonald, *A Woman's Civil War: A Diary, with Reminiscences of the War, from March 1862,* ed. Minrose C. Gwin (Madison: University of Wisconsin Press, 1992), 108. *Harper's Weekly* agreed with McDonald that the northern people had almost reached a breaking point: "They have borne, silently and grimly, imbecility, treachery, failure, privation, loss of friends and means, almost every suffering which can afflict a brave people. But they cannot be expected to suffer that such massacres as this at Fredericksburg shall be repeated" (quoted in McPherson, *Ordeal By Fire,* 305).

21. Edmund Ruffin, *The Diary of Edmund Ruffin,* ed. William Kauffman Scarborough, 3 vols. (Baton Rouge: Louisiana State University Press, 1972–89), 2:518–19; Anne S. Frobel, *The Civil War Diary of Anne S. Frobel of Wilton Hill, Virginia,* ed. Mary H. Lancaster and Dallas M. Lancaster (Florence, Ala.: Birmingham Printing and Publishing, 1986), 105–6.

22. Mary Jones to Col. Charles C. Jones, Jr., December 19, 1862, quoted in Robert Manson Myers, ed., *The Children of Pride: A True Story of Georgia and the Civil War* (New Haven: Yale University Press, 1972), 1001; Jones, *Diary,* 1:214 (entry for December 16, 1862). Some northern soldiers also praised Lee after Fredericksburg. A Georgian talked with Federal pickets who said "if they had such generals as Lee and Jackson they could crush the rebellion, but as it is they are satisfied they will never succeed" (anonymous to "Dear Frank," December 30, 1862, quoted in Mills Lane, ed.,

"Dear Mother: Don't grieve about me. If I get killed, I'll only be dead.": Letters from Georgia Soldiers in the Civil War [Savannah, Ga.: Beehive Press, 1977], 210).

23. Ruffin, *Diary*, 2:518–19. Ruffin did not exaggerate conditions in the North. For example, Senator Charles Sumner of Massachusetts, a leading Radical Republican, wrote on December 21 that "there has been a terrible depression here & I recognise it throughout the country." Two weeks later Sumner insisted on the removal of Lincoln's key advisers—though he confessed seeing "great difficulties in organizing a true & strong Cabinet" (Charles Sumner to Henry W. Longfellow, December 21, 1862, and Charles Sumner to Orestes A. Brownson, January 4, 1863, in Charles Sumner, *The Selected Letters of Charles Sumner*, ed. Beverly Wilson Palmer, 2 vols. [Boston: Northeastern University Press, 1990], 2:133, 138).

24. Catherine Ann Devereux Edmondston, *"Journal of a Secesh Lady": The Diary of Catherine Ann Devereux Edmondston, 1860–1866*, ed. Beth Gilbert Crabtree and James W. Patton (Raleigh: North Carolina Division of Archives and History, 1979), 321. George Templeton Strong's diary confirms Edmondston's comments about Stanton. "It is generally held that Stanton forced Burnside to this movement against his earnest remonstrance and protest," wrote the New Yorker on December 18, 1862. "Perhaps Stanton didn't. Who knows? But there is universal bitter wrath against him throughout this community, a deeper feeling more intensely uttered than any I ever saw prevailing here. Lincoln comes in for a share of it" (George Templeton Strong, *The Diary of George Templeton Strong: The Civil War, 1860–1865*, ed. Allan Nevins and Milton Halsey Thomas, 4 vols. [New York: Macmillan, 1952], 3:281).

25. Lucy Rebecca Buck, *Sad Earth, Sweet Heaven: The Diary of Lucy Rebecca Buck during the War between the States, Front Royal, Virginia, December 25, 1861–April 15, 1865*, ed. William P. Buck (Birmingham, Ala.: Cornerstone Publisher, 1973), 157.

26. Kate Stone, *Brockenburn: The Journal of Kate Stone, 1861–1878*, ed. John Q. Anderson (Baton Rouge: Louisiana State University Press, 1955), 168; Robert Garlick Hill Kean, *Inside the Confederate Government: The Diary of Robert Garlick Hill Kean*, ed. Edward Younger (New York: Oxford University Press, 1957), 33, 35.

27. Henry Robinson Berkeley, *Four Years in the Confederate Artillery: The Diary of Private Henry Robinson Berkeley*, ed. William H. Runge (Chapel Hill: University of North Carolina Press [for the Virginia Historical Society], 1961), 37–38; Green B. Samuels to Kathleen Boone Samuels, December 18, 1862, quoted in Carrie Esther Spencer, Bernard Samuels, and Walter Berry Samuels, eds., *A Civil War Marriage: Reminiscences and Letters* (Boyce, Va.: Carr Publishing, 1956), 150.

28. Edward E. Sill to "Dear Sister," December 20, 1862, Edward E. Sill Papers, William R. Perkins Library, Duke University, Durham, N.C. (repository hereafter cited as DU); Susan Leigh Blackford and others, comp. and eds., *Letters from Lee's Army, or Memoirs of Life in and out of the Army in Virginia during the War Between the States* (New York: Charles Scribner's Sons, 1947), 146, 148. Blackford's remarks about Fredericksburg are undated, but he almost certainly wrote them before the end of December 1862.

29. James T. McElvaney to "My Dear Mother," December 19, 1862, typescript in the collections of Fredericksburg and Spotsylvania National Military Park Library, Fredericksburg, Va. (repository hereafter cited as FSNMP); James K. Edmondson to "My darling wife," December 17, 1862, quoted in James K. Edmondson, *My Dear Emma: War Letters of Col. James K. Edmondson, 1861–1865*, ed. Charles W. Turner (Verona, Va.: McClure Press, 1978), 115; Charles Kerrison to "Dear Uncle Edwin," December 18, 1862, Kerrison Family Papers, University of South Carolina, Columbia, S.C.

30. David Winn to his wife, December 18, 1862, quoted in Lane, *Letters from Georgia Soldiers*, 201; S. W. Branch to his mother, December 17, 1862, quoted in ibid., 200; William Beverley Pettit to "My Dear Wife," December 16, 1862, quoted in Charles W. Turner, ed., *Civil War Letters of Arabella Speairs and William Beverley Pettit of Fluvanna County, Virginia, March 1862–March 1865*, 2 vols. (Roanoke: Virginia Lithography & Graphics, 1988–89), 1:80.

31. U.S. War Department, *The War of the Rebellion: A Compilation of the Official Records of the Union and Confederate Armies*, 127 vols., index, and atlas (Washington, D.C.: GPO, 1880–1901), 21:634 (hereafter cited as *OR*; all references are to series 1); William Nelson Pendleton to [?], December 17, 1862, quoted in Susan P. Lee, *Memoirs of William Nelson Pendleton, D.D.* (1893; reprint, Harrisonburg, Va.: Sprinkle Publications, 1991), 247; Heros Von Borcke, *Memoirs of the Confederate War for Independence*, 2 vols. (1866; reprint, New York: Peter Smith, 1938), 2:147.

32. James E. B. Stuart to Mrs. Stuart, December 14, 1862, and Stuart to G. W. C. Lee, December 18, 1862, quoted in James E. B. Stuart, *The Letters of General J. E. B. Stuart*, ed. Adele H. Mitchell (n.p.: Stuart-Mosby Historical Society, 1990), 284–85; Edward E. Sill to "Dear Sister," December 20, 1862, Edward E. Sill Papers, DU; Benjamin Edward Stiles to "dear Aunt," December 21, 1862, Mackay-Stiles Collection, MS #470, Southern Historical Collection, Wilson Library, University of North Carolina, Chapel Hill, N.C. (repository hereafter cited as SHC).

33. William H. Hill Diary, December 17, 1862, Mississippi Department of Archives and History, Jackson, Miss. Testimony from Federal sources corroborates Confederate claims of demoralization in the Army of the Potomac. Henry Livermore Abbott of the 20th Massachusetts, a Democrat who supported bringing McClellan back to the army, stated that the "army isn't worth a brass farthing in the way of fighting now. . . . The strongest peace party is in the army. If the small fry at Washington want to hear treason talked, let them come out to the army" (Henry Livermore Abbott to "My Dear Carry," December 21, 1862, in Henry Livermore Abbott, *Fallen Leaves: The Civil War Letters of Major Henry Livermore Abbott*, ed. Robert Garth Scott [Kent, Ohio: Kent State University Press, 1991], 155). Writing the same day as Abbott, artillerist Charles S. Wainwright tried to be more upbeat but still conveyed a depressing picture: "In the army the effect has been, as far as I can see, to take all life out of it: it is not really demoralized, but every bit of the enthusiasm which was so marked as we came down through Loudoun County is gone. Very little is said about Burnside, but neither officers nor men have the slightest confidence in him" (Charles S. Wain-

wright, *A Diary of Battle: The Personal Journals of Colonel Charles S. Wainwright, 1861–1865*, ed. Allan Nevins [New York: Harcourt, Brace & World, 1962], 148–49).

34. Philip H. Powers to his wife, December 25, 1862, Lewis Leigh Collection, U.S. Army Military History Institute, Carlisle Barracks, Pa. (repository hereafter cited as USAMHI); Blackford, *Mine Eyes Have Seen the Glory*, 211–12; Milo Grow to [?], December 17, 1862, quoted in *Milo Grow's Letters from the Civil War* (Lake Seminde, Ga.: Privately printed for the Grow family reunion, 1986), 7.

35. Henry Herbert Harris to "Dear Sister," December 26, 1862, typescript at FSNMP; Irvin Cross Wills to his brother, January 1, 1863, quoted in *Three Rebels Write Home: Including the Letters of Edgar Allan Jackson (September 7, 1860–April 15, 1863), James Fenton Bryant (June 20, 1861–December 30, 1866), Irvin Cross Wills (April 9, 1862–July 29, 1863), and Miscellaneous Items* (Franklin, Va.: News Publishing, 1955), 81. A soldier in the Iron Brigade described similar conditions. "Soldier's are all discouraged," wrote Henry Matrau. "We think that this war is never going to be ended by fighting[,] for the North & the South are to[o] evenly matched. No troops ever fought better than did our's the other day at Fredericksburg, but to no avail" (Henry Matrau to his mother, December 22, 1862, in Henry Matrau, *Letters Home: Henry Matrau of the Iron Brigade*, ed. Marcia Reid-Green [Lincoln: University of Nebraska Press, 1993], 39).

36. William Britton Bailey to "Dear Brother," December 17, 1862, HCWET-Coco Collection, USAMHI; John Andrew Ramsey to his cousin, December 17, 1862, John Andrew Ramsey Papers (#3534), SHC.

37. W. R. M. Slaughter to "My Dear Sister," January 4, 1863, MSS 25L 1575B, Virginia Historical Society, Richmond, Va.

38. James J. Archer to R. H. Archer, January 2, 1863, and James J. Archer to "My Dear Mother," January 12, 1863, quoted in C. A. Porter Hopkins, ed., "The James J. Archer Letters," part 1, *Maryland Historical Magazine* 56 (June 1961): 140–41; Elisha Franklin Paxton to his wife, January 17, 1863, quoted in Elisha Franklin Paxton, *The Civil War Letters of General Frank "Bull" Paxton: A Lieutenant of Lee and Jackson*, ed. John Gallatin Paxton (Hillsboro, Tex.: Hill Junior College Press, 1978), 71.

39. Shepherd Green Pryor to Penelope Tyson Pryor, December 23, 1862, quoted in Shepherd Green Pryor, *A Post of Honor: The Pryor Letters, 1861–1863*, ed. Charles R. Adams, Jr. (Fort Valley, Ga.: Garret Publications, 1989), 296; Francis W. Dawson to "My dear Mother," April 23, 1863, quoted in Francis W. Dawson, *Reminiscences of Confederate Service, 1861–1865*, ed. Bell I. Wiley (1882; reprint, Baton Rouge: Louisiana State University Press, 1980), 192. H. A. Ogden's famous print of Lee at Fredericksburg portrays almost precisely the cast and scene described by Dawson.

40. Freeman, *R. E. Lee*, 2:462. See n. 1 from the introduction, above, for a brief discussion of this quotation.

41. Bryan Grimes, *Extracts of Letters of Major-General Bryan Grimes, to His Wife, Written While in Active Service in the Army of Northern Virginia*, comp. Pulaski Cowper (1883; reprint, Wilmington, N.C.: Broadfoot, 1986), 26–27.

42. *OR* 21:555.

43. R. E. Lee to Mrs. Lee, December 16, 1862, quoted in Robert E. Lee, *The Wartime Papers of R. E. Lee*, ed. Clifford Dowdey and Louis H. Manarin (Boston: Little, Brown, 1961), 365; Robert E. Lee, Jr., *Recollections and Letters of General Robert E. Lee* (1904; reprint, Wilmington, N.C.: Broadfoot, 1988), 87.

44. Henry Heth, "Letter from Major-General Henry Heth, of A. P. Hill's Corps, A. N. V.," in *Southern Historical Society Papers*, ed. J. William Jones and others, 52 vols. and 3-vol. index (1877–1959; reprint, Wilmington, N.C.: Broadfoot, 1990–92), 4:153–54 (hereafter cited as *SHSP*). Lee made his comments about Fredericksburg in the context of a discussion of Confederate public opinion relating to Gettysburg.

45. R. E. Lee to James A. Seddon, January 10, 1863, in Lee, *Wartime Papers*, 388–89.

46. Questions about Lee's decision to remain on the defensive after the thirteenth persisted after the war. He paraphrased his official report in answering queries from William M. McDonald in April 1868: "The plain of Fredericksburg is completely commanded by the heights of Stafford. . . . To have advanced the whole army into the plain for the purpose of attacking General Burnside, would have been to have insured its destruction by the fire from the continued line of guns on the Stafford hills. It was considered more wise to meet the Federal army beyond the reach of their batteries than under their muzzles, and even to invite repeated renewal of their attacks. When convinced of their inutility, it was easy for them, under cover of a long, dark and tempestuous night, to cross the narrow river by means of their numerous bridges before we could ascertain their purpose" ("Letter from General R. E. Lee," in *SHSP*, 7:445–46).

47. R. E. Lee to Jefferson Davis, September 8, 1862, quoted in Lee, *Wartime Papers*, 301.

48. R. E. Lee to Mrs. Lee, April 19, 1863, quoted in ibid., 437–38.

49. For a systematic—and disapproving—analysis of Lee's penchant for the offensive, see chap. 4 of Alan T. Nolan, *Lee Considered: General Robert E. Lee and Civil War History* (Chapel Hill: University of North Carolina Press, 1991). For a more sympathetic interpretation, see Gary W. Gallagher, " 'Upon Their Success Hang Momentous Issues': Generals," in *Why the Confederacy Lost*, ed. Gabor S. Boritt (New York: Oxford University Press, 1992).

50. Heth, "Letter from Major-General Heth," 154.

51. Anonymous letter to "Dear Frank," September 30, 1862, quoted in Lane, *Letters from Georgia Soldiers*, 208; Jones, *Diary*, 1:223.

Barbarians at Fredericksburg's Gate

THE IMPACT OF THE UNION ARMY

ON CIVILIANS

WILLIAM A. BLAIR

Fredericksburg residents quickly grasped the significance of the two cannon shots that cracked across the cold, crisp dawn of December 11, 1862. Southern artillerists fired the guns to alert the Army of Northern Virginia to prepare against attack and to let civilians know that the moment so long dreaded finally had come. Townspeople had spent a sleepless night fretting over what to pack, justifiably worried about what would happen to property left behind. As the echo of the shots died, people carrying bedding and household goods filled roads leading to woods behind the Confederate army. Shortly after noon, after a morning of sporadic artillery firing, more than 140 Union guns opened on the town, creating a smoke screen through which bursting shells winked like "a countless swarm of fire-flies." The destruction outraged a populace still naively believing that civilians and their property should remain exempt from carnage. The next day Federal soldiers added a more personal stamp to the violation by breaking into homes and public buildings, rifling belongings, parading in dresses stripped from wardrobes, and smashing furniture during an orgy of looting that only seemed to confirm the stereotype of the barbaric Yankee.[1]

The sacking of Fredericksburg scarred the town and its inhabitants. For months awestruck visitors remarked about the devastation. Surviving photographs show skeletons of buildings standing amidst rubble—scenes suggestive of European cities bombed during World War II. This visit from the Federal army was neither the first nor the last. Standard accounts of the war ignore an earlier Federal occupation from late April to August 1862, during which the mayor and eighteen other community leaders had been held as political hostages. The townspeople experienced a war more complicated

Buildings in Fredericksburg damaged by artillery fire.
National Archives

than the familiar description of a conflict moving in discrete stages from limited to total, with strategic targets gradually expanding from armies to civilians. On the Confederacy's frontier a hard war occurred as soon as Union troops encountered Confederate loyalists, with depredations escalating after Maj. Gen. George B. McClellan's failure on the Peninsula. In their wake the invaders left destruction in northern Virginia as extensive as in the more celebrated areas of the Deep South touched by Sherman's army.[2]

The Union army affected Fredericksburg's civilians in several ways over the short term. The Federals first violated private property, helping themselves to fence rails and crops. Far more serious from a southern perspective, many slaves fled their masters and briefly turned Fredericksburg into a collection point for contrabands from across northern and central Virginia. This flight had repercussions for Confederate manpower, as well as necessitating adjustments within households to compensate for the loss of labor.

An occupying force also inevitably sparked confrontations over the loyalty of civilians. Arrests occurred, especially in response to persecution of unionists. Finally, the Union army provoked a more complex response than simply eroding the southern will to fight. Whenever northern soldiers burned fence rails or shelled homes of relatives, the gesture sent shock waves beyond a particular locale, adding vengeance to the list of why Confederates fought. "No victory of the war has ever done me so much good," one Virginia soldier wrote in December 1862. "I *hate* them worse than ever in the first place, and then their destruction of poor old Fredericksburg! It seems to me that I dont do anything from morning to night but hate them worse & worse."[3]

The war also affected civilians in countless ways over the long term, the most enduring of which revolved around the revolutionary consequences of emancipation. The Union army destroyed much of northern Virginia's resources, leaving the Fredericksburg region in an economic hole with neither labor nor cash to assist the climb back out. Real estate value declined by nearly one-quarter in the 1860s, but personal property, which included slaves, plummeted more than $11 million, or by 85 percent. The freeing of 11,000 slaves accounted for more than half of the latter loss. Emancipation involved more than economics, as southerners adjusted to new social arrangements affecting everything from politics to the layout of homes.[4]

To track these changes it is necessary to look at the late antebellum period, when Fredericksburg remained a prosperous town but one with its greatest days past. Established in colonial times as a mercantile center on the fall line of the Rappahannock River between the Tidewater and the Piedmont, the town suffered with most of Virginia during the tobacco depression of the 1840s. The people of the Old Dominion rebounded during the 1850s by increasing production of wheat, corn, and other grains and by encouraging small manufacturing—principally iron stimulated in part by the building of canals and railroads. New transportation links tied more of the state to markets, allowing more people to participate in the decade's tobacco boom. When economic recovery came, the Northern Neck already had changed from a landscape primarily of large plantations to one of smaller farms with more diversified agriculture. The area provided important services in processing wheat into flour and fattening cattle, both of which made their way to northern markets. Fredericksburg's leaders also entertained hopes in 1860 that a forthcoming shoe factory would enhance the area's economic potential. The region thus at first appears to resemble Stephen Ash's description of a "third South" that, like Middle Tennessee, "gazed Janus-like toward the egalitarian, nonslaveholding South of the yeoman farmer and toward the plutocratic, plantation South of the cotton nabobs." But antebellum Virginia was a modern slave society, consciously struggling with how to keep pace with the free states in material progress without undercutting the peculiar institution.[5]

Fredericksburg itself lay between counties with different economic features. Bordering the town toward the south and west, Spotsylvania County featured more traditional plantation agriculture, while across the river to the northeast Stafford County contained smaller landholdings. Slaves constituted 45 percent of the region's total population but nearly 60 percent in Spotsylvania, which also had a higher concentration of wealth, fewer heads of households, more slaveowners, and a smaller free black community. With 39 percent of its population slaves, Stafford emphasized subsistence crops. Neither county ranked particularly high in agricultural production, but both fell within the top fifth of counties in value of manufactured goods. Fed by farms along the Northern Neck, Stafford's ten mills churned out respectable quantities of wheat and corn meal; however, nearly 70 percent of the county's manufacturing jobs came through shad and other fishing. Largely because of Fredericksburg, carpentry led Spotsylvania's manufacturing output and provided the greatest employment. The town supported the region's diverse needs through a sizable number of merchants, shopkeepers, and artisans, although its total population numbered only 5,000 residents, 1,291 of them slaves.[6]

Despite economic diversity the area contained little full-fledged commercial agriculture or industrial capitalism. Like most of Virginia, the region consisted of loosely connected neighborhood economies of farms and family manufactories. Tobacco and wheat linked farmers to markets beyond the community, but the needs of daily life—shoes, barrels, milled flour, leather goods, and so on—typically were met through neighborhood resources in which custom dictated the cost of services. Trust rather than cash played a central role in exchanges: merchants might carry for years a customer who could not pay, or they might accept fees in trade. Although railroads somewhat disrupted these practices by expanding markets and stimulating a cash economy, old practices held sway. In 1860 a fellow southerner saw little entrepreneurial enthusiasm among the town's shopkeepers, whom he likened to tabby cats sunning themselves in front of stores. "The advent of a customer seemed to embarrass and disturb them," he noted; "yet, with a sort of lofty Castilian politeness, they waited on him, and then returned to sunning themselves again. . . . Nowhere in town are they a busy, fussy people."[7]

Only the edges of Virginia sustained incursions by the enemy during the first ten months after secession, yet the Union army sent rippling effects far into the interior. Instead of moving with agricultural cycles or a community's habitual pace, life on the home front danced to a military waltz. Troop movements set the rhythm, even if occurring several counties away. Although no Federal soldiers appeared in Fredericksburg until April 1862, the threat of northern advances stimulated a shift in population as slaveowners moved their property to safer places within Virginia.[8] Throughout the Old Dominion the fear of Union invasion closed schools, spurred refugees to hunt for secure areas, and canceled church services. Battles brought wounded to towns of any size, where homes and public buildings became makeshift hospitals. This caused concern over dysentery, typhoid, and smallpox as well as requiring police to handle loitering soldiers and hangers-on who typically accompanied an army.

The Union army permanently stepped across the Potomac in late February and except for brief periods maintained a presence in northern Virginia for virtually the rest of the war. Because the Lincoln administration crafted no official policy for treatment of southern civilians until April 1863, the behavior of an army largely depended upon the mood of officers. No Virginian could be sure what fate awaited because soldiers harbored fewer reservations than their leaders about destroying civilian property. Fence rails, lumber, and a variety of crops and foodstuffs served as more frequent targets than homes or buildings. The shock of seeing Union soldiers take whatever they wanted without permission was enough to unsettle civilians, especially when arrests of community leaders followed.[9]

As the Federal army neared Fredericksburg in mid-April, the man who would be its first Union provost marshal feared matters would get out of control. The troops "burned fences & ran riot," Brig. Gen. Marsena R. Patrick wrote in his diary, adding, "I found both Officers & men running into private homes & playing the mischief generally." Partly to protect property but also to maintain discipline among the soldiers, Patrick stationed guards at each

*Brig. Gen. Marsena
Rudolph Patrick.
National Archives*

home with orders to shoot their colleagues who tried to enter. This stopped
rampant looting but not the systematic consumption of wood and crops.
After the war fence rails, lumber, and cordwood dominated lists from unionists in Stafford County who filed claims for damages from Federal soldiers.
The precedent and potential existed for soldiers to escalate matters as far as
officers would allow.[10]

Extending from April 19 to the last day of August,[11] the first occupation of
Fredericksburg began with Union officers controlling their men and limiting
damage to the town. Troops serving under Irvin McDowell in the Department of the Rappahannock constituted the first occupying force, and most of
their generals still viewed acts against property as vandalism rather than a

way to cripple the war-making capability of the Confederacy. Control of depredations also played to self-interest: officers feared that pillaging made troops more difficult to control. Provost Marshal Patrick treated soldiers and residents with equal strictness and was replaced in late May by men of similar feelings—Maj. Gen. Rufus King and, later, Maj. Gen. John F. Reynolds, under whom Union troops continued to guard property. Except for soldiers used as police, the rest of the army was restricted from town. Civilians and soldiers alike needed passes to travel to and from Fredericksburg. Reynolds also placed an 8:00 P.M. curfew on the stores, hotels, and other public places to battle the prostitution, drinking, and smuggling that proliferated. Citizens appreciated the efforts. When Reynolds was captured on the Peninsula during the Seven Days, Fredericksburg civilians lobbied officials in Richmond for his release in consideration of his tenure as military governor.[12]

This does not mean that life passed peacefully in Fredericksburg. Tensions flared as the occupation emboldened the unionists who remained. Among them was the Reverend James W. Hunnicutt, who had suspended publishing the Fredericksburg (Va.) *Christian Banner* on May 9, 1861, because secessionists threatened his life. Federal occupation revived the paper, while forcing suspension of the Fredericksburg *News* and the *Virginia Herald*. Over the next several months Hunnicutt directed a verbal onslaught against the evils of secession, alleging that a small group of elites had misled poorer whites. Actions of townspeople spoke otherwise. Women turned their backs on Union soldiers, and repression of unionists worsened in Spotsylvania County and other areas where Federals exerted weaker control. Threatened earlier with possible arrest by Confederate authorities, unionist Benjamin Armstrong finally gave up as community pressure forced him to leave Spotsylvania for the North in May. Even where Federal troops roamed, unionists faced difficult times because of the prevalence of secessionist sentiment within the region. "The people in Fredericksburg are secesh of the first water," General Reynolds observed, "the first almost we have seen of the real F.F.V.'s [First Families of Virginia]."[13]

The character of the occupation changed in July. The incompetence of George B. McClellan, commander of the Army of the Potomac, placed civilian property at greater risk. His defeat on the Peninsula infuriated northerners who increasingly called for a sterner war. Many of the officers in the Army of the Potomac had been handpicked by McClellan and were Democrats committed to a limited war, which placed them at odds with the new mood. Lincoln tapped a westerner, Maj. Gen. John Pope, to command a new Army of Virginia to protect Washington and to campaign in northern Virginia. Apart from other attributes, Pope was a Republican who believed in making Confederates pay.[14]

Almost immediately life grew more difficult for civilians in northern Virginia. Pope followed his appointment with edicts in mid-July that Federal troops must subsist off the countryside through which they traveled, reimbursing civilians at the conclusion of the war only if the claimant could prove loyalty to the Union. Practically speaking this meant the value of the goods was lost forever. In Fredericksburg General Patrick feared the worst: "Our men know every house in the whole country, and . . . they now believe they have the perfect right to rob, tyrannize, threaten & maltreat any one they please, under the Orders of Gen. Pope." By the month's end the army had devastated nearby Culpeper and Orange counties. One Confederate official noted that the acts brought "our men to such a pitch of exasperation that, when the day of battles comes, there will be, must be terrible slaughter."[15]

Pope followed these measures with another policy equally infuriating to southerners when he demanded that Union officers administer oaths of allegiance to people in occupied territories and prosecute under military law those who would not comply. Some Fredericksburg civilians pondered whether to flee with slaves, horses, and other valuables before the army seized them. Had Pope and the occupation lasted longer, Confederate loyalists would have faced the prospect of losing everything they owned. As it was, Union officers began pressuring civilians into taking the oath—a process interrupted by Lee's advance into Maryland.[16]

Previous treatment of Fredericksburg civilians appeared far too lenient in this new climate, bringing public criticism of the responsible military commanders. Reports of illicit trade conducted with stolen Union goods also angered northern civilians and officials who heard of Confederates reaping financial advantage. Pope castigated Brig. Gen. Rufus King; Secretary of War Edwin M. Stanton removed one provost marshal; and U.S. Senator Benjamin F. Wade vented irritation before the Senate over rumors that McDowell protected the corn and fencing of a southerner near Belle Plain. Most of the charges proved groundless (although some illicit trade had occurred), and a military court of inquiry in January 1863 cleared McDowell of wrongdoing.

The general never apologized for his actions, maintaining that respect for property helped prosecution of the war. "There is no need to destroy what you may afterward want yourself," he told the court. "Whether the growing grain was the property of Union men or not I protected it. In either case the army would need it. The same with houses; to burn and destroy simply because the property belongs to the enemy and will irritate him can have no effect on the war, except to strengthen the feeling which causes it to be maintained on the other side."[17]

For Fredericksburg residents the changes in northern mood fostered greater restrictions on personal liberties. It became more difficult, for example, to secure passes for travel or business. Perhaps the most notorious Union action was the imprisonment of nineteen community leaders, including Mayor Montgomery Slaughter. These civilians served as political hostages pending the exchange of seven Union prisoners the Confederate government had removed from the area. Marsena Patrick selected the first four to be arrested on July 22. Three more were seized on July 29; the remainder, on August 13. All were released September 24 after the exchanges were made. Although authorities treated the prisoners well, the episode raised considerable outcry, which amused unionists who viewed the arrests as tit for tat. "There is a great fuss made of the arrest of secessionists," Hunnicutt editorialized in his *Christian Banner*, "but when Union men were seized and hurried off to prison, nothing was said against the course of action pursued by the Confederate authorities. This was all right: there was no sympathy for the poor wives and children and friends of these Union men."[18]

African Americans understandably viewed the first occupation of Fredericksburg as a boon. Five months before Lincoln issued his preliminary emancipation proclamation, slaves risked that Union officers would allow them to remain free rather than, as the slaveowners alleged, return contrabands to masters or ship them to Cuba. As early as April 25 one resident recorded in her diary, "The negroes are going off in great numbers, and are beginning to be very independent and impudent. We hear that our three are going soon. I am afraid of the lawless Yankee soldiers, but that is nothing to my fear of the negroes if they should rise against us." "Matters are getting worse and worse here every day with regard to the negroes," she added the next month. "They are leaving their owners by the hundred and demanding wages." Citizens attempted to band together by agreeing not to hire out their own slaves or contract for others, but nothing slowed the migration.[19] More slaves seized the chance to flee masters as the occupation wore on and Fredericksburg became a destination for contrabands from across the Northern Neck and central Virginia. By mid-June Hunnicutt estimated that as many as 200 African Americans arrived in Fredericksburg each day. Although this number may have been high because Hunnicutt hoped to underscore the repercussions of secession, Marsena Patrick affirmed that a steady flow of contrabands came into town and only increased as the summer went on. On one day in August the provost marshal sent fifty contrabands North. He also had to establish quarters that month in which fugitives waited a day or two before being sent by rail to Washington. The effect was dramatic on a southern countryside that depended on the labor of slaves. On July 19 a cavalry officer scouting in nearby Caroline County made a typical observation when he noted that an acquaintance "has lost seven of his negro men; gone over to the enemy. Everybody here has lost some of their force."[20]

Filled with paternalistic notions of kind masters and happy slaves, Virginians could not embrace the obvious conclusion that most slaves hated life under the peculiar institution and wanted their freedom. Masters instead explained their losses by charging Union officers with stealing southern property. Hunnicutt's *Christian Banner* pointed out the contradiction in this thinking. After listing the counties from which the contraband had come (which included most of those surrounding Spotsylvania but also Madison and Albemarle), he asked on July 2, "Did the 'Yankees' go to all these different localities and 'steal away the negroes'? No: the negroes *voluntarily* leave their homes and come to Fredericksburg. What does all this argue? The problem is practically and literally demonstrated that the slaves of Virginia have an idea of *freedom* and a wish to obtain it, and are determined *to be free*." That African Americans pursued their own best interests was reaffirmed after the war by the widow of a free black resident of Stafford County who pressed the family's claim for damages. Asked the standard question which side her husband supported during the war, she replied, "I don't know—not particularly neither side. Well, he was for himself, a free man, and he wanted to continue to be a free man."[21]

Even a unionist like Hunnicutt bemoaned the beginning of the end of slavery in Virginia. Freedom disturbed the accustomed order in the South and would create a "deplorable state of anarchy and confusion." He clarified the importance of slavery by placing the peculiar institution ahead of land in a hierarchy of values. When a handsome carriage pulled into Fredericksburg filled with contraband women and children who had fled from Caroline County, the behavior of the occupants angered Hunnicutt, who thought they fanned themselves like aristocrats from the first families of Virginia. He believed from twenty to thirty contrabands formed the group, all of whom had fled the same master. The lot, he estimated, had been worth about $25,000—a loss that boggled the mind, especially because they had "all gone in a single night." A world in which slavery formed the basic component of social and economic hierarchy threatened to come apart at a dizzying rate.[22]

On the last day of August Federal soldiers burned a temporary bridge and other buildings and goods. Residents had heard of a battle near Manassas and reckoned that the Federals were withdrawing. "Every body was in the streets that Sunday night," Betty Herndon Maury recorded, "and as the soldiers went over the bridge and applied the torch to the piles of tarred lumber, such a shout and cheer was raised by the people as old Fredericksburg had never heard before."[23] The retreat proved the last gasp for unionists, many of whom fled with the army, and checked the flow of contrabands, who quickly left town in expectation of the return of the Confederate army. "The flames, the water, the illumination, the trees and the dark night," wrote one correspondent, "together made a splendid celebration of the restored independence of the subjugated Confederates." The writer particularly delighted in the spectacle of African American fugitives carrying bags and bundles, bandboxes and chests. Little did he know that his description presently would apply to the town's Confederate civilians.[24]

The second major contact of Fredericksburg civilians with the enemy dwarfed the first not only in destruction of property but also in the dislocation of townspeople. Many became refugees from the first sight of the Union army. Maj. Gen. Edwin V. Sumner, commander of the Right Grand Division of Ambrose E. Burnside's Army of the Potomac, encouraged their departure by demanding on November 21 that the mayor and common council surrender the town by 5:00 P.M. or face an artillery barrage. Sumner justified this order with the standard claim of shots fired at Union soldiers from homes, but he also displayed an awareness that the first occupation had prompted criticism of officers considered too lenient toward the rebels. "Your mills and manufactories are furnishing provisions and the material for clothing for armed bodies in rebellion against the Government of the United States," Sumner wrote. "Your railroads and other means of transportation are removing supplies to the depots of such troops."[25] Townspeople avoided shelling and surrender by arguing that the shots had been fired by Confederate military personnel. The civilians promised no more shots would be fired or materiel produced for the Confederate army. R. E. Lee supported this position, indicating he would neither occupy the town nor use it for military purposes unless the enemy threatened to move in. Lee also engineered the evacuation of civilians. "I was moving out the women & children all last night & today," he wrote his wife on November 22. "It was a piteous sight. But they have brave hearts. What is to become of them God only knows."[26]

As train cars of refugees departed, the first incident occurred that reinforced Confederate notions about the enemy. Through some mistake, Federal artillery on Stafford Heights fired a few rounds at the final car. The shelling ended quickly and apparently without casualties, but the repercussions continued as the story circulated widely as an example of the atrocities one could expect from Yankees. A North Carolina woman wrote, "Was [there] ever greater cowardice, more unmanly or baser conduct? They do indeed 'war on woman & the dead.' " Women and children evicted from homes into the cold Virginia weather dominated public and private discourse, playing upon notions that women should be exempt from such hardships.[27]

Not surprisingly, civilians returned to town during the more than three weeks that passed before Burnside's men built pontoon bridges across the Rappahannock. Virginia faced increased privations, with men from both the Union and Confederate armies seizing provisions. Soldiers traveling through northern Virginia and points immediately south and west of Fredericksburg often commented on the thoroughness of devastation. Refugees thus encountered little relief unless they could reach the homes of relatives or friends. Richmond and other cities offered the best hope for safety and subsistence, but even there the winter featured hardships that would lead to bread riots by women the following March. Returning home offered the best prospects for Fredericksburg residents to coax whatever they could from neighborhood markets and to protect their remaining possessions.

The Federal bombardment on December 11 consequently caught a number of civilians in town who had tired of false alarms and decided to ride

Federal bombardment of Fredericksburg, December 11, 1862.
Robert Underwood Johnson and Clarence Clough Buel, eds., Battles and
Leaders of the Civil War, *4 vols. (New York: Century, 1887–88), 3:112*

out any forthcoming storm in their cellars. Sporadic shelling opened early
in the morning and continued in fits and spurts until a lull toward noon
during which shaken residents fled to Confederate lines. Mississippi soldiers
in William Barksdale's brigade of Lafayette McLaws's division had sparked
the artillery action by picking off Union engineers building pontoon bridges
over the river. As they withdrew, Confederate pickets supplied covering fire
for civilians, some of whom fled in ambulances scrounged from the army.
Around 12:30 P.M. the massive Federal barrage began. The shelling set fire to
homes, sending at least one family scurrying from the basement to spend the
rest of the day huddled in their garden. Smoke formed slender pillars that
stretched to the sky and fanned out into a black canopy. Remarkably, only
four residents died. Although most buildings sustained damage from can-

nonballs and shell fragments, the worst destruction occurred to the structures nearest the river in which the Mississippians had posted themselves.[28]

The greatest jolt to sensibilities came on December 12 as the Federal soldiers marched through town. Overwhelming testimony from both sides confirms that rampant pillaging occurred and that it was encouraged by Union officers of at least company grade. The men had stacked arms and cartridge boxes in two neat rows along the streets running parallel to the Rappahannock River before beginning to collect ammunition and other military stores and to settle into quarters in homes and shops. Matters quickly escalated to a point that astounded even the soldiers who participated in the looting. Stores were gutted, and soldiers trashed whatever could not be carried off. They entered homes, stripped clothing from bureaus, defaced walls with their unit numbers, and tossed contents into the streets. "I may add," a Union surgeon wrote his sister, "that I could have furnished your house better than it is now without taking a single piece of furniture from any house—I would take only that which I found in the street." Another witness reported that soldiers lounged in covered armchairs, while on Princess Anne Street a ragged group gathered around a piano to sing and dance: "I couldn't help thinking of 'Nero fiddled while Rome was burning.' "[29] The scene infuriated Marsena Patrick, who had to lash a soldier with a riding whip before the man would obey an order to drop his haul of carpeting and bedding. Patrick also arrested officers caught with goods hanging from their saddles.[30]

Although few soldiers likely attempted to fathom what lay behind the furious assault on civilian property, Edmund Ruffin viewed the sacking of Fredericksburg as part of a broader process that indicated a change in the sentiments of the Federal government and military officers. "Previously, & generally, wherever the Yankee troops had access & sway, there was widespread robbery & no little of wanton destruction of private property," the old secessionist mused on December 20. "But recently, judging by effects, it would seem as if the Yankee government & military commanders had expressly authorized & ordered that the country shall be plundered & laid waste, & every moveable either carried off or destroyed. Such has been the procedure in North Carolina & in Mississippi, under recent Yankee army movements, as well as at Fredericksburg, & sundry other places in Va— indeed nearly wherever they have occupied long enough for such work."[31]

While Ruffin overstated the unanimity of northern opinion, he was probably correct in thinking that the destruction achieved its proportions because officers condoned the pillaging. Soldiers always conducted as many depredations as officers would allow. Why they did so in Fredericksburg could be attributable to a number of reasons. They knew that northern civilians favored greater punishment of secessionists and had witnessed the castigation of McDowell for treating Confederate property too leniently. The popular McClellan's removal from the Army of the Potomac in November also may have demoralized followers or loosened discipline in general. Given these circumstances, controlling the soldiers might have seemed more trouble than it was worth. Also, the officers themselves may have undergone a transition similar to civilians on the home front, with Fredericksburg presenting an opportunity to vent frustrations over the prosecution of the war. A more definitive answer awaits further research.[32]

The sacking of the city fired spirits of Virginians during a bleak time on the home front. The year preceding the battle of Fredericksburg had featured a steady slide in the civilian standard of living. Privations had begun by the fall of 1861, and more serious suffering occurred as the Union army advanced into Virginia and seized crops stockpiled by farmers. Newspaper editors throughout the state urged readers in the fall of 1862 to establish programs to donate food and wood so the poor could survive a difficult winter. The draft also irked civilians and soldiers alike: fall 1862 through spring 1863 was the time in which the greatest number of wealthier civilians bought their way out of conscription by employing substitutes. In this season of discontent the Confederate army supplied badly needed hope with its victory on December 13 at Fredericksburg, and outrages perpetrated by Union soldiers provided one piece in a complex mosaic of southern identity.[33]

Almost immediately word of the depredations spread throughout Virginia and the South. Newspaper correspondents from Georgia and South Carolina wrote vivid accounts of the destruction that stressed the violation of women— not sexual assaults, per se, but the blundering of soldiers through bedrooms and other traditional domains of women. Accounts unanimously told of Union soldiers donning women's garb and parading in the streets. Next in frequency came religious images, as correspondents told how churches were shelled and Bibles burned. All told, the writers embellished the existing stereotype of the greedy Yankee with additional traits of the enemy as violators of property, women, and church.[34]

Federal soldiers looting Fredericksburg, December 12, 1862.
Library of Congress

The destruction itself gave ample cause to hate Union soldiers, but the pillaging added to the intensity of feelings in Confederate hearts. "The thefts committed in the sack of Fredericksburg by persons who called themselves gentlemen are astonishing to us Southrons," wrote North Carolinian Catherine Edmondston. One Virginian estimated only twenty-five or so buildings had been permanently destroyed, but he and others could not help noting the personal belongings that littered the streets.[35] The waste in general incensed southerners and helped harden attitudes against Yankees among soldiers and civilians alike. A soldier from Georgia wrote home: "It was a pitiable sight to see the women & children those dreadfully cold nights streaming along the roads from the city stopping at every fire to keep from freezing with nothing in the world but what they had on their backs, many of them brought up to enjoy every luxury. . . . I do believe after seeing all I have I could murder the devils in cold blood." A South Carolinian writing from the city on April 1, 1863, was disturbed by the "vandalism of an uncivilized and inhuman mob of belligerents" and wished a day of retribution soon would come that would force "these miscreants" to repent for the destruction.[36]

News of Yankee barbarities elsewhere prompted responses similar to those triggered by events in Fredericksburg. After hearing a friend from Memphis tell about the rape of a southern woman, a Virginian exhorted in October 1863, "Shoot them, dear husband, every chance you get. Hold no conference with them. They are devil furies who thirst for your blood and who will revenge themselves on your helpless wife and children. It is God's will and wish for you to destroy them. You are his instrument and it is your Christian duty. Would that I may be allowed to take up arms, I would fight them, until I died."[37]

Donations that almost immediately poured into the city attested to the strong feelings provoked by the plundering of Fredericksburg. Soldiers collected money from within their units to distribute to the needy. Occasionally donations came from other parts of the Confederacy, but most often from within Virginia. In James Longstreet's corps in Lee's army Virginians changed their minds and transferred $1,391 raised for the relief of Charleston to help "the sacked, pillaged, and destroyed city of Fredericksburg." Editors noted the generosity of soldiers and encouraged citizens throughout the state to follow suit. "Fredericksburg has been sacrificed to win a great victory which has saved Virginia and saved Richmond from the foe," one wrote. "Let no man pretend to rejoice at the victory who does not do his part in this work of benevolence."[38] By February 1863 donations of $1,103.60 had come in from Lexington, Virginia; $1,000 from Staunton; $6,800 from Lynchburg; and $10,000 from the Richmond city council. Total donations amounted to roughly $170,000, a considerable sum in 1863 dollars. Barter or gifts in kind probably boosted this total. For example, the president of the Richmond, Fredericksburg & Potomac Railroad promised to refund the costs of transportation for furniture and effects of civilians who had begun evacuating under the enemy's order in November.[39]

The rest of the war brought more battles and privations to Fredericksburg, although nothing quite like the destruction of 1862. The town remained between two armies, with the Federals in Stafford County and the Confederates just across the Rappahannock. The presence of soldiers—no matter which side—meant a continual drain on local resources. Even General Lee admitted that his men at times preyed on civilians: "The farms and gardens have been robbed, stock and hogs killed, and these outrages committed, I am sorry to say, by our own army to some extent, as well as by the Federals."[40] Residents struggled to keep food on the table, which increased the importance of gardening, dairying, and other areas of farm work traditionally conducted by women. Others turned to the river to supplement diets with fish. Those behind enemy lines traded goods for Yankee supplies, some to profit from resale in Richmond but more merely to survive. When a Confederate enrollment officer complained about the extent of this trade in the Northern Neck of Virginia, Secretary of War James Seddon cautioned against cracking down. All trade with the enemy, Seddon admitted, was illegal, but "situated as the people to a serious extent are, beyond the power of active protection by us, and cut off from supplies through their regular avenues of trade . . . by the enemy, some barter or trading for the supply of their necessities is almost inevitable and excusable."[41]

When the Union army withdrew, it left a new form of commerce that benefited some residents. One Fredericksburg man admitted after the war that he regularly went to Chancellorsville to buy the clothing of Union soldiers—some discarded by the wearer, some stripped from the dead. He took the clothing to Essex County to trade for corn. "Any number of families jest lived on what they got from the Union armies in that way," he told his northern visitor, adding that one blanket could typically be exchanged for a half-bushel of meal.[42] This trade lasted about a year, beginning in June 1863 with the withdrawal of the Union army from Stafford Heights during the Gettysburg campaign. A resident recalled that "it was ridiculous to see the very ordinary white people of that county, whom nobody had ever known to wear a coat, in the heat of July & August never without a light blue Army overcoat," adding that the traffic in tools, supplies, sutler's stores, and other goods encouraged a certain prosperity because of prices that Richmond residents paid. While surveying near Fredericksburg in September 1864 a Confederate engineer was surprised at how well some lived amidst the desolation. "Indeed I believe that so far as I can observe Fredericksburg is the cheapest place I have been to in the Confederacy," he wrote, "and I know it is the case in Stafford that the people, especially the poorer classes are better off than they have been during the war."[43]

This man's final assessment probably held true for a narrow area confined to Stafford County. More often people were impressed by the devastation and impoverishment in the region and with the knowledge that recovery would not come soon because of the lack of slave labor. The war also had undermined the neighborhood economy: in September 1864 a Confederate purchasing agent for Spotsylvania was forced to buy grain from the Shenandoah Valley instead of locally to feed the needy.[44]

Two more indignities inflamed passions among Fredericksburg's civilians against the Yankee barbarian. On May 8, 1864, roughly sixty Federal soldiers came to town. Most had been wounded but still bore weapons. Citizens demanded their surrender, turning the prisoners over to Confederate authorities. In retaliation Union officials arrested an equal number of the city's residents. A committee of two led by Mayor Montgomery Slaughter—himself a former political hostage—negotiated an exchange for their release by July 8.[45] Not long afterward Union gunboats ascended the Rappahannock River, stopping about four miles from Fredericksburg at the mansion of Col. John Seddon. A brother of the Confederate secretary of war, Seddon recently had died, but soldiers still evicted the widow, an eighty-year-old mother, five children, and a sister before burning the home. The Union military ordered the destruction as a reprisal for the similar treatment of Maryland governor Augustus Bradford's home during the Maryland campaign of Lt. Gen. Jubal A. Early. A Richmond editor predictably omitted mention of this while decrying the Union act.[46]

From then on, events passed more peacefully in the town, which even returned to the control of a Confederate provost marshal on September 9, 1864, after the Union army shifted to Petersburg.[47] By October of that year the population of the town had fallen from its prewar 5,000 to perhaps 600 to 800 people, chiefly women and children. When a Florida man toured the area that autumn, he reported that the "evidence of the enemy's vandalism begins a few miles out of Richmond, and increases every step as it advances towards the Rappahannock." Upon alighting at the train depot at Hamilton's Crossing below Fredericksburg, he was struck by the extent of the destruction.

> A few trees remain upon the hills near the site of the depot, but there is not a fence nor an inhabited house all the way to Fredericksburg. A few cattle may be seen grazing on the rich plains which bear no crops now but crops of luxuriant weeds. . . . There are no hands at work in the fenceless fields— no signs of animated life about the deserted houses—the drowsy crow of the cock, the neighing of the horses, the cawing of the crow, and the laughter of the children in the yard, and the 'wo haw' of the plow driven, are no longer heard in this blasted region. All is still as death for miles and miles under the sweet and autumnal sun.[48]

Burned depots and bridges also evoked for this observer memories of Georgia during the Atlanta campaign—although with crucial differences. The land, he noted, bore deeper scars in Virginia: rifle pits, redoubts, and entrenchments indicated that armies had remained in fixed positions for longer stretches.[49] Other factors made the depredations in Virginia different from those in Georgia and the Carolinas. Acts against civilians in northern Virginia occurred over longer duration—like a steady rain shower with periodic storms, versus the hurricanelike shock of Sherman's march from Atlanta to Savannah. Civilians around Fredericksburg had greater ability to salvage homes or secure protection from pillaging during the period in which officers held divided minds over how to treat Confederate loyalists. Awaiting future study is whether there was any regional difference in the impact on morale from depredations. Sherman's march through Georgia has been credited with undermining the will of civilians to fight, yet Fredericksburg's experience suggests that morale rebounded to an extent and that depredations at times fed the desire for vengeance. The timing of these acts—toward the beginning or end of the conflict—may have determined their impact. Ultimately Fredericksburg points to the destruction of the South's resources and the capture of Lee's army as more decisive factors in Confederate defeat.[50]

The loss of property in the Fredericksburg region was considerable, but buildings could be repaired. The human upheaval lasted longer. Emancipation guaranteed a sweeping adjustment in all phases of life—economic, political, and social. As hinted above, the economic impact alone could be mind boggling. Agriculturally the region did not show signs of returning to prewar levels of production until at least 1880, although some enterprises—such as wheat growing—took even longer. With the largest number of slaves Spotsylvania County changed the most dramatically, as personal property declined 92.5 percent, from $5.5 million in 1860 to $421,132 in 1870. These figures represent both trauma for slaveholders and opportunity for former slaves: emancipation allowed 1,170 freedpeople to become heads of households, altering the landscape as large farms gave way to smaller ones.[51]

Other aspects of the war's impact on the population, both white and black, have received little attention. Census figures indicate that the white population recovered from wartime losses, although whether this resulted from new births or migration into the area requires further study. Women outnumbered men in Virginia before the war, and in 1880 they continued to do so by a margin of 21,106. Corresponding changes to family life are unknown, especially the dynamics of female responsibilities within households and whether women delayed marriages or had trouble finding spouses.[52] Meanwhile African Americans declined by 50 percent in the Fredericksburg region, mirroring demographic patterns in the state. The region's freedpeople likely joined thousands who sought better economic opportunity than the eastern portions of Virginia could offer. Cities such as Charlottesville, Lynchburg, Petersburg, and Richmond drew freedpeople like magnets, but economic depression and harsh measures by employers chased more than 100,000 to other portions of the South where higher wages prevailed. Many followed the railroads, perhaps anticipating the pattern of later migrant pickers by sending money back home with the intention of returning to Virginia. Others left for good to reconstitute families broken before the war by the sale of slaves to the Cotton South.[53]

Statistics cannot reveal the sense of personal dislocation felt by Virginians who had supported the Confederacy. Privations continued despite the war's end. With commission merchants refusing to extend credit for the promise of future crops, cash replaced trust in most exchanges. For women charged with maintaining food and clothing for households, this immediate postwar transition could be especially trying. Vegetable gardening, dairying, and poultry raising—all identified as women's work—for a while became more important for family subsistence. A year after the war ended, a Charlottesville woman noted that her circle discussed chickens and little else. Slaveholding women faced the most drastic adjustments, for their farms and households had been structured on the premise of having servants. A Campbell County woman underscored to a northern friend what this meant: "Our domestic arrangements are so entirely different to what they are with you that it will take some time for us to get fixed to do our own house work or to do with a few servants. For instance, my kitchen is about forty five yards from the dwelling house; my spring about two hundred yards, and other things to correspond. We have no wood house, washing machine, cooking stove,—in short, none of the conveniences that you Northern people have been so long accustomed to, and worse than all, we have no money to fix these things." The effects of emancipation thus penetrated the most mundane aspects of Virginia life.[54]

Such disruption to prewar lives resulted in no widespread expression of unhappiness with the Confederate effort to gain independence, however. At least in Fredericksburg, war weariness did not necessarily equate with abandonment of the southern cause. The Union army did narrow the choices of Virginia's poorer people, whose conflicts with planters and other elites probably grew during the war. But deserting the army often meant giving up the best chance to protect one's home. The blending of front and home front—and the depredations by the enemy—possibly fueled commitment to the war for most Virginians. This was not necessarily decisive in the construction of Confederate identity for residents of the Old Dominion, but the unifying effect of an opposing army is a factor largely ignored in recent scholarship.

Union depredations also provided memories that gave Confederates common ground in the postwar world, undergirding the southern distinctiveness that C. Vann Woodward defined so well. Fredericksburg residents and much of the Confederacy experienced defeat, occupation, and impoverishment that made their lives more akin to the lives of Europeans than people of the northern United States. Woodward's epic study of the post-Reconstruction South underscored this with a quotation from Arnold J. Toynbee remembering Queen Victoria's Diamond Jubilee in England. The procession Toynbee witnessed as a boy made him believe his country was atop the world, ready to stay there forever—except for this nagging thing called history that "is something unpleasant that happens to other people." Like Woodward, Toynbee recognized that southerners in the United States had a different experience. Fredericksburg civilians, and their counterparts throughout the South, knew that history had happened to them.[55]

Acknowledgments

The author acknowledges the generous help of Robert K. Krick, who shared a wealth of materials on the experience of Fredericksburg during the war.

Notes

1. Edward Porter Alexander, *Fighting for the Confederacy: The Personal Recollections of General Edward Porter Alexander*, ed. Gary W. Gallagher (Chapel Hill: University of North Carolina Press, 1989), 170–71; S. J. Quinn, *The History of the City of Fredericksburg, Virginia* (Richmond: Heritage Press, 1908), 86–88; Sumter (S.C.) *Tri-Weekly Watchman*, January 5, 1863; Jane H. Beale, *The Journal of Jane Harrison Beale* (Fredericksburg, Va.: Historic Fredericksburg Foundation, 1979), 69.

2. For a similar argument and the historiography of a hard war, see Mark Grimsley, "Conciliation and Its Failure, 1861–1862," *Civil War History* 39 (December 1993): 317–35. A recent work also stressing violence that erupted from the start is Charles Royster's *The Destructive War: William Tecumseh Sherman, Stonewall Jackson, and the Americans* (New York: Knopf, 1991). For a viewpoint that questions whether the war ever became a total one, see Mark E. Neely, Jr., "Was the Civil War a Total War?," *Civil War History* 37 (March 1991): 5–28.

3. B. Lewis Blackford to Father, December 23, 1862, Blackford Papers, box 6, folder 83, Southern Historical Collection, Wilson Library, University of North Carolina, Chapel Hill, N.C. (repository hereafter cited as SHC). On Confederate nationalism, see Drew Gilpin Faust, *The Creation of Confederate Nationalism: Ideology and Identity in the Civil War South* (Baton Rouge: Louisiana State University Press, 1988); Richard E. Beringer and others, *Why the South Lost the Civil War* (Athens: University of Georgia Press, 1986), 64–81; and Paul D. Escott, *After Secession: Jefferson Davis and the Failure of Confederate Nationalism* (Baton Rouge: Louisiana State University Press, 1978). For revenge as a motivation among Confederate soldiers, see James M. McPherson, *What They Fought For, 1861–1865* (Baton Rouge: Louisiana State University Press, 1994), 18, 21–24.

4. Cynthia Musselman, "The Economic Impact of the Civil War on the City of Fredericksburg, Spotsylvania County, and Stafford County" (unpublished study, 1984), 6–7, at Fredericksburg and Spotsylvania National Military Park Library, Fredericksburg, Va. (repository hereafter cited as FSNMP). Scholarship stressing the revolutionary aspect of the Civil War because of its impact on slavery includes Joseph P. Reidy, *From Slavery to Agrarian Capitalism in the Cotton Plantation South: Central Georgia, 1800–1880* (Chapel Hill: University of North Carolina Press, 1992); James M. McPherson, *Abraham Lincoln and the Second American Revolution* (New York: Oxford University Press, 1990); Eric Foner, *Reconstruction, 1863–1877: America's Unfinished Revolution* (New York: Harper & Row, 1988); Barbara Jeanne Fields, "The

Advent of Capitalist Agriculture," in *Essays on the Postbellum Southern Economy*, ed. Thavolia Glymph (Arlington: Texas A&M University Press, 1985), 73–94; Harold D. Woodman, "Sequel to Slavery: The New History Views the Postbellum South," *Journal of Southern History* 43 (November 1977): 523–54. Many owe a debt to the pioneering work in W. E. B. DuBois's *Black Reconstruction in America, 1860–1880* (1935; reprint, New York: Atheneum, 1992).

5. Stephen V. Ash, *Middle Tennessee Society Transformed, 1860–1870: War and Peace in the Upper South* (Baton Rouge: Louisiana State University Press, 1988), 9–10; George Fitzhugh, "Make Home Attractive," *DeBow's Review*. June 1860, 625–26. On the economy in general, see Lewis C. Gray, *History of Agriculture in the Southern United States to 1860*, 2 vols. (Washington, D.C.: Carnegie Institution, 1933), 2:916, 919–20; Emmett B. Fields, "The Agricultural Population of Virginia, 1850–1860" (Ph.D. dissertation, Vanderbilt University, Nashville, Tenn., 1953), 39–40; Anne Lenore Stauffenberg, "Albemarle County, Virginia, 1850–1870: An Economic Survey Based on the U.S. Census" (M.S. thesis, University of Virginia, Charlottesville, Va., 1973), 10, 18, 40–42; Fredericksburg *Herald* assessment of wheat crop in the *Democrat* (Abingdon, Va.), May 14, 1859; Avery Craven, *Soil Exhaustion as a Factor in the Agricultural History of Virginia and Maryland, 1606–1860* (Urbana: University of Illinois Press, 1926). A Confederate staff officer observed about Fredericksburg during the war: "A dwindling trade had thinned the population and quieted its ambitions." See G. Moxley Sorrel, *Recollections of a Confederate Staff Officer*, ed. Bell I. Wiley (1959; reprint, Wilmington, N.C.: Broadfoot, 1987), 123. For the concept of a modern slave society and the dilemma of slaveholders and progress, see James Oakes, *Slavery and Freedom: An Interpretation of the Old South* (New York: Knopf, 1990), and Eugene D. Genovese, *The Slaveholders' Dilemma: Freedom and Progress in Southern Conservative Thought, 1820–1860* (Columbia: University of South Carolina Press, 1992).

6. Musselman, "Economic Impact," 12–13 and appendices detailing the economic impact on the town and region; U.S. Bureau of the Census, *Eighth Census of the United States*, 4 vols. (Washington, D.C.: GPO, 1865), 3:630–31.

7. Fields, "Agricultural Population of Virginia," 163; Elizabeth Fox-Genovese and Eugene D. Genovese, *Fruits of Merchant Capital: Slavery and Bourgeois Property in the Rise and Expansion of Capitalism* (New York: Oxford University Press, 1983), 48–53; Faust, *Confederate Nationalism*, 52–54; Steven Hahn, *The Roots of Southern Populism: Yeoman Farmers and the Transformation of the Georgia Upcountry, 1850–1890* (New York: Oxford University Press, 1983), 50–58, 70–77; Fitzhugh, "Make Home Attractive," 626. The term *neighborhood economy* is borrowed from Laurel Thatcher Ulrich, *A Midwife's Tale: The Life of Martha Ballard, Based on Her Diary, 1785–1812* (New York: Vintage, 1991), 33.

8. John Washington, "Memorys of the Past," Library of Congress, Acc. No. 16,842, typescript version at FSNMP.

9. Grimsley, "Conciliation and Its Failure," 328; Daniel E. Sutherland, "Introduction to War: The Civilians of Culpeper County, Virginia," *Civil War History* 37 (June

1991): 123–24. On enemy depredations in the northern Piedmont in general, see Jedediah Hotchkiss to wife, July 27, 1862, reel 4, frames 443–44, microfilm edition, Jedediah Hotchkiss Papers, Library of Congress, Washington, D.C.

10. Marsena Rudolph Patrick, *Inside Lincoln's Army: The Diary of Marsena Rudolph Patrick, Provost Marshal General, Army of the Potomac*, ed. David S. Sparks (New York: Thomas Yoseloff, 1964), 69. For claims allowed unionists in Stafford County, see Southern Claims Commission, boxes 398–99, RG 216, National Archives, Washington, D.C. (repository hereafter cited as NA).

11. Although the town surrendered to Federal forces on April 19, most of the Union army remained in Stafford. Official occupation began when the provost marshal established headquarters in town on April 27. Discrepancy exists in accounts of when the Federal soldiers withdrew. A Richmond resident heard reports of the withdrawal as early as August 26, although this appears to have been only the beginning of the Federal movements. See John B. Jones, *A Rebel War Clerk's Diary at the Confederate States Capital*, 2 vols. (1866; reprint, [Alexandria, Va.]: Time-Life Books, 1982), 1:150.

12. Patrick, *Inside Lincoln's Army*, 88; James W. Hunnicutt, *The Conspiracy Unveiled: The South Sacrificed; or, the Horrors of Secession* (Philadelphia: J. B. Lippincott, 1863), 440–42; Quinn, *History of Fredericksburg*, 75; Moncure D. Conway, "Fredericksburg First and Last," *Magazine of American History* 17 (June 1887): 453; Edward J. Nichols, *Toward Gettysburg: A Biography of General John F. Reynolds* (1958; reprint, Gaithersburg, Md.: Butternut Press, 1986), 80, 85–86. For the intercession of Fredericksburg civilians on behalf of Reynolds, see U.S. War Department, *The War of the Rebellion: A Compilation of the Official Records of the Union and Confederate Armies*, 127 vols., index, and atlas (Washington, D.C.: GPO, 1880–1901), ser. 2, 4:796–97 (hereafter cited as *OR*; all references are to series 1 unless otherwise noted).

13. Patrick, *Inside Lincoln's Army*, 73; Hunnicutt, *Conspiracy Unveiled*, v, xi; Benjamin Armstrong Claim, Spotsylvania County, December 14, 1874, Southern Claims Commission, box 397, no. 12474, RG 216, NA; Reynolds quoted in Nichols, *Toward Gettysburg*, 86. By the end of November a southern soldier estimated that only six unionist families remained in Fredericksburg. See Thomas Reeder to Sister, November 28, 1862, South Caroliniana Library, University of South Carolina, Columbia, S.C.

14. Patrick, *Inside Lincoln's Army*, 104–5; Wallace J. Schutz and Walter N. Trenerry, *Abandoned by Lincoln: A Military Biography of General John Pope* (Urbana: University of Illinois Press, 1990), 93–94; Quinn, *History of Fredericksburg*, 75–76; Grimsley, "Conciliation and Its Failure," 331.

15. *OR* 12(2):50–52; Patrick, *Inside Lincoln's Army*, 108, 110; Jones, *Diary*, 1:146–47.

16. A unionist commented that the orders by Pope to swear allegiance to the United States came to the people of Fredericksburg "like a thunderbolt from a clear sky on the citizens of this community." See Hunnicutt, *Conspiracy Unveiled*, 418–19; Betty Herndon Maury, *The Civil War Diary of Betty Herndon Maury*, ed. Robert A. Hodge (Fredericksburg, Va.: n.p., 1985), 65.

17. *OR* 12(1):289–98, 293; Patrick, *Inside Lincoln's Army*, 112; Conway, "Fredericksburg First and Last," 456.

18. Lucille Griffith, ed., "Fredericksburg's Political Hostages: The Old Capitol Journal of George Henry Clay Rowe," *Virginia Magazine of History and Biography* 72 (October 1964): 395–429; W. Harrison Daniel, ed., "The Prison Diary of William F. Broaddus," *Virginia Baptist Register* 21 (1982): 998–1018; Quinn, *History of Fredericksburg*, 77–79; Hunnicutt, *Conspiracy Unveiled*, 414.

19. Maury, *Diary*, 52, 55. For other comments by Maury concerning fleeing slaves, see 60, 66, 67.

20. Hunnicutt, *Conspiracy Unveiled*, 354–55, 379; Patrick, *Inside Lincoln's Army*, 114–15; Washington, "Memorys of the Past," 73; Susan Leigh Blackford and others, comp. and eds., *Letters from Lee's Army, or Memoirs of Life in and out of the Army in Virginia during the War Between the States* (New York: Charles Scribner's Sons, 1947), 93.

21. Hunnicutt, *Conspiracy Unveiled*, 379; Emily Jane Grayson testimony, June 9, 1877, John Grayson Claim, Stafford County, Southern Claims Commission, box 399, no. 6923, RG 216, NA.

22. Hunnicutt, *Conspiracy Unveiled*, 354–55, 430–31.

23. Maury, *Diary*, 68.

24. Quinn, *History of Fredericksburg*, 81–82; Richmond *Daily Dispatch*, September 18, 1862.

25. *OR* 21:783.

26. Robert E. Lee, *The Wartime Papers of R. E. Lee*, ed. Clifford Dowdey and Louis H. Manarin (Boston: Little, Brown, 1961), 343. Also concerning this truce, see *OR* 21:784–85; Quinn, *History of Fredericksburg*, 84–86; and Edmund Ruffin, *The Diary of Edmund Ruffin*, ed. William Kauffman Scarborough, 3 vols. (Baton Rouge: Louisiana State University Press, 1972–89), 2:497.

27. Catherine Ann Devereux Edmondston, *"Journal of a Secesh Lady": The Diary of Catherine Ann Devereux Edmondston, 1860–1866*, ed. Beth Gilbert Crabtree and James W. Patton (Raleigh: North Carolina Division of Archives and History, 1979), 308; Robert A. Moore, *A Life for the Confederacy: From the War Diary of Robert A. Moore, Pvt., C.S.A.*, ed. James W. Silver (1959; reprint Wilmington, N.C.: Broadfoot, 1987), 117; Mary Elizabeth Massey, *Refugee Life in the Confederacy* (Baton Rouge: Louisiana State University Press, 1964), 5, 61; Quinn, *History of Fredericksburg*, 86–87; Alfred M. Scales, "The Battle of Fredericksburg," in *Southern Historical Society Papers*, ed. J. William Jones and others, 52 vols. and 2-vol. index (1877–1959; reprint, Wilmington, N.C.: Broadfoot, 1990–92), 40:205.

28. Catherine Thom Bartlett, *My Dear Brother: A Confederate Chronicle* (Richmond: Dietz Press, 1952), 75; Beale, *Journal*, 69; Conway, "Fredericksburg First and Last," 460–61; Quinn, *History of Fredericksburg*, 88–89; William W. Teall, "Ringside Seat at Fredericksburg," *Civil War Times Illustrated* 4 (May 1965): 26; Wm. H. S. Burgwyn Diary, December 11, 1862, typescript at FSNMP (original at North Carolina

Department of Archives and History, Raleigh, N.C.); *OR* 21:190–91; Alexander, *Fighting for the Confederacy*, 170–71.

29. Abraham Welch to Sister Mary Ann, December 27, 1862, Abraham Welch Papers, SHC; Letter of Lt. Samuel S. Partridge, 13th New York, Fredericksburg, December 17, 1862, FSNMP. For other reports of looting, see Darius N. Couch, "Sumner's 'Right Grand Division,'" in *Battles and Leaders of the Civil War*, ed. Robert Underwood Johnson and Clarence Clough Buel, 4 vols. (New York: Century, 1887–88), 3:108; Atlanta *Southern Confederacy*, December 27, 1862; Capt. Benjamin Edward Stiles to Aunt, Fredericksburg, December 21, 1862, Mackay-Stiles Collection, SHC.

30. Patrick, *Inside Lincoln's Army*, 189.

31. Ruffin, *Diary*, 2:515.

32. On soldier attitudes concerning destruction, see Bell I. Wiley, *The Life of Billy Yank: The Common Soldier of the Union* (1952; rev. ed., Baton Rouge: Louisiana State University Press, 1971), 203; Grimsley, "Conciliation and Its Failure," 328.

33. Blackford et al., *Letters from Lee's Army*, 139; Ruffin, *Diary*, 2:500; Lynchburg *Virginian*, October 6, 1862; Richmond *Daily Enquirer*, December 23, 1862. On substitutions, see Record of Exemptions, 1862–63, Virginia, chap. 1, vol. 251, RG 109, NA.

34. Atlanta *Southern Confederacy*, December 27, 1862; Lynchburg *Virginian*, December 20, 1862; Richmond *Daily Enquirer*, December 23, 1862; Richmond *Daily Whig*, December 22, 1862; Augusta (Ga.) *Chronicle & Sentinel*, January 10, 1863; H. W. R. Jackson, *The Southern Women and the Second American Revolution: Their Trials, &c., Yankee Barbarities Illustrated* (Atlanta: Intelligencer Steam-Power Press, 1863), 49–50.

35. Edmondston, *"Journal of a Secesh Lady,"* 322; Blackford et al., *Letters from Lee's Army*, 149. Also see L. Minor Blackford, *Mine Eyes Have Seen the Glory* (Cambridge, Mass.: Harvard University Press, 1954), 213–14.

36. Capt. Benjamin Edward Stiles to Aunt, December 21, 1862, Mackay-Stiles Collection, SHC; *Daily Southern Guardian* (Columbia, S.C.), April 8, 1863.

37. Charles W. Turner, ed., *Civil War Letters of Arabella Speairs and William Beverley Pettit of Fluvanna County, Virginia, March 1862–March 1865*, 2 vols. (Roanoke: Virginia Lithography & Graphics, 1988–89), 1:155.

38. *OR* 51(2):665–66; Richmond *Daily Enquirer*, December 23, 1862.

39. George Graham Morris, "Confederate Lynchburg, 1861–1865" (M.A. thesis, Virginia Polytechnic Institute and State University, Blacksburg, Va., 1977), 62–63; Louis H. Manarin, ed., *Richmond at War: The Minutes of the City Council, 1861–1865* (Chapel Hill: University of North Carolina Press, 1966), 275; Quinn, *History of Fredericksburg*, 93; Massey, *Refugee Life*, 252–53; Richmond *Daily Dispatch*, January 1, 1863; Richmond *Daily Enquirer*, January 2, 1863.

40. *OR* 29(2):823–24.

41. Moore, *Life for the Confederacy*, 146; *OR*, ser. 4, 2:334–35.

42. J. T. Trowbridge, *The South: A Tour of Its Battlefields and Ruined Cities, a Journey Through the Desolated States, and Talks with the People* (Hartford, Conn.: L. Stebbins, 1866), 115.

43. Anonymous, "Reminiscences of the Civil War," Civil War Collection, Maryland Historical Society, Baltimore, Md. (historians at FSNMP have identified the author as Edward L. Heinichen); R. L. B. to Mother, September 20, 1864, box 6, folder 87, Blackford Papers, SHC.

44. John W. Geary to Mary, July 28, August 3, 1863, Geary Papers, Pennsylvania Historical Society, Philadelphia, Pa.; James M. Holladay to James A. Seddon, September 13, 1864, Letters Received/Confederate Secretary of War, roll 130, file no. H458, RG 109, NA.

45. Quinn, *History of Fredericksburg*, 100–107.

46. Ruffin, *Diary*, 3:525–26; *OR* 43(1):998–99; Charles Kingsley to Frank E. Kingsley, August 6, 1864, Kingsley Letter, Virginia Historical Society, Richmond, Va.; Richmond *Examiner*, August 11, 1864.

47. Capt. H. S. Doggett of the 30th Virginia served as Confederate provost marshal and commander of post, effective September 9, 1864. See his testimony in Joseph B. Ficklin Claim, Stafford County, Southern Claims Commission, box 399, no. 5365, RG 216, NA; Robert K. Krick, *30th Virginia Infantry*, 2nd ed. (Lynchburg, Va.: H. E. Howard, 1985), 94.

48. Mobile *Register*, November 26, 1864.

49. Ibid.

50. While not quite making the specific argument above, scholars have recently questioned the prevailing tendency to view the defeat of the Confederacy as resulting from internal factors. Two works in particular have restored the Union army to the equation for Confederate defeat. See James M. McPherson, *Battle Cry of Freedom: The Civil War Era* (New York: Oxford University Press, 1988), 854–59, and Gabor S. Boritt, ed., *Why the Confederacy Lost* (New York: Oxford University Press, 1992). For a study that reveals how the Union found the strategy through which to use its resources, see Herman Hattaway and Archer Jones, *How the North Won: A Military History of the Civil War* (Urbana: University of Illinois Press, 1983). Another work suggesting how depredations could reinforce Confederate hatred is George C. Rable, *Civil Wars: Women and the Crisis of Southern Nationalism* (Urbana: University of Illinois Press, 1989), 158–59.

51. Musselman, "Economic Impact," appendices W–Z.

52. Ibid.; Stanton *Spectator*, January 25, 1881; Joan Firor Scott, *The Southern Lady: From Pedestal to Politics, 1830–1930* (Chicago: University of Chicago Press, 1970), 106–9, 124–33.

53. William Cohen, *At Freedom's Edge: Black Mobility and the Southern White Quest for Racial Control, 1861–1915* (Baton Rouge: Louisiana State University Press, 1991), 93–95; Lynda Joyce Morgan, *Emancipation in Virginia's Tobacco Belt, 1850–1870* (Athens: University of Georgia Press, 1992), 144–45, 207–8; Alrutheus Ambush Taylor, *The Negro in the Reconstruction of Virginia* (Washington, D.C.: Association for the Study of Negro Life and History, 1926), 88–93, 100–103.

54. Louisa A. Minor Diary, April 22–28, 1866, and Sarah P. Payne to Mary [M.

Clendenin], September 30, 1865, Payne Letters, both in Alderman Library, University of Virginia, Charlottesville, Va.

55. C. Vann Woodward, "The Search for Southern Identity," in *The Burden of Southern History*, by C. Vann Woodward (Baton Rouge: Louisiana State University Press, 1960), 16–25, and C. Vann Woodward, *Origins of the New South, 1877–1913* (Baton Rouge: Louisiana State University Press, 1951), viii.

Morale, Maneuver, and Mud

THE ARMY OF THE POTOMAC,

DECEMBER 16, 1862 – JANUARY 26, 1863

A. WILSON GREENE

The 6th Wisconsin Infantry, members of the fabled Iron Brigade, protected the far left of the Army of the Potomac during and immediately after the battle of Fredericksburg. This veteran regiment largely escaped the bloodletting on December 13, 1862, but it witnessed the portion of the Union defeat experienced by its First Corps comrades and heard tales of the calamity on the northern end of the field. Lyman C. Holford of the 6th remembered receiving orders at 11:00 P.M. December 15 to fall in line and move upstream along the Rappahannock River toward Fredericksburg. "Then the thought struck me," Holford told his diary, "that we were on the retreat. Not a word was uttered above the lowest kind of whisper and in silence broken only by the crackling of dry weeds, we took our departure from the most dangerous part of Dixie."[1]

Holford and the nearly 100,000 other soldiers in the Army of the Potomac now ventured into another perilous province. This district's dimensions stretched beyond Marye's Heights, the canal ditch valley, and Prospect Hill, killing zones during the battle of Fredericksburg. It encompassed the most menacing territory encountered during a democratic war: the realm of public opinion. During the next six weeks the army's leadership, both military and civilian, and its morale would be tested as never before. Within an arena of political intrigue unsurpassed by any Civil War military organization, the Army of the Potomac would try twice to redeem its fortunes squandered in futility and carnage below the ridges south and west of Fredericksburg.

On December 16 Maj. Gen. Ambrose E. Burnside explained the origin and conduct of his evacuation from Fredericksburg. "The army was withdrawn to this side of the river because I felt the positions in front could not be carried, and it was a military necessity either to attack or retire," he told General in Chief Henry W. Halleck. "A repulse would have been disastrous to us."[2]

Although Burnside indicated that he executed his retreat in secret and without loss, Halleck and the country knew that in its largest context the Fredericksburg campaign had been a dismal failure. The army had barely spread its collective blankets over the cold soil of Stafford County when the effort to assign blame sprang from pens and voices all over the North. President Abraham Lincoln adopted a conciliatory if implausible official explanation of the Federal defeat. He reassured the vanquished Army of the Potomac that their attempt on December 13 "was not an error, nor the failure other than an accident." Lincoln's assessment of the army's casualties as "comparatively . . . small" rendered his message to the army even more transparently disingenuous.[3]

Soldiers and officers in the field declined to dismiss their recent sacrifice as the product of fate. They instinctively knew that their repulse at Fredericksburg stemmed from some conscious decision that drew them into the teeth of Robert E. Lee's unshakable defense. Lincoln's explanation left many with the belief that the government had forced Burnside to initiate the ill-advised battle. One Union officer testified that he thought "the interference of the Administration had changed certain victory into disaster. I deprecated politics when it was allowed to interfere with the management of armies." William Orr of the 19th Indiana wrote his wife less than a week after the battle that "there is some mad Reckless fanatical, Demagouges at Washington who have got control of the president, the Secretary of War, & of Gen. Halleck, who are running the machine, and they are running it into the ground." The army's provost marshal, Brig. Gen. Marsena R. Patrick, confided to his diary on December 21 that "the papers say, that the whole Cabinet resigns. . . . The news is too good to be true. . . . May it be confirmed!"[4]

Those who blamed politicians for the battle of Fredericksburg cited "intolerable and wicked blundering" in Washington characterized by an unreasonable determination to move against the Confederate capital regardless of military circumstances. Implicit in this argument was the belief that political dictates somehow forced army commander Burnside to cross the Rappahannock and offer battle against his will. "I say now that I do not blame 'Sides' for the Fredericksburg disaster," wrote Capt. Jacob W. Haas of the 96th Pennsylvania, "but I do blame . . . Abolitionists at home for crying out 'on to Richmond' until at last he succumbed." The *New York Times*, even while recommending resumption of an offensive campaign, thought it "plain that the direct assault upon Fredericksburgh Heights should have never been ordered by the Government against the settled judgment of General Burnside." The *Times* also demanded a congressional investigation of the battle, which the Joint Committee on the Conduct of the War promptly conducted, eventually concluding that Maj. Gen. William B. Franklin's conduct on the Union left led to the unhappy results on December 13.[5]

Not everyone shared the urge to deflect blame for Fredericksburg from the army commander's shoulders. Samuel S. Partridge of the 13th New York wrote that "after six days and six nights of terrific cannonading and terrible musketry, after an expenditure of several millions of dollars worth of ammunition, after the loss of thousands of lives, the inflictions of thousands of wounds, and the effusion of thousands of quarts of blood, we stand just where we did one week ago today. How are you Mister Burnside?" Union colonel Regis de Trobriand thought that following the battle "the troops had lost their confidence in [Burnside]." A soldier in the 7th Rhode Island adjudged the army as sympathetic with General Burnside's misfortune but doubting his capacity as a general. But others like Col. Robert McAllister of the 11th New Jersey found reason to praise Burnside's conduct of the retreat and opted to defer ascribing responsibility for the battle itself. "Who is to blame I don't know," wrote McAllister, "time will tell us all."[6]

That time arrived on December 23. The *New York Times* published on page one a letter from Burnside to Halleck intended to end any speculation about who masterminded the fiasco at Fredericksburg. "For the failure in the attack, I am responsible," conceded Burnside. "The fact that I decided to move from Warrenton on to this line, rather against the opinion of the President, Secretary of War, and yourself, and that you left the whole movement in my hands, without giving me orders, makes me responsible."[7]

Burnside drafted this remarkable mea culpa in response to reports brought to him from Washington by Dr. William H. Church, his medical director. Church paraphrased conversations he had overheard and produced northern newspapers assigning responsibility for events on the Rappahannock to Lincoln, Secretary of War Edwin M. Stanton, and General Halleck. Burnside immediately vowed to set the record straight by drafting a note to the Associated Press for public distribution. His staff persuaded him to modify these plans. Burnside agreed instead to consult with the president and present the letter as official correspondence to Halleck, although his staff thought their chief should not have ignored the roles of superiors in devising the Fredericksburg strategy. To the relief of Lincoln and the delight of Stanton, Burnside shared his letter with the press after personally informing the president of his intentions.[8]

Burnside's selflessness no doubt restored some degree of confidence in the administration. Historian Allan Nevins calls the general's behavior "sportsmanlike," and Burnside's biographer, William Marvel, cites evidence to indicate that the gesture worked "a wonderful effect" on the country's morale. But the impact of Burnside's letter on public perceptions of the military situation in Virginia would prove problematical.[9]

Many in the North grew despondent over the butcher's bill at Fredericksburg. Joseph Medill of the Chicago *Tribune* believed "the feeling of utter hopelessness is stronger than at any time since the war began. The terrible bloody defeat of our brave army . . . leaves us almost without hope. . . . Sometimes I think nothing is left now but to fight for a boundary." *Harper's Weekly* averred that "the loyal North is filled with sickness, disgust and despair" over the outcome at Fredericksburg. Republicans feared conservative Democrats could manipulate the country's angst into a peace movement that might sweep the administration from office and end the war upon terms dictated from Richmond.[10]

Morale within the Army of the Potomac, according to traditional interpretation, suffered equally. Burnside's command, wrote historian T. Harry Williams, "was a seething mass of discontent and demoralization." The chronicler of the Fifth Corps agreed: "The dark days had come, when dissatisfaction, discouragement, home sickness, and many other ills of camp life prevailed."[11]

A number of reasons account for the army's apparently flagging esprit. Its proximate cause stemmed from the outcome on December 13. A New Hampshire soldier thought the battle of Fredericksburg "had depressed the spirit, crushed the hopes and destroyed the effective power of the regiment." Edmund Halsey of the 15th New Jersey noted that "the memory of our defeat throws a gloom over the camp. We look to a retreat to the Potomac line." "The disaster at Fredericksburg affects us all deeply," observed Brig. Gen.

Alpheus S. Williams on December 19, adding, "I am as discouraged and blue as one well can be, as I see in these operations much that astonishes and confounds me and much that must discourage our troops and the people."[12]

The Army of the Potomac had been defeated before. In fact, with the exception of its drawn battle at Antietam, it had known nothing but defeat. What made the experience at Fredericksburg seem so debilitating? First, the magnitude and one-sidedness of the affair left little room for redefinition. With the exceptions of Meade's and Gibbon's brief successes on the southern end of the field, the Federal attacks clearly miscarried. The human cost of that failure, in raw as well as relative numbers, left many soldiers certain that the sacrifice of their comrades had gained nothing.[13]

Such disappointment unleashed resentments unrelated to the battle. For instance, some of the regiments had received no wages since the summer. "Our paymaster has never shown his face yet," complained Lt. James Carman of the 107th Pennsylvania. "On the first of January there will be six months pay due me ($600.63)." The perception grew in some army quarters that the administration sent its unpaid troops into slaughter while plundering the public treasury. Moreover, the lack of money created a hardship on army dependents. "Men are discouraged that their families are in want and, of course, have no hart [sic] to work or fight," wrote Colonel McAllister. "If the government would only pay the troops, all would be right."[14]

More than any other factor, doubts about the army's leadership fractured morale. "This army seems to be overburdened with second rate men in high positions," wrote Maj. Rufus R. Dawes of the 6th Wisconsin. "Common place and whiskey are too much in power for the most hopeful future. This winter is, indeed, the Valley Forge of the war." Lt. Theodore Dodge of the 119th New York recorded on December 20 that "I have no faith in our Leaders. . . . I am glad to see that the government has begun to dismiss Officers who fail in their duty; we have so much trash in the way of officers from our mode of recruiting that many need to be dismissed." Pvt. William Hamilton of the 2nd Pennsylvania Reserves agreed: "It is about time something was done to relieve us if not of duty at least of our immediate commanders."[15]

Thomas M. Covert of the 6th Ohio Cavalry described the dubious executive style of his commanding officer in a letter to his wife: "We are under a dutchman by the name of Di Cesnola and we call him desplonada. He is a fool or a coward. He will get the brigade out and scout our side of the picketts [*sic*] all night or go a mile or so from camp and make us dismount and hold our horses all night. I tell you there is some cussing at . . . times. I hope some of our picketts will shoot him for he will never get close enough to the rebs to get shot."[16]

Alex Hamilton of the 72nd Ohio summarized the feelings of many northern soldiers in December 1862: "I tell you Sam we ain't got no generals worth a dam." As might be expected, the army's top general attracted the most criticism. "For the first time, the Army of the Potomac could be said to be really demoralized," wrote newspaper correspondent William Swinton. "The cause of all this could not be concealed; it was a lack of confidence in General Burnside." Maj. Gen. Carl Schurz found the origin of dissatisfaction with Burnside in the general's willingness to accept sole blame for the outcome at Fredericksburg. While Schurz admitted that Burnside's public expression of responsibility "found a response of generous appreciation in public opinion . . . the confidence of the army in his ability and judgment was fatally injured."[17]

How much of this anti-Burnside feeling manifested itself remains in doubt. Brig. Gen. John Cochrane remembered that Burnside's qualities as a commander dominated conversation around every campfire, while Col. Charles S. Wainwright wrote that "very little is said about Burnside, but neither officers nor men have the slightest confidence in him. It is singular how plainly this is apparent, and yet I cannot point out how it is shown, unless it is by a universal distaste to talk about the future."[18]

Some soldiers expressed their feelings about army leadership with their feet. "It troubles me to see the spirit [in the army] worse than it was before," wrote Walter Carter on December 24, "and it certainly does not inspire us to hear men say they will never fight when they can skedaddle." Estimates of desertions vary, but there can be no question that a number of Federals left the ranks. The overwhelming majority of the troops remained with the army in December 1862, but some lost faith in the prospects for victory. James R. Coye of the 76th New York reported on December 17 a widespread attitude "that our army are sick of fiting & want to stop fiting. . . . i can tel you my mind is that they never will be whipped & i hope that something will turn up to settle up the matter for i want to get home and so does every one els." Joseph B. Osborn of the 26th New Jersey told his father that "every soldier out here believes [the war] can not be settled by fighting." Jacob Haas agreed: "I think sometimes we will never be able to conquer the 'Rebs'. . . . I do wish I could think that we can end this war fighting, but am afraid that our blood and treasure has been lavished in vain."[19]

The army's perception of Burnside suffered from one additional factor: he was not George B. McClellan. The Army of the Potomac belonged to the Young Napoleon from that summer day in 1861 when he arrived to resurrect it from its first defeat at Bull Run until November 1862 when Lincoln replaced him with Burnside. Coming as it did after the army's perceived victory at Antietam, McClellan's removal left many in the ranks mistrustful of future events. The battle of Fredericksburg fueled those doubts until they erupted into an orgy of rhetoric in late December.

"The recent battle was only a murder, for which the commander in chief [Halleck] and A. E. Burnside are responsible," wrote Eugene Carter of the 8th U.S. Infantry. "'Little Mac' will have to be called upon again. . . . When George was commander-in-chief, everything went as merry as we could wish to have it, but from the moment they commenced to interfere with him, we have had nothing but disaster. . . . If George B. McClellan should come here again in command of this army, I believe the soldiers would go crazy with joy." Veterans such as William H. Brown of the 44th New York unfavorably compared Burnside's style of warfare as displayed at Marye's Heights with McClellan's reduction of the Yorktown defenses by siege. Similarly, Dexter Macomber of the 1st Michigan Cavalry asked, "Is it better for a General to stare ahead and loose [sic] or gane [sic] a battle with a great loss of men [or] to go safe and sure, well prepared and calculated with science and discipline[?] Then let us have the long head of our Little Mac." Theodore Dodge remembered talking to a group of 100 wounded men in Falmouth after the battle who agreed that McClellan knew better than to lead his soldiers against the sunken road. "Give us back McClellan is the cry of the army," reported Rueben W. Shell of the 7th Pennsylvania Reserves.[20]

Such evidence clearly points to lagging morale and an unrequited affection for George McClellan following Fredericksburg. Yet everyone in the army did not perceive its spirit to be crippled or think Burnside must give way to a recoronated Young Napoleon. Maj. Gen. Edwin V. Sumner's testimony to the Joint Committee on the Conduct of the War about "a great deal too much croaking" in the army is often cited as proof of the army's disaffection. Less familiar is another of his statements before the committee: "I consider that within a few days, with sufficient exertion, this army will be in excellent order again." On December 19 the Left Grand Division's commander, William B. Franklin, informed the congressmen that the army "is not demoralized at all." Burnside himself told the committee that his army's condition remained good and its efficiency unimpaired.[21]

Officers of lesser rank concurred with this assessment. On December 28 Robert McAllister pronounced the army "in a very good condition—not demoralized—but all tired of war. Yet they will fight to the last." Robert G. Carter echoed McAllister's opinion the same day in a letter home: "I want just one good show, one hack at them where I can reach them; when our army can be victorious; and that's what we want—a victory! . . . I am still patriotic and full of hope." The *New York Times* rejected suggestions that troops were unmotivated, stating that "the morale of the army is excellent, the men being . . . anxious to be again led to battle by their commander." Rhode Islander Daniel R. Ballou suggested that the perception of an army "hopelessly demoralized or wrapped in a cloud of gloom and dejection, existed principally in the prejudiced imaginations of disaffected subordinates."[22]

Burnside's personal secretary, Daniel Larned, described the general's demeanor as "oppressed but by no means discouraged." The army commander found solace in supportive communication from Lincoln, Stanton, and others in official Washington. Larned also documented "no end to the letters of sympathy & expressions of confidence" Burnside received following publication of his letter accepting blame for the battle. "I have rode through many of the camps since the fight, and I have yet to see the demoralization and disorganization spoken of by several citizens & correspondents of the press— some degree of depression did exist for some days after the fight, but there is not a regiment that will not heartily cheer and fight for Burnside whenever & wherever he says."[23]

Even admiration for McClellan did not percolate through the entire army. William R. Williams of the 82nd Pennsylvania, a unit in the scarcely pro-Burnside grand division of William B. Franklin, wrote his wife on December 26: "This talk about McClellan not losing the battle if he had been in command is all bosh. The men never have nor cannot fight better than they did under Burnside. If those men who think and talk so much of McClellan will only recruit an army for him, maybe we could get along better. They had better enlist under McClellan and fight for their country and their little God than stay in their comfortable homes and talk of army movements of which they know no more than does a mule of astronomy."[24]

William Swinton wrote after the Civil War about the problem of assessing morale. "Nothing is more difficult," he insisted, "than to indicate, in precise terms, that complex of qualities, passions, prejudices, and illusions, that at any given time make up what is expressively called the morale of an army." Much later the great chronicler of the Army of the Potomac, Bruce Catton, agreed that "there are few ventures which offer as many chances for error as this business of trying to determine exactly how an army feels and what it proposes to do about it."[25] Nevertheless, an assessment of army morale is central to any analysis of the Army of the Potomac during the period following Fredericksburg.

Kenneth P. Williams offers persuasive evidence that the well-documented carping of officers and enlisted men in December 1862 did not equate with irredeemable despair. Williams concluded that the "complaints and criticisms of the soldiers [were not] necessarily an indication that the army lacked battle effectiveness. . . . The hardships and requirements of which soldiers complain one week may be the very things which they boast and brag about the next." Measuring absenteeism provides one concrete means of gauging morale. The army's truancy rate on November 10, 1862, three days after Burnside assumed command, stood at 26.1 percent. On January 20, 1863, the proportion of absent men had actually declined to 25.9 percent. "Burnside had taken over from McClellan an army in poor spirits," concluded Williams.[26] It is logical to expect that the crushing repulse at Fredericksburg did nothing to enhance the army's attitude. That is not to say, as Williams demonstrates, that the Army of the Potomac lay supine in Stafford County bereft of the fortitude to mount new efforts to whip the rebels. Indeed, its commander intended to do just that.

On Christmas morning the *New York Times* proclaimed in bold headlines, "The Army not Going into Winter Quarters. A Probable Speedy Movement in Some Direction." The *Times* correspondent accurately described Burnside's intention, although the general confronted a number of options and had not revealed his preferred course of action. Two subordinates, however, embraced one alternative so fervently that they advanced their idea over Burnside's head directly to the president. Left Grand Division commander Franklin and Sixth Corps chieftain Maj. Gen. William F. "Baldy" Smith wrote

Lincoln on December 20 advocating a movement against the Confederate capital via the Peninsula, McClellan's approach the previous spring. Citing supply problems with the overland route and the numerous natural defensive positions available to Lee, Franklin and Smith suggested massing a quarter of a million men east of Richmond by means of water transport. Once ashore on both sides of the James, this mighty host would either overwhelm the Confederate defenders or invest the capital.[27]

Franklin and Smith's detailed proposal (they even specified how much underwear the soldiers should pack) had merit and found support among other high-ranking officers. Unfortunately for them, Abraham Lincoln remained unconvinced. "The difficulties you point out are obvious and palpable," replied the president on December 22. "But now, as heretofore, if you go to James River, a large part of the army must remain on or near the Fredericksburg line, to protect Washington."[28] An aggressively led force of more than 200,000 men operating against Richmond and Petersburg simultaneously in the winter of 1863 creates an intriguing image. However, the actual significance of Lincoln's exchange of views with Franklin and Smith is the revelation of an atmosphere that encouraged subordinate officers to debate grand strategy with the commander in chief without first consulting the commander of the army.

While Franklin and Smith entertained visions of the Chickahominy, Burnside devised his own offensive scheme. Shortly after completing his interviews with the Joint Committee on the Conduct of the War, he ordered engineers to scout crossing points below Fredericksburg. He selected a spot near the Seddon House, some six or seven miles downriver from town, for his main effort, and had artillery positions sited and wood cut for corduroying roads. His plan included executing a feint above the city that might be converted to an assault if circumstances permitted. He also intended to launch a cavalry raid across the upper Rappahannock leading eventually all the way to Suffolk.[29]

Brig. Gen. William W. Averell, who commanded the Center Grand Division's cavalry brigade, contrived the mounted portion of Burnside's strategy. Indulging an idea he had nurtured for months, Averell would use 2,500 men supported by an infantry division to breach the Rappahannock at Kelly's Ford, twenty-five miles upstream from Fredericksburg. The core of his command, 1,000 picked men from nine regiments, would gallop through central

Virginia; cross the James River west of Richmond, destroying canals and bridges along the way; and reunite with Federal forces 150 miles away in the southeastern corner of the state. The rest of Averell's troopers would proceed toward Warrenton, Culpeper, or back from the Rapidan to confuse pursuing Confederates about the mission's real objectives.[30]

Burnside met with Averell on December 27 to approve his segment of the plan. Shortly thereafter Burnside issued orders to his infantry commanders to be prepared on twelve hours' notice to distribute three days' cooked rations and sixty rounds of ammunition to their men and load a week's worth of supplies onto wagons.[31] Less than a fortnight after abandoning Fredericksburg the Army of the Potomac poised ready to test Lee's defenses once again.

On December 30 Col. James Barnes's division of the Fifth Corps marched upstream to support Averell's river crossing. The following morning Col. Charles A. Johnson's brigade scattered a tiny complement of Confederate cavalry at Richard's Ford and marched six miles upstream to Ellis' Ford, where it recrossed the Rappahannock. Johnson's would be the only Federals to penetrate the southside of the river during the entire operation.[32]

Burnside's offensive did not fail; it simply never began. On the afternoon of December 30 a dispatch from Lincoln arrived at army headquarters: "I have good reason for saying you must not make a general movement of the army without letting me know." Burnside immediately instructed Averell to postpone the raid and tell his infantry supports to "return leisurely to their camps." Burnside further commanded Averell to entrap Confederate cavalry that had been raiding in northern Virginia, a mission Averell correctly identified as futile. "I will try and intercept the rebel cavalry referred to, but think that I may be too late, from having wasted some time in the project which you order me to postpone," replied Averell. "It can never be undertaken again," he added with an unmistakable tone of disappointment.[33]

Averell's chagrin no doubt originated in large part from his arrested opportunity for glory, but did Burnside's grander operation, of which Averell's raid formed but a fraction, enjoy any chance of success? Certainly some at the time believed it did. Maj. Gen. John G. Parke, Burnside's chief of staff, told a congressional panel in January that "had there been an attack, from the preparations which were made, I have every reason to believe that it would have been successful." According to Fifth Corps commander Maj. Gen. George G.

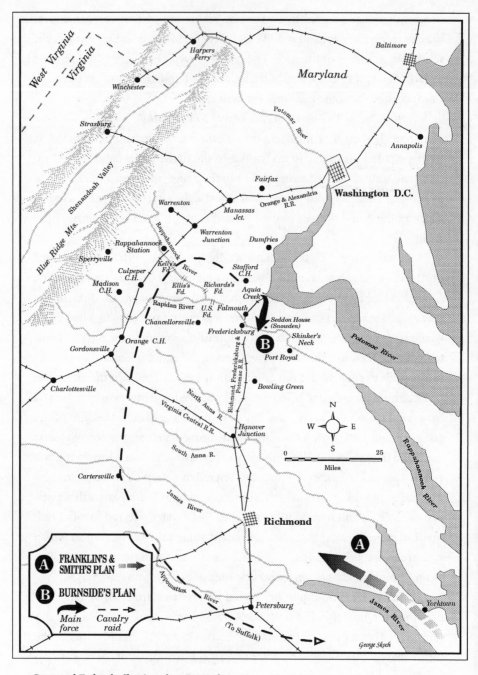

Proposed Federal offensives, late December 1862

Meade, Burnside had managed to keep his specific plans for a downriver crossing secret from his own lieutenants as late as December 30; presumably, the enemy also remained in the dark. From the historian's perspective, Kenneth Williams and Bruce Catton agree that the army's morale was equal to the test Burnside proposed to administer.[34]

Yet the Army of Northern Virginia continued to present a major obstacle to Burnside. Lee's force, which entered winter quarters on December 20, had built heavy fortifications along the hills behind Fredericksburg and remained vigilant for any renewed Union offensive.[35] Whether the Federal notion of bridging the river below town; seizing the Richmond, Fredericksburg & Potomac Railroad; and turning Lee's right flank would have worked remains debatable.

At least two Union officers considered the endeavor doomed. "It was . . . my military belief," said Brig. Gen. John Newton, "that with the best troops in the world we would have failed at that time." His subordinate, John Cochrane, shared this view.[36] These pessimistic assessments eventually carried more influence than might be expected from a division and brigade commander. In fact, Newton and Cochrane bore indirect responsibility for scuttling Burnside's plans.

Both men knew something of politics. The forty-year-old Newton grew up in Norfolk, Virginia, and graduated second in the West Point class of 1842. His father served fourteen terms in Congress, so Newton was no stranger to the Washington political milieu. Nor was the forty-nine-year-old John Cochrane, who had represented a New York district in Congress from 1857 to 1861 as a states' rights conservative and officially attended both Democratic presidential conventions in 1860.[37]

Newton, his corps commander Smith, and grand division commander Franklin met regularly after the battle of Fredericksburg and quickly discovered a shared impression of the army's condition. "I became painfully aware," Newton stated later, "that the troops of my division and of the whole army had become exceedingly dispirited. . . . From all that I heard I was decidedly of the opinion that the dissatisfaction of the troops arose from a want of confidence in General Burnside's military capacity." Newton requested a leave of absence ostensibly to visit his family in Washington, but he told Smith and Franklin that he also intended to call on "some of the prominent members of Congress and others," perhaps even the president, to in-

*Brig. Gen.
John Newton.
Francis Trevelyan
Miller, ed.,* The
Photographic History
of the Civil War, *10 vols.
(New York: Review of
Reviews, 1911), 10:179*

form them of the woeful state of the Army of the Potomac. Like most generals in the Potomac army, Newton knew little about Burnside's plans to cross the Rappahannock beyond the rumor that such an endeavor was imminent. Despite this likelihood of battle, Newton received Franklin's permission to leave his command, confident that he could rejoin his troops before any advance.[38]

Newton informed Cochrane of his impending journey and invited the brigade commander to come along. Cochrane had some petty personal business in Washington, but his real motivation was a desire to convey to civilian officials his concerns about the anticipated offensive: "Believing that if a crossing was attempted, and it should be unsuccessful for any reason, the

Brig. Gen.
John Cochrane.
Francis Trevelyan
Miller, ed., The
Photographic History
of the Civil War, *10 vols.*
(New York: Review of
Reviews, 1911), 10:223

influence of the disaster upon the cause of the whole country would be ruinous[,] . . . I expressed my opinion that it was a duty which I owed myself and my country . . . to make clear to those in authority" the situation at the front.[39]

As the better connected of the two, Cochrane suggested meeting with Senator Henry Wilson of Massachusetts, chairman of the Senate Military Committee, and Congressman Moses F. Odell of New York, a member of the Joint Committee on the Conduct of the War. The officers arrived at Washington's Metropolitan Hotel on the afternoon of December 30, and while Newton waited, Cochrane searched in vain for Wilson and Odell, both of whom had left town because Congress stood in recess.

Undaunted, the brigade commander sought an audience with the president. Repairing to the White House, Cochrane spotted Lincoln and Secretary of State William H. Seward emerging from a meeting. Seward greeted his New York political colleague warmly, and Cochrane related the purpose of his visit and requested that Seward arrange an interview with Lincoln. The secretary promptly complied. Cochrane returned to the Metropolitan, where he collected Newton for the visit to the president.[40]

Lincoln received his visitors, and as the senior officer Newton opened the conversation. He recognized the "delicate position" he occupied and began with a description of the rumored advance across the Rappahannock and the doubts expressed by many of the army's officers about its likely success. "It occurred to me that it would look too much like interference with General Burnside if I was to tell the President that the troops had no confidence in him," admitted Newton, so he dissembled on that point, hoping Lincoln would draw his own conclusions about army morale. Lincoln interpreted Newton's presentation as an attempt by a subordinate to influence the authority of his commander. Sensing that he had lost control of the dialogue, Newton quickly backpedaled. Cochrane then confirmed Newton's characterization of the army's condition, "its murmurs of discontent, its daily canvass of the merits of its commander," and the doubtful outcome of another river crossing near Fredericksburg. "As for me," Cochrane added, "Mr. President, to have withheld from you these facts, I should not have ranked at any criminal grade below treason."[41]

Newton and Cochrane both testified that their mission mollified Lincoln, who thanked the generals for their time and predicted that "good will come from this." Later that day Lincoln instructed Burnside to postpone the army's offensive, the upriver portion of which had already commenced. Unaware of what prompted Lincoln's message, Burnside inferred it was a reaction to events in distant theaters. In any event, the general withheld orders for the infantry advance and hastened to Washington to ascertain the source of Lincoln's concern.[42]

Lincoln bluntly told his commander on December 31 that two of his officers had painted a grim picture of the army's prospects on the Rappahannock. "I was so much surprised at the time at what I heard that it did not make an active impression on my mind as to the exact words," remembered Burnside. Lincoln would not reveal the identities of his informers, so Burnside proceeded to provide a detailed description of his plans for a coordinated crossing downstream from Fredericksburg. The president remained unsure of the wisdom of Burnside's approach and wished to consult with Halleck and Secretary of War Stanton.[43]

Before these two men arrived, Burnside admitted that his failure at Fredericksburg had eroded the army's confidence in him and that he ought to be replaced. Lincoln asked how the army felt about Stanton and Halleck; Burnside replied that considerable dissatisfaction also existed regarding those two officials. Once Stanton and Halleck appeared, the four men debated Burnside's strategy without reaching a consensus, beyond Halleck's agreeing with his subordinate that the two anonymous informants ought to be arrested or dismissed from the service.[44]

Burnside returned to the Willard Hotel and, acknowledging the army's lack of faith in him, wrote Lincoln an offer to resign his command. He also reiterated that "the Secretary of War has not the confidence of the officers and soldiers" and "the same opinion applies with equal force in regard to General Halleck." At a meeting with the president, Halleck, and Stanton the next day, Burnside handed Lincoln his letter; the president read it without comment. The four men then resumed their discussion of Burnside's plan, with Halleck particularly waffling about its advisability. The meeting concluded without agreement concerning future activities at Fredericksburg. Burnside returned to the army brimming with understandable fury about the duplicity of the unnamed officers who had seen Lincoln. He also revealed in casual conversation his expressions to the president about attitudes toward Stanton and Halleck, leaving the inadvertent impression that he had spoken about them in their presence. This misunderstanding led to a bitter round of correspondence later in the year in which Franklin and Halleck concluded that Burnside was a liar.[45]

Lincoln remained troubled by the strategic irresolution of his meetings with Stanton, Halleck, and Burnside. Shortly after the conclusion of the New Year's Day conference, the president asked the general in chief to join Burnside on the Rappahannock, examine the ground, confer with the officers, and assess their spirits. "In a word," said Lincoln, "gather all the elements for forming a judgment of your own, and then tell General Burnside that you do approve or that you do not approve his plan. Your military skill is useless to me if you will not do this."[46]

Halleck replied immediately through Stanton. "I am led to believe that there is a very important difference of opinion in regard to my relations toward generals commanding armies in the field," he stated, "and that I cannot perform the duties of my office satisfactorily at the same time to the President and to myself." He then requested to be excused from his post. Halleck reasoned that his presence at the front would undermine Burnside's independence, ignoring the army commander's manifest need for his superior's endorsement as a prerequisite to his campaign. Lincoln thus entertained requests for relief from his general in chief and the commander of the Army of the Potomac on the same day, hardly a propitious beginning to the new year.[47]

Burnside faced his own dilemma. He wished to execute the plan he had devised in late December but recognized that at least some of his lieutenants mistrusted his leadership. Even worse, the administration declined to help him shoulder responsibility for an offensive. The predicament resolved itself when Burnside became aware of the enemy's probable knowledge of his proposed operation: "When I returned to my camp I found that many of the details of the general movement were already known and was told by [Gen. Alfred Pleasonton] that the details of the cavalry movement were known . . . in the city of Washington to some sympathizers with the rebellion. . . . Of course, I then abandoned the movement in that distinct form, intending to make it in some other form within a few days."[48]

Newton and Cochrane's interview with Lincoln thus foiled a major offensive by the Army of the Potomac. Halleck's impotence helped ensure that Burnside's troops would not attack across the Rappahannock in early January. While it may not be possible to determine with any precision whether these men robbed Burnside of victory or spared the army another Fredericksburg-style debacle, we can draw conclusions about the propriety of their actions.

Halleck's vacillation marked him as unfit for his high office. It is difficult not to conclude that he lacked the moral courage to accept even partial responsibility for his principal army's destiny. Newton and Cochrane, on the other hand, took it upon themselves to interfere with decisions rendered three or four steps up the military ladder. Neither their essentially selfless motives nor the democratic freedom of expression that flourished in volunteer Civil War armies condones their actions. As citizens of the republic, Newton and Cochrane had every right to visit their president for redress of grievances. As generals in the Army of the Potomac, their role was to obey orders and see to the discipline and efficiency of their units through the chain of command.

William Franklin and Baldy Smith were not blameless in the affair, either. No direct evidence links Newton and Cochrane's meeting at the White House with instructions from their superiors, but both major generals knew the disgruntled brigadiers represented potential political mischief. Franklin and Smith already had expressed opposition to further operations along the Rappahannock line. It is unlikely they would permit two of a division's three general officers to leave the army on the eve of such an offensive unless they foresaw that the departure might result in cancellation of the movement.[49]

This episode contributed to the unhappy termination of each of these officer's careers with the Army of the Potomac. Cochrane resigned during the winter, complaining that "the virus of the Chickahominy fevers had sharpened the tooth of chronic malady," but appeared again in 1864 as John Frémont's running mate on the short-lived anti-Lincoln Republican ticket. Smith and Franklin left the army for less important commands, and Congress failed to confirm Newton's promotion to major general despite that officer's creditable service as a corps commander at Gettysburg. He finished the war in charge at Key West and the Dry Tortugas.[50]

The army's rank and file remained fundamentally ignorant of the political chicanery in Washington and at various headquarters. They concerned themselves instead with preparing serviceable habitations and enduring the spartan realities of life at the front. Many units returned to encampments they had occupied prior to the battle only to find that their temporary homes had been sacked. "In our absence," observed Lt. Thomas Francis Galwey of the 8th Ohio, "the camp followers—'Dog robbers' and 'Pot Wholloppers,' they are called—had pillaged our comfortable huts, leaving them nothing but mere shells." While cursing the "lazy hounds" who had dismantled their old quarters for firewood, the soldiers employed varying degrees of skill in reerecting their "chebangs." "As none of us had been educated for architects," wrote Eugene Carter, "many [of the huts] were crude indeed. Each seemed to vie with the other, however, as to who should set up the best 'coop.'" One popular interior decorating technique involved liberating the colored fashion plates from ladies's magazines for use on cabin walls. "As hardly any women, excepting the gaunt half-starved natives, were ever seen, their images at least were put where the boys could feast their eyes upon them," explained Galwey.[51]

The troops also sought solace in alcohol. On December 24 the various commissaries issued whiskey to all who applied for it. The result, according to signal officer Louis Fortescue, "was the Army of the Potomac was as drunk as an owl. We had a gallon on Christmas Eve and . . . Whiskey punches flowed like rain." Fortescue sobered up sufficiently the next day to visit friends at several headquarters, among them those of generals Daniel E. Sickles and Joseph Hooker. Everybody, including "the gentleman who so suddenly stopped Barton Key's heart [Sickles]," appeared "considerably elevated."[52]

Picket duty presented the men's most taxing obligation during these late December days. A typical division assumed responsibility for about one and one-half miles of Rappahannock shoreline, but each regiment might go on picket only once every nine days. Those soldiers would make blanket rolls and fill their haversacks with food, knowing they would receive no rations while at the front. Officers established picket posts of thirty men each at quarter-mile intervals, with the remainder of their commands resting at some convenient nearby point. The men maintained particular vigilance after dark.[53]

For the troops back in camp, daily life became a dull routine. The soldiers drilled, held reviews for officers, wrote letters home, tinkered with the chimneys in their huts, and passed idle time in games of cards or dice. At night, bugle calls stilled the bivouacs while sentinels paced the margins of dying cook fires. "Here I am this dark, nasty, rainy, gusty, cold, disagreeable day, in my own tent, in my comfortable old clothes . . . in my muddy boots and in happiness," wrote Samuel Partridge on January 6. "Here I am amid the clanger of bugles, the roll of drums, the shrieking of fifes, the glitter of bayonets, the gleaming of rifles, the angry looking cannon, the thousands of men, the myriad of nasty, dirty, terrible, horrible, awful things that make and are made by an army. . . . On the whole I am glad to be here."[54]

Others in the Army of the Potomac shared this grudging contentment with Partridge. "I feel differently about the war and the state of the country now from what I did . . . before," wrote Lt. Col. William F. Draper of the 36th Massachusetts on January 9. "The influences of our defeat here begin to wear off and our victory in the west [Stones River] gives our affairs a more hopeful aspect." Allen Landis of the 116th Pennsylvania assured his parents on New Year's Day that he was not "very much discouraged and Homesick. . . . There is no use in getting low spirited out here." The correspondent of the Cleveland *Plain Dealer* reported on January 5 that at a troop review of the Third Corps "the men presented a fine appearance, and gave evidence of a high state of discipline." Staff officer Larned informed his sister on January 11 that he was "actually 'spiling' for a fight—I know we could knock the rebels endways."[55]

This is not to suggest that a complete metamorphosis of morale had engulfed the army. Familiar protestations regarding lack of pay, miserable living conditions, and unqualified officers still resonated around campfires. "I am tired of this way of carrying on war and if this army lies here much longer there will not be over half their number left on account of desertions," wrote John Morton of the 17th Michigan on January 13. "Nearly all the soldiers are disgusted with Lincoln's mode of warfare and if I ever get the chance there will be one less in the Northern army." "I am heartsick at what I see around me," agreed John T. Boyle of the 96th Pennsylvania. "The men have caught the infection from the officers and seem to have lost much of their fire and energy." Pvt. Edwin O. Wentworth of the 37th Massachusetts hoped to be taken prisoner and paroled to avoid further fighting. "You know," he added superfluously, "I am sick of war." Charles Gibson of the 14th Indiana objected to the geographical origins of his comrades. "I am tired of this army," he wrote, "too many Yankees. I would like to be with troops from our own state."[56]

George B. McClellan's popularity in the army remained high. "Many wish that Genl. McClellan would quietly slip round among the soldiers and then proclaim himself for a . . . military dictator," stated William Hamilton. "We must have McClellan back with unlimited and unfettered powers," thought Brig. Gen. Gouverneur K. Warren. "His name is a tower of strength to every one here."[57]

A desire for McClellan's restoration did not necessarily indicate a corresponding antipathy toward Burnside. "You don't know how the whole army loves Genl. McClellan and longs for his return," Col. McAllister wrote his wife on January 14. "I am honest in my conviction that he is the man for the times." Yet McAllister had "nothing to say against Burnside. I think he is a good man." The Washington *Daily Intelligencer* admitted in its January 12 edition that while "the army, almost to a man, are for McClellan," there was "no feeling against Burnside, but on the contrary, one of kindness."[58]

To be sure, Burnside's image remained tarnished among some of his soldiers. During a review of the Second Corps, for example, a regimental commander reminded his men to cheer when "Burney" rode by. A witness heard the soldiers respond with a chorus of noes, and Burnside went by without accolades. Gideon Welles probably stated the case as accurately as anyone: "There are rumors that the army is much demoralized, that the soldiers do not give their confidence to Burnside, doubt his military capacity, and that some of the generals are cool. There is, I think, some truth and some exaggeration in all these reports."[59]

A corollary of the pro-McClellan syndrome found voice in opposition to Lincoln's Emancipation Proclamation. It is difficult to gauge how much Little Mac's opinions on abolition and its relationship to war aims influenced his former troops, but army correspondence in January contained countless expressions of dismay with the administration's new policy. "We thought we were fighting for the stars and stripes," growled James Kelaher of the 9th New York, "but we find out it is for the d— nigger. They are getting so sacy [sic] that you cannot get a civil answer from one of them. I wish we were let have our way of it we would kill every one of them." Kelaher's virulence reached an extreme, but few northern soldiers found inspiration in fighting to free the slaves. "I care not if the Niggers eat the Whites or the Whites kill the Niggers, just so that the war be ended," said Jacob Haas. Theodore Dodge complained that the proclamation meant "we are fighting, not for the Union but for the nigger. I however am not fighting for the Nigger. I fight because having once gone into it I will not back out." Jonathan Hutchison of the 15th New Jersey commented that "since Abe Lincoln issued his proclamation I never before seen so much discontent in the army."[60]

Those flames of discontent, whatever their origin, burned brighter because some senior officers fanned them. T. Harry Williams described the camp at Falmouth as "a hive of deceit and conspiracy and gossip." Officers such as William B. Franklin undermined Burnside's authority, probably with the hope that McClellan would return to command. Burnside did not enjoy the partisan allegiance of the army's Republicans to offset this McClellanism. Worst of all, Joseph Hooker worked tirelessly behind the scenes in quest of his own elevation. Hooker frequently characterized Burnside as incompetent and sometimes castigated the administration's management of the war as well. On January 3 Burnside ordered the arrest of division commander William Thomas Harbaugh Brooks for insubordination, a concrete manifestation of the disease that ran deep through the army's corpus.[61]

Atop this unsteady foundation Burnside focused on a new way to challenge Lee. Encouragement to pursue such an endeavor came from various sources. Quartermaster Gen. Montgomery C. Meigs urged Burnside on December 30 to undertake a fresh offensive, while, ironically, a few blocks away Newton and Cochrane sowed seeds with Lincoln that would stymie any such operation. Meigs spoke forcefully about the dangers inherent in keeping the troops idle: "Every day's consumption of your army is an immense destruction of the natural and monetary resources of the country," argued the supply officer. "The country begins to feel the effect of this exhaustion, and I begin to apprehend a catastrophe."

Meigs mentioned the natural inclination of subordinates to temporize and urged Burnside to take unilateral responsibility for planning an offensive. Meigs suggested that Burnside move the army "bodily up the Rappahannock, cross the river, aim for a point on the railroad between the rebels and Richmond, and send forward cavalry and light troops to break up the road and intercept retreat." If another strategy seemed preferable, Meigs urged Burnside to adopt it. "But rest at Falmouth is death to our nation—is defeat, border warfare, hollow truce, barbarism, ruin for the ages, chaos!" The popular press echoed these sentiments. The *New York Times*, for example, observed in January that "an army idle, disintegrates by disease, desertion, resignation, and death. It can only be stimulated and made equal to great deeds by constant action. . . . The soldiers of the Army of the Potomac deserve prompt leading to 'military success,' and the country needs and demands it as much as they desire and deserve it."[62]

These imprecations received a sympathetic hearing at army headquarters. On January 5, just a few days after returning to Falmouth from his unhappy interviews with Lincoln, Burnside wrote the president of his intention to renew the offensive: "I am still of the opinion that the crossing should be attempted, & I have accordingly issued orders to the Engineers and Artilery [*sic*] to prepare for it." But Burnside freely admitted that most of his generals disagreed with this approach. For that reason and because he understood Lincoln's desire to be involved in strategic planning, Burnside submitted an undated resignation for the president's use "if my movement is not in accordance with the views of yourself and your military advisors." Burnside presented his offer to step down not to force Lincoln's hand, but as a sincere effort to garner support for his offensive.[63]

A somewhat different impulse inspired Burnside's letter to General Halleck on the same day. He advised the general in chief of his intention to cross the Rappahannock and the submission of his standing resignation, adding, "I do not ask you to assume any responsibility in reference to the mode or place of crossing." Burnside did ask his superior to explain the available options, particularly in regard to their impact on events in other theaters. "You will readily see that the responsibility of crossing without the knowledge of this effect, and against the opinion of nearly all the general officers, involves a greater responsibility than any officer situated as I am ought to incur."[64]

Halleck replied on January 7 at some length. He agreed that the army should try to pass the Rappahannock, but oddly labored to absolve himself of blame for December's results at Fredericksburg. More admirably, Halleck averred that the army's true objective should be Lee's destruction, not the capture of Richmond, and endorsed an offensive. "The chances are still in our favor to meet and defeat the enemy on the Rappahannock, if we can effect a crossing in a position where we can meet the enemy on favorable or even equal terms," counseled Halleck. "I therefore still advise a movement against him."

This no doubt provided some comfort to the beleaguered Burnside. But he had asked Halleck not so much for strategic validation as for guidance about how to execute his proposed operation. Here the general in chief equivocated. "It devolves upon you to decide upon the time, place, and character of the crossing which you may attempt," wrote Halleck. "I can only advise that an attempt be made, and as early as possible." The following day Lincoln wired Burnside endorsing Halleck's approval of a new offensive but cautioning that neither the government nor the country demanded rash action. The president added a lukewarm vote of confidence: "I do not yet see how I could profit by changing the command of the A. P. & if I did, I should not wish to do it by accepting the resignation of your commission."[65]

Burnside acted immediately to formulate a specific design. He notified Averell on January 6 that "your whole plan of movement will be changed" and asked to see the cavalryman, presumably to consult on possible crossing points and counterintelligence measures. He ordered his provost marshal and civilian operatives as well as the cavalry to analyze enemy preparations and note all relevant terrain features on the Union side of the river. A citizen named McGhee arranged to slip across the Rappahannock to communicate with northern sympathizers about Confederate dispositions. On the river's left bank Burnside conducted his own explorations. "The General is working day & night on plans—studying maps—and off on reconnaissance—much has to be done by him personally," recorded Secretary Larned. Sgt. Wyman S. White of the 2nd U.S. Sharpshooters spotted his chief near Falmouth on January 15, "riding almost unattended along near the river and seemed to be reconnoitering the country on the Fredericksburg side. I wondered what his thoughts were."[66]

By the middle of the month Burnside had developed a mature plan. He would move most of his army upstream, as Meigs had suggested, and span the Rappahannock at Banks and United States fords, four and ten miles upriver from Fredericksburg, respectively. A diversionary force would bluff a crossing below the city near Muddy Creek, scene of the intended offensive canceled by Lincoln in December. He built and corduroyed roads and ordered Brig. Gen. Henry J. Hunt to select numerous positions for artillery to neutralize Confederate fire and support the infantry during its passage of the Rappahannock.

Burnside issued orders on the sixteenth to begin the march the following day. He postponed the movement, however, in order to verify reports that Lee had shifted troops to the west. By January 18 Burnside's spies confirmed that a substantial Confederate force blocked United States Ford but that Banks Ford remained relatively defenseless. The general therefore opted to convert his movement to United States Ford into a feint and concentrate instead on crossing the river at Banks Ford. The operation would commence on January 20.[67]

On the eve of the offensive three of Burnside's grand divisions—Sumner's, Hooker's, and Franklin's—occupied camps between Falmouth and White Oak Church. Cavalry prowled up- and downstream as far as Warrenton and King George Court House. Franz Sigel's Reserve Grand Division, consisting of the Eleventh and Twelfth Corps, assumed positions farther north at Stafford Court House and Fairfax.

Burnside selected Hooker's Center Grand Division to form the army's right and cross the river just above Banks Ford. A Third Corps division would assist the engineers in laying pontoon bridges. Franklin's Left Grand Division would cross simultaneously on two bridges a little below Banks Ford. The Second Corps followed by the Ninth, Sumner's command, would

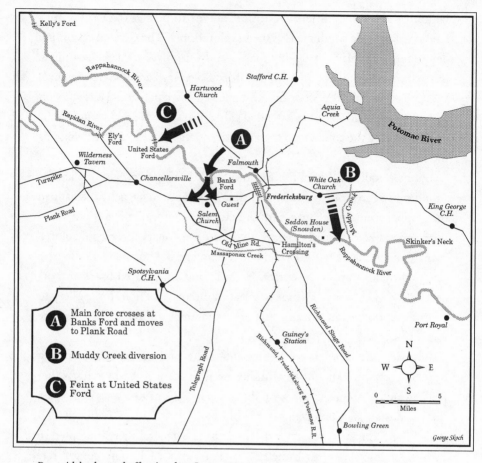

Burnside's planned offensive, late January 1863

shadow Franklin in reserve. Sigel received instructions to shift one Eleventh Corps division between Falmouth and Hartwood, ten miles upstream from Fredericksburg, and to leave one to protect the Richmond, Fredericksburg & Potomac Railroad back to Aquia Landing. His remaining division would bear responsibility for the downriver charade planned at Muddy Creek. Maj. Gen. Henry W. Slocum's Twelfth Corps would march south to Stafford Court House. Hunt would move 41 batteries, 184 guns, to positions between Falmouth and Banks Ford in support of the infantry.

Once across the river Burnside expected Franklin and Hooker to seize the high ground in their immediate front and move south to the Orange Plank Road. With Franklin's force blocking that highway near the Guest House, barely one mile west of Marye's Heights, the Union commander anticipated that Lee would either attack or retreat south via the Telegraph Road. Hooker would be in supporting distance at Salem Church to assist Franklin should Lee assault, with Sumner also available. In case of Confederate flight, Hooker could pursue using the Old Mine Road. "I need not impress upon you the importance of a most vigorous attack," Burnside intoned. On January 20 he issued General Orders No. 7, which announced to the army that "the auspicious moment seems to have arrived to strike a great and mortal blow to the rebellion, and to gain that decisive victory which is due to the country." The army went in motion late that morning.[68]

Opinions in the army varied widely about the timing of the movement. Most troops knew nothing about Burnside's aborted plans in December, the Newton-Cochrane episode, or the current preparations for an upstream crossing. When the initial order to advance appeared on January 16, therefore, many soldiers expressed surprise at the prospect of a mid-winter operation. For some, that surprise turned to deep skepticism or outright opposition. "The utmost dissatisfaction almost insubordination, was shown . . . here at the prospect of an attack," wrote Lt. Henry Ropes of the 20th Massachusetts. "Regiments openly said they would not cross a bridge, the 42nd New York of our Brigade hooted at the order, even the 15th Mass. cheered for Jefferson Davis and groaned for President Lincoln." "It would be idle to conceal the fact that our soldiers enter upon this campaign with less zeal and spirit than have characterized them in past conflicts," thought the *New York Times*. As evidence of this attitude an entire Third Corps picket detail of 315 men deserted during the night of January 20, leaving only their abandoned rifles stuck lock-deep in the ground.[69]

The proposed movement bore only partial responsibility for such sentiments. Factors that had demoralized the army during the previous six weeks also persisted. But many of the soldiers doubted the wisdom of an offensive that might reprise the bloodbath at Fredericksburg. "Every one seems to feel that it is a hopeless task to try to dislodge the enemy from their works," wrote the lieutenant colonel of the 24th New York. Blatant opposition of officers such as Franklin and Hooker to Burnside's plan percolated through their staffs to men in the ranks. Artillerist Wainwright remembered on January 20 that "on the march today the disaffection produced by Franklin's and others' talk was very evident. The whole army seems to know what they have said, and their speeches condemning the move were in the mouths of everyone."[70]

Wainwright's assessment was not literally true. The Fifth Corps commander, George Meade, had advocated an offensive since early in the month. "I am tired of this playing war without risks," he told his wife. "We must encounter risks if we fight, and we cannot carry on war without fighting." On January 18 he predicted that "if this programme is carried out, I believe we shall be successful. . . . The army is in good condition, though there are those who insist its morale is not good, but of this I see no signs." John H. Pardington of the 24th Michigan felt less sanguine than Meade but remained determined to do his duty in the anticipated battle: "I hope . . . victory will crown our arms this time. . . . Anything to put down this Rebellion." Lieutenant Carman summarized the primary concern of most men in the Army of the Potomac on January 19, whether they approved or rejected Burnside's strategy: "I hope this will not be such a blunder as the last slaughter was."[71]

The outcome of Burnside's new offensive would be determined at least in part by the Confederate reaction. Burnside's escape across the Rappahannock on December 16 had disappointed Lee, who remained vigilant in expectation of another Federal effort. "I presume he is meditating a passage at some other point," Lee told the secretary of war. Jackson's corps marched downstream toward Port Royal, the location Lee initially identified as Burnside's most likely destination. One of Maj. Gen. Lafayette McLaws's brigades occupied Fredericksburg itself; southern infantry erected rifle pits, and artillerists placed batteries along the length of their lines. To discover Federal intentions Lee sent cavalry on Christmas Day probing through Dumfries and Fairfax before returning via Culpeper with more than 200 prisoners and twenty-five wagons. These were the marauders Burnside hoped Averell would snare after Lincoln canceled his own offensive.[72]

As the days passed without a Union advance, Lee contented himself with improving his fortifications from United States Ford to Port Royal while dispatching cavalry beyond the enemy flanks to keep Burnside off balance. Lee informed Jefferson Davis on January 13 that "for several days past there have been general indications of some movement by the army of Burnside, but nothing sufficiently definite to designate it if true." He had detached some troops toward North Carolina but replaced them with fresh men and remained convinced that the Army of the Potomac still presented an imminent danger.[73]

Beginning on January 18 Lee took steps to counter a movement against his left flank. As the Federals noted, he shifted additional forces to United States Ford but also reinforced Banks Ford, "these being the points apparently threatened." On the twentieth Lee had sufficient information to confirm Burnside's intention to use Franklin and Hooker in an upstream crossing but speculated the targets might be Kelly's Ford or Rappahannock Station. Longstreet issued orders to resist passage of the river and subsequently sent Pickett's division to Salem Church to hold the high ground west of Fredericksburg that Burnside had instructed Hooker to occupy. The Confederates also plowed the ground near possible Union crossing points to facilitate the production of mud. In sum, though the Confederates lacked an entirely accurate picture of Burnside's plans, they would not be entirely unprepared if the Federals appeared on the Rappahannock above Fredericksburg.[74]

The Unionists broke camp late on the morning of Tuesday, January 20, "under threatening weather, with a chilly wind blowing from the east." Whatever their individual attitudes might have been, collectively the soldiers impressed various witnesses with the alacrity of their marching and their apparent good spirits. Units covered four, six, or eight miles before finding bivouacs in the piney woods back from the river. Scarcely had night fallen when the first drops of a cold rain sent a shudder through the shelterless army, the harbinger of a storm that would define an unfortunate chapter of the Potomac army's history. "It does not describe the situation by simply saying it rained," stated a member of the 44th New York. "The wind blew a gale and rocked the trees spitefully. The night was very dark." A solid sheet of near-freezing precipitation, the product of a classic Atlantic coast nor'easter, descended with a vengeance on the Virginia countryside, wrapping the Army of the Potomac in its merciless grip.[75]

The night of January 20–21, 1863, would never disappear from the memories of Union troops who endured it. "It was a dismal night; one of those sleepless nights when everything has a funeral aspect, in which the enthusiasm is extinguished; in which the courage is worn out, the will enfeebled, and the mind stupefied," recalled one northern officer. A New Yorker recollected that "our blankets were wet through and we found ourselves lying in a pool of ice-cold water. No one got a wink of sleep, and all, in that cheerless wilderness, of trees and mud, agreed that it was the most tedious night that we had ever passed."[76]

Burnside's timetable suffered along with his men. He expected the engi-

The Mud March.
Editor's collection

neers to begin their bridge construction by 7:30 A.M. on January 21, but at 4:00 A.M. an aide from Brig. Gen. Daniel P. Woodbury reported that the rain had paralyzed the pontoon train and retarded the artillery needed to support a crossing. Burnside informed his subordinates of the delay but took no steps to cancel the offensive. In fact, an optimistic atmosphere still prevailed at army headquarters. "Had we not been visited by this terrible storm last night & today," wrote the loyal Larned to a friend in New York, "you would have had stunning news . . . this Evg . . . though I hope the ball will open tomorrow."77

Larned also noted that "it does not take more than an hours rain to make these roads utterly impassable," a phenomenon that elicited considerable commentary from incredulous Yankees. "Virginia mud is a clay of reddish color and sticky consistence," observed a Maine officer, "which does not appear to soak water, or mingle with it, but simply hold it, becoming softer and softer, and parting with the water wholly by evaporation." Chaos ensued when thousands of feet and hundreds of vehicles attempted to move across such surfaces.[78]

A Fifth Corps soldier thought "a statement of the awful condition of the roads might exhaust all the adjectives in the English language and yet not exaggerate the actual condition of things." Horses, mules, wagons, pontoons, caissons, limbers, and, according to Pennsylvania lieutenant James W. Latta, even the occasional Union officer became hopelessly mired. "It was no un-common thing to see twenty horses hitched to a cannon usually drawn by four sticking fast on a road as level as a floor," said William Hamilton. Troops joined the toiling beasts in attempting to extract wagons, ambulances, and guns. A droll engineer officer requisitioned "50 men, 25 feet high, to work in mud 18 feet deep." Mules drowned in mud holes, soaked soldiers struggled with ropes in futile attempts to drag pontoon boats toward the river, and wagons sank so deeply that only their tops showed above grade. "I don't know . . . how the world's surface looked after the flood in Noah's time," wrote General Williams, "but I am certain it could not have appeared more saturated than does the present surface of the Old Dominion."[79]

General Woodbury informed Burnside that although he could span the river by the morning of the twenty-second, he advised abandoning the cam-paign. "There can be no doubt as to the enemy's knowledge of our loca-tion and intentions," cautioned the engineer. "Our camp-fires last night pre-sented . . . the appearance of a large sea of fire. . . . The rain has prevented surprise, and changed our condition entirely." Burnside, however, was not ready to forsake his initiative. After passing the same sleepless night suffered by his men, he ate a quick breakfast of tea and toast and, accompanied by a handful of staff officers, rode upstream to superintend his army. He plodded through the muck all day, positioning batteries, encouraging troops in their fatigue duties, and selecting locations for new roads. That afternoon an army surgeon spotted Burnside riding through a camp, virtually alone and covered with mud—a tragic figure. The general returned to his tent at 5:00 P.M. to endure another restless night under canvas and a driving rain.[80]

Exposure to the unrelenting elements continued to dampen the army's spirits. "It would be hard to tell which was the meanest . . . time the Army of the Potomac ever had," reflected one soldier after the war, "but for mud, rain, cold, whiskey, drowned-out men, horses, mules, and abandoned wagons and batteries, for pure undulterated [sic] demoralization . . . and downright cussedness, this took the cake." The troops manifested displeasure in various ways, including taking "French leave." "Hundreds of men, being entirely discouraged, broke to the rear and started toward the north and home," remembered Wyman White, "not because they were not patriotic but because they were discouraged beyond endurance." Burnside employed cavalry to catch these poor wretches as they slogged their way toward the Potomac. Some units received an ill-advised whiskey ration on January 22, causing a donnybrook in Johnson's brigade between the 118th Pennsylvania and the 22nd Massachusetts. A disgusted New Jersey soldier thought "two-thirds of the [army's] prominent officers were drunk."[81]

Confederates on the southern bank did their best to contribute to their enemy's malaise. "Say! Yanks! We'll be over in the morning and haul your guns and pontoons out of the mud for you," shouted a sarcastic rebel picket. "We'll build your bridges, and escort you over." The southerners erected boards or hung tents from trees visible from the opposite shore on which they had written, "Burnside Stuck in the Mud of the Sacred Soil." Disaffected officers such as Hooker and Franklin expressed deepening opposition to continuing the offensive, opinions they shared freely with anyone who would listen. These two grand division commanders primarily responsible for the scheduled attack told Burnside on January 22 that they measured the odds against success at nineteen to one. Hooker informed a reporter that he considered his superior incompetent and the government in Washington "played out" and in need of a dictator.[82]

Under such meteorological, spiritual, and military conditions Burnside concluded that the campaign could not continue. On January 22 he ordered the army to return to its camps. He also telegraphed the weak-kneed Halleck requesting a meeting, inviting the general in chief to visit the front or volunteering to go to Washington. Halleck characteristically refused to budge from his desk at the capital but agreed to see Burnside if the latter thought it advisable to travel.[83]

First, however, the general would have to extricate his command, no mean feat under the prevailing circumstances. The movement commenced on the morning of January 23, the entire army helping to corduroy roads and free equipment mired in the mud. Although the rains eventually ceased, the return march proceeded more slowly than the trek upriver because of horrible road conditions. Troop morale continued to slide, discipline disintegrated, and order vanished. "The mud was deep, the day was gloomy and the men were discouraged," wrote Surgeon Stevens of the 77th New York. "They straggled badly. Regiments were not to be distinguished. The whole column became an unorganized crowd, pressing toward the old camps."[84]

The army's vanguard began to appear around Falmouth on January 24. An officer leading a picket detail opposite Fredericksburg left a vivid picture of the bedraggled troops as they arrived:

There were thousands of stragglers, without any organization, and completely demoralized. . . . Near where I was on picket was a small station and depot of supplies for the Army. There was lots of whiskey here in barrels, and the heads were knocked in and the men helped themselves, and drank it by the pint. . . . Many of the men were drunk. They . . . were the worst lot of men I ever saw together. Many of them had thrown their arms away, and the hill[s] between the station and their camps were covered with men; some very drunk, straggling towards their camps, and cursing Burnside and everybody else, I guess. It looked as though the enemy could have crossed the river at that time, and captured the whole Army.[85]

Troops who had not marched upriver also received a liquor ration. Their inebriation merely added to the "pandemonium." Some of the lubricated men greeted returning comrades with the rhetorical question, "I say ole feller, has the [auspicious] moment arrived?"—an inquiry that elicited invitations to visit "a place where the climate is popularly supposed to be somewhat warmer than that of the West Indies." Pennsylvanian James Coburn summarized the endeavor that had already been dubbed the Mud March: "We have won another of those 'signal victories' for which the Army of the Potomac has become renowned. We have been hub & axle deep in the 'sacred sile of the Old Dominion.' Pontoons, artillery, baggage, ammunition, commissary stores, horse, man, mules & niggers—but we got out again!"[86]

Coburn's dual expression of relief and cynicism suggests that he harbored post facto doubts about the offensive's potential success. He shared this contemporary view with men like Lyman Holford, who wrote on January 25, "I believe that the weather saved Burnside[']s army from another defeat for I never saw so many straglers [sic] in any march we have yet made. If we had got into a fight not more than one half of the army would have been on hand in time to take any part in it." Franklin considered the rain "Providential interference in our behalf," and twenty years after the war Maj. Gen. Darius N. Couch thought, "To start off in the mud as we did with the army in its discouraged state was perfect folly." Historian Bruce Catton concluded that "the winter campaign was a complete triumph of unreason, and it would be useless to judge it by the standards of sensible men."[87]

Not everyone appraised the enterprise similarly. Brig. Gen. Andrew A. Humphreys, a division commander in the Fifth Corps, thought that "if we had marched a day earlier, and could have attacked the enemy's intrenchments in that storm we should have carried them. It would have been a glorious fight." Artillerist Wainwright remembered both Henry Hunt and First Corps commander Maj. Gen. John F. Reynolds expressing confidence in the plan, and the popular press spoke glowingly of the army's chances had not the elements intervened. Isaac Newton Durboraw provided a common soldier's perspective on January 25: "I am sorry it turned out as it did for I was in hopes we would whip the Grey-Backs and give them another trial for their Capitol. This time no General can be censured for all the troops were on the ground ready for the pontoons but they stuck fast in the mud."[88]

"The plan was based on the presumption that we would take the enemy unawares, at least so far as the place of crossing was concerned," remarked George G. Meade, "and I believe, but for the storm, we should have succeeded in this." Burnside's chief of staff, General Parke, told a congressional panel that the army had preserved the element of surprise until the tempest arrested its progress. Lee's correspondence with Richmond confirms this. Although the Confederate commander had taken prudent steps to counter a crossing above Fredericksburg, he remained in doubt about Burnside's specific intentions. On January 21 he wired President Davis that "I think it is certain that some movement is contemplated by General Burnside, but whether it is toward Richmond or into winter quarters is not so clear. . . . I have discovered yet no preparations for crossing the Rappahannock." Two days later he told the president he had detected Federals downstream from Fredericksburg and speculated that the troops above the fall line might be heading west to rendezvous with Maj. Gen. Robert H. Milroy in the Shenandoah Valley.[89]

This does not mean Lee remained ignorant of Federals opposite Banks Ford. Amateur rebel sign makers possessed no greater evaluative powers than their commander. But the gray chieftain's reports to Davis do indicate that Burnside's stratagem of appearing simultaneously at widely scattered locations along the river left Lee less than certain about if and where a blow might fall. The Army of Northern Virginia defended a much longer stretch of the Rappahannock on January 20 than it had on December 13, proportionately compromising its ability to concentrate quickly. Had his bridges been in place as scheduled early on the morning of January 21, with Union artillery providing a blanket of covering fire for four infantry corps to storm the south bank, it is reasonable to believe Burnside could have effected a lodging in Spotsylvania County. Questions regarding the determination and competency of Franklin's and Hooker's leadership, Lee's reaction, and the weather, however, render subsequent success less certain.[90]

The Mud March wrung much of the remaining spirit out of the Army of the Potomac. "It must be confessed that our failure at Bank's [sic] Ford had done much to demoralize the army and destroy the confidence in the commanding general so absolutely necessary to success," wrote Dr. Stevens. "When we had failed at Fredericksburg, the men were as willing as ever to try again under the same commander . . . but an army must have success." "This army will be a source of great trouble to the government if things go on this way much longer," agreed Col. William Draper. "Discipline in the old regiments . . . is merely a name and the new regiments are easily infected with the spirit of the old." Marsena Patrick succinctly told his diary, "We are all disgusted."[91]

More than the battle of Fredericksburg, operations during January 20–24 eroded the men's trust in their commander. "The army returned, giving groans for Burnside," reported Samuel Partridge. Joseph H. Law of the 148th Pennsylvania testified, "The boys is al down on burnside. . . . the rebs holows a cros to us on picket and make fun of us they say that burney stuck in the mud they say that they have a lame corporal that they will trad[e] us for burnside." Alpheus Williams summed up his thoughts on January 24: "I think the commander has very little confidence in himself and the army generally reciprocates the feeling."[92]

As in December, it would be an exaggeration to ascribe all the army's disaffection to its feelings about Burnside. Some of the same complaints that littered soldier correspondence in the weeks before the Mud March defined their unhappy sentiments during the last days of January. Displeasure with incompetent line officers, the Emancipation Proclamation, perfidiousness in Washington, and general war weariness mingled with residual McClellanism to undermine morale.

G. D. Mace of the 147th New York exalted that his "wooden Capt." had resigned his commission, warning his uncle on January 28 to beware of enlisting under an officer who was not willing to serve in the ranks "nor one who is an exhorter or Preacher or any other Hyppocrite. They come here for the pay alone and care nothing for their men or their country." Joseph Osborn described stragglers breaking their rifles across trees on the march back to camp, swearing "they would move no further to fight for the niger," and Harry W. Roose of the 31st New Jersey spoke plainly of the administration's policy of organizing black units: "Should there be a regiment of niggers sent here, the whole army would throw away its arms—for we consider this a white man's country and that there are just enough of those who feel an interest in its perpetuity to put down the rebellion, but who will not be trifled with." William Hamilton marveled at "how fast Lincoln is converting this corps into good Democrats." George McClellan remained the chief Democrat and martyred hero to much of the army. "Ever since the removal of McClellan . . . things have taken a downward course," said Dayton E. Flint of the 15th New Jersey. "The shrieking politicians . . . have made a graveyard of Virginia."[93]

The persistent nay-saying practiced by Franklin, Smith, Hooker, and lesser officers nurtured the discontent of the men. In fact some observers placed responsibility for the army's pessimism squarely on the shoulder straps of such faithless leaders. "A good deal has been said of the demoralization of the army," wrote Henry J. Raymond. "The word is too strong. It does not apply to the mass of the army at all. But it does apply to a good many of the officers [who] are demoralized in every sense of the word and they are the source of discouragement . . . to the ranks." Without naming names but clearly referencing Hooker, Franklin, and engineer Woodbury, Raymond hypothesized that some officers rejoiced in the collapse of Burnside's offensive: "They had committed themselves openly and publicly to the opinion that it would fail: perhaps it would be unreasonable to expect that they should work with any excess of vigor to secure the failure of their own predictions."[94]

These strong words suggested treason. Although Burnside avoided using that term, he recognized the malodorous influence some of his subordinates exercised over their troops. As the army returned to its camps around Falmouth, he took a positive step toward eradicating the cancer that had been infecting his command.

That measure, styled General Orders No. 8, had been germinating in Burnside's psyche since his visit to Washington on New Year's Eve. He realized then that as long as disloyal officers felt unrestrained in criticizing or interfering with his plans, he could never create the environment necessary for success. He deferred taking action against any subordinates in early January, however, because such internal disruption might postpone a renewed offensive until spring. Burnside wagered that he could defeat Lee despite his flawed officer corps.[95]

Burnside recognized on January 22 that his campaign had stalled, and mindful of continuing carping from Hooker, Franklin, and others, he decided to act. Perhaps Burnside's desire to see Halleck that day stemmed in part from a wish to consult with the general in chief about troublesome subordinates. After all, Halleck had shared Burnside's outrage at Newton and Cochrane's visit with the president. When Halleck declined to bestir himself, Burnside turned to Henry Raymond of the *Times*, an intimate around army headquarters, and spoke of his intention to step down. Raymond remonstrated that the aborted offensive had been militarily sound but "thwarted in its execution by the insubordination of your generals." The journalist suggested that Burnside should instead order the dismissal of the guilty parties and, if not sustained in this by the government, then resign with good cause.[96]

Burnside embraced this idea, and when Franklin and Smith dropped by for lunch on January 23, he let slip that "in a day or two you will hear something that will surprise you all." That day he dictated four fateful paragraphs calling for the cashiering of four generals and the transfer of four others. The document descended most severely on Joe Hooker:

Having been guilty of unjust and unnecessary criticisms of the actions of his superior officers, and of the authorities, and having, by omissions and otherwise, made reports and statements which were calculated to create incorrect impressions, and for habitually speaking in disparaging terms of other officers [Hooker] is hereby dismissed [from] the service of the

United States as a man unfit to hold an important commission during a crisis like the present, when so much patience, charity, confidence, consideration, and patriotism are due from every soldier in the field.

Burnside imposed the same penalty on W. T. H. Brooks, whom he had arrested earlier in the month, and on Newton and Cochrane, whom Burnside had deduced to be Lincoln's December informants. Franklin, Smith, two Ninth Corps generals, and an officer on Franklin's staff would be relieved from duty with the Army of the Potomac. The orders specified that the dismissals would be subject to Lincoln's approval.[97]

When Burnside showed his handiwork to Raymond, the newspaperman heartily agreed with its sentiments and pronounced the measure to be "the best step taken during the war." Pleased by this reaction Burnside told his adjutant general to issue the order at once. Raymond then suggested that an outraged Hooker might "attempt to raise a mutiny among his troops." The usually mild-mannered Burnside replied that should Fighting Joe try anything of the sort, he would "swing him before sundown."[98]

But a staff officer, perhaps medical director Church, prompted Burnside to rethink his position. General Orders No. 8 presented the president with an ultimatum: either Lincoln approved the document or Burnside would resign. Officially issuing the orders would paint Lincoln into a public corner from which he could not escape without either making Burnside a martyr or alienating the country's Hooker/Franklin contingent. Burnside affirmed that he had no desire to embarrass the president. He would visit Lincoln and personally transmit the orders without making them public.[99]

Burnside knew Lincoln possessed the authority to purge the army of officers. The president had exercised this power more than 100 times, so the legality of Burnside's directive was never an issue. Though the thorough house cleaning demanded by General Orders No. 8 would jolt the Army of the Potomac, such a shakedown must occur if the commander in chief expected Burnside to succeed.

At 8:50 P.M. on the twenty-third, Burnside wired the White House requesting an audience that night: "I have prepared some very important orders, and I want to see you before issuing them. Can I see you alone if I am at the White House after midnight?" The general then boarded an ambulance with Larned, Raymond, and a servant and headed for the railroad that would deliver them to Aquia Landing, whence a steamboat would take them up the

Potomac. The ambulance driver, who suffered nearsightedness and partial deafness, lost his way within the first quarter-mile. Eventually this poor fellow managed to plunge his vehicle over an embankment and into a declivity full of dead mules.

Burnside and his companions righted the ambulance and again trundled down the murky road. At one point an artillery wagon, axle-deep in Virginia mud, blocked the highway, and Burnside personally assisted in removing this obstacle. These misadventures consumed three hours, and the weary entourage at last reached the Falmouth depot on the Richmond, Fredericksburg & Potomac to discover that the train reserved for Burnside's use had been diverted to clear a wreck up the track. The general asked the telegraph operator to summon the train, but when the man failed to do so, Burnside and his party, guided by a borrowed lantern, set out afoot along the rails. After two hours they finally encountered the engine, which, after turning around to facilitate the arrest of the incompetent telegrapher, chugged up to Aquia. By the time Burnside reached Washington, the sun had risen on a new day.[100]

He went directly to the White House and presented the president with General Orders No. 8 and his personal resignation. Burnside explained that conditions within the army had reached a point where Lincoln must either endorse the orders or accept his abdication. The president understood his options but expressed a desire to "consult with some of my advisors about this." He asked Burnside to spend the day in Washington, but the general opted to return to his command. After a quick repast at Willard's Hotel, Burnside bid adieu to Raymond, and he and Larned caught a 9:30 A.M. boat down the Potomac.

The exhausted general spent some four hours in camp before reembarking on what proved to be a mercifully uneventful trip to Washington. When he called on Lincoln about midnight, the sleepy chief executive ordered him to Willard's for a decent night's rest. Burnside returned to the White House at 6:00 A.M. on January 25, but the president did not yet receive him. Lincoln had scheduled a meeting with Stanton and Halleck and wished to inform them of the situation before seeing Burnside. Once the pair arrived, Lincoln explained to them, without divulging the specifics of General Orders No. 8, the choice Burnside had offered. He then announced his decision to relieve Burnside and replace him with Hooker.[101]

After breakfast the general returned to the executive mansion. Lincoln related the outcome of his deliberations, and Burnside said he "was willing to accept that as the best solution of the problem; and that neither [Lincoln] nor General Hooker would be a happier man than I would be if General Hooker could gain a victory." "I then said to him, 'I suppose, Mr. President, you accept my resignation, and all I have to do is to go to my home.'" Lincoln kindly protested that he needed Burnside's services elsewhere and, in the presence of Stanton and Halleck, offered him command of troops in the Carolinas. Burnside declined in deference to the incumbents, so the president graciously invited Burnside to apply for the thirty days' leave he craved, reserving the right to reassign him thereafter. Later that day the president issued General Orders No. 20 relieving not only Burnside but also Sumner and Franklin and elevating Hooker to command of the army.[102]

Historians have disagreed about the process that led Lincoln to select Hooker. Certainly Fighting Joe himself did nothing to discourage his candidacy, despite his assertion that "no being lives who can say that I ever expressed a desire for the position. It was conferred upon me for my sword, and not for any act or word of mine indicative of a desire for it." He had been in Washington earlier in the month boasting to reporters about how he would handle affairs if placed in army command, and his every expression in camp served to undermine Burnside's authority. Hooker also had struck a political alliance with Secretary of the Treasury Salmon P. Chase, perhaps as early as the autumn of 1862. Chase coveted the presidency and, quite correctly, recognized that a popular military hero might become a potent rival. Hooker's rejection of White House aspirations endeared him to Chase, who thus became his patron in the Lincoln cabinet.[103]

Edwin Stanton's chief clerk, Charles F. Benjamin, provided a detailed published account of the debate that led to Hooker's promotion. Benjamin claimed that both Stanton and Halleck favored Maj. Gen. William S. Rosecrans, the recent victor at Stones River, Tennessee, as Burnside's successor, but a reluctance to import a man from the West limited the field to candidates already in the Potomac army. Because of Sumner's advancing age and Franklin's link with responsibility for the Fredericksburg fiasco, the options narrowed to Hooker and corps commanders Reynolds and Meade. Benjamin claimed that Lincoln authorized Halleck to inquire about Reynolds's willingness to assume command. Reynolds supposedly demanded a higher degree of independence than exercised by any previous field commander, thus eliminating himself from consideration. The influence of Chase and his friends, professed Benjamin, tipped the scales in Hooker's favor.[104]

The problem with Benjamin's account is an absence of corroboration. In fact Halleck stated categorically that "the removal of General Burnside, and appointment of General Hooker, was the sole act of the President. My advice was not asked at all in the matter, and I gave no opinion whatever." Stanton may have shared his doubts about Hooker's capacity and his preference for Rosecrans, Reynolds, or Meade with his clerk; indeed, Benjamin stated that the secretary of war wished to resign when Lincoln named Hooker. But apart from Benjamin's testimony there is no reason to believe that Lincoln discussed the selection of Burnside's replacement with anyone.[105]

Henry Raymond stayed in Washington on January 24 and used the opportunity to speak with Lincoln at a social affair that evening. Although Raymond could not know what the president would do the next day, he candidly informed him of Hooker's disloyalty and "habitual conversation." Lincoln drew the journalist aside and admitted that he was aware of Hooker's behavior and attitude. "The trouble is," said Lincoln, "he is stronger with the country today than any other man." Raymond inquired how long Hooker might maintain that strength once reports circulated about his character. "The country would not believe it," replied the president, "they would say it is all a lie."[106]

One of Burnside's top three lieutenants and an officer with a nickname to match his reputation as an aggressive and competent leader, Hooker appeared in many ways an obvious choice for Lincoln. He had forged his creditable war career solely within the Army of the Potomac but outside McClellan's Democratic clique. There is no reason to doubt that the qualifications Lincoln outlined in his brilliant January 26 letter to Hooker—bravery, military skill, self confidence, ambition, and avoidance of politics—formed the basis for Fighting Joe's promotion—those qualities and a lack of attractive alternatives.[107]

Hooker's appointment elicited a mixed reaction. His biographer asserts that "the great majority of the rank and file who knew Hooker for the fighter he was" greeted his ascension with delight." That may be overstating the case. While many common soldiers appreciated Hooker's style and willingness to share the dangers of battle with his men, he enjoyed no more instant popularity than had Burnside. "The news was received without any demonstration

*Maj. Gen.
Joseph Hooker.
Francis Trevelyan
Miller, ed.,* The
Photographic History
of the Civil War, *10 vols.
(New York: Review of
Reviews, 1911), 10:169*

on the part of the troops," reported Lyman Holford. Men such as Theodore Dodge admired Hooker but wondered if the general could handle army command better than Burnside, Franklin, or Sumner. In certain army quarters Hooker stood in particularly low esteem. Some of the Pennsylvania Reserves, for example, "heartily hate[d]" Fighting Joe because he had criticized their performance during the Seven Days.[108]

The army's officers enjoyed a more intimate acquaintance with Hooker and generally viewed their new commander with skepticism. George Meade wrote his thoughts on January 26: "My opinion [of Hooker] is more favorable than any other of the old regular officers, most of whom are decided in their hostility to him. I believe Hooker is a good soldier; the danger he runs is of subjecting himself to bad influences, such as Dan Butterfield and Dan Sickles, who, being intellectually more clever than Hooker, and leading him to believe they are very influential, will obtain an injurious ascendancy over him and insensibly affect his conduct."[109]

Hooker's intemperance and questionable moral character also disturbed some Federal officers. Radical newspapers supported the choice, while the conservative journals withheld judgment. Few Confederates lost sleep with Hooker as their new opponent. One southern general stated, "Hooker is a fool, and always was, and that's a comfort."[110]

Burnside's dismissal also generated a range of reactions. Some soldiers expressed relief at the departure of the man who had led them to slaughter at Fredericksburg and muddy disgrace in Stafford County. Typical was Pennsylvanian A. S. Bright, who wrote on January 27 that "the only good news I have heard for some time is that Burnsides [*sic*] has been relieved of the command. . . . It is too good to be true." Wyman White declared Burnside's removal "a pleasant surprise to most of the men." The *New York Times* assessed soldier reaction to Burnside's ouster as "so stunning as to elicit no reply, or one of greatest wonder and surprise." On January 26 a Pennsylvania soldier simply asked, "What next?"[111]

Some of the men, such as A. S. West of the 1st Pennsylvania Cavalry, defended their deposed leader, refusing to equate their unhappy fate with Burnside's leadership: "Burnside was not to blame for the inclemency of the weather. . . . The removal of B is causing a great deal of dissatisfaction among soldiers." Frederick Pettit of the 100th Pennsylvania, a Ninth Corps unit, wrote on January 28, "We think Burnside did all he could do and cannot understand why he was relieved of the command. Burnside appeared much like Washington to the troops that [k]new him best." Even those like Walter Carter, who confessed their general may have lacked qualifications for army command, called Burnside "a noble man" who had done his best.[112]

Burnside returned to Falmouth after his interview with Lincoln. He stopped at Sumner's headquarters on the way to deliver the orders that, to "Bull" Sumner's satisfaction, unburdened the elderly warrior of further association with the army. He then repaired to his headquarters and steeled himself to draft the official directive naming Hooker as the army's new commander. The words that appeared as General Orders No. 9 on January 26 were vintage Burnside. They acknowledged the disappointments of the previous two months while praising the "courage, patience, and endurance" of the troops themselves. They also transferred power in a fashion designed to minimize any bitterness his partisans might feel. "Be true in your devotion to your country and the principles you have sworn to maintain," Burnside encouraged his troops, "give to the brave and skillful general who has so long been identified with your organization, and who is now to command you, your full and cordial support and co-operation, and you will deserve success." Burnside did not promise that Hooker's generalship would deliver that success.[113]

Early on the morning of January 26 Hooker arrived at Burnside's tent and formally accepted army command. He immediately issued General Orders No. 1, which, with some irony, recognized that he required "the cheerful and zealous cooperation of every officer and soldier in this army" to deliver victory. He made reference to Burnside at the end of the communique, merely wishing that general "the most cordial good wishes for his future" and thus mercifully sparing readers then and now from digesting even one hypocritical adjective.[114]

Secretary Larned reported that Burnside desired "to avoid any demonstration" as he exited the army. The general did, however, request that some favorite officers visit his quarters before he decamped. Larned told Mrs. Burnside that her husband "addressed [these officers] in a few words and took formal leave of all by shaking hands." Other witnesses described a more animated scene.

Col. Zenas R. Bliss of the 7th Rhode Island reported to army headquarters on the morning of the twenty-sixth not as Burnside's invited guest but as president of a court-martial. About 9:00 A.M. he approached Burnside's lodgings, which stood at the head of a little street formed by the tents of his staff, "and saw the General in his shirt sleeves standing in the door of his tent, with a tumbler and a bottle of champagne in his hands." Burnside cheerfully asked the colonel to join him for some wine. Bliss just as cheerfully accepted. Upon entering Burnside's abode the colonel noticed that empty liquor bottles covered the floor. "Is this the usual morning custom at Army Headquarters," he inquired, "or what is the meaning of this celebration?" A startled Burnside, who assumed the army grapevine if not General Orders No. 9 would have informed field officers of the change in command, told the colonel of his removal. Burnside's visitor expressed regret. "Well, Bliss," replied the general, "they will find out before many days, that it is not every man who can command an army of one hundred and fifty thousand men."[115]

Marsena Patrick recalled Burnside's remarks at the farewell reception as being made with "some feeling," perhaps a function of ninety additional minutes of "Oh Be Joyful." Signal officer Fortescue claimed to overhear the general bid goodbye to his friends with the words, "Farewell Gentlemen[,] there are no pleasant reminiscences for me connected with the Army of the Potomac." By early afternoon Burnside, accompanied by Sumner, departed for Washington, ending the shortest tenure any man would experience at the head of the Army of the Potomac.[116]

Conventional wisdom has deemed that tenure a failure. Counting his intention to cross the Rappahannock on pontoons in November, Burnside mounted four unsuccessful attempts in nine weeks to move "on to Richmond." Historians usually rate his conduct of the Fredericksburg campaign as grossly incompetent. His leadership during the next six weeks appears in the literature as a virtual caricature, to the extent it has been studied at all, epitomized by endurance of the army's ultimate indignity in the Mud March.

Is Ambrose Burnside responsible for the barren record compiled by the army he led? To some extent the answer is no. The general himself enumerated a number of conditions beyond his control which, in his view, contributed to his disappointing record:

> I was the first officer to take charge of [the army] after its first commander had been relieved. I had not been identified with it in the Peninsular campaign, and was unacquainted with a large portion of its officers. The season was very far advanced, which rendered all military movements precarious. The army had not been paid for several months, which caused great dissatisfaction among the soldiers and their friends at home . . . and in short, there was much gloom and despondency throughout the entire command. When to this is added the fact that there was a lack of confidence on the part of many of the officers in my ability to handle the army, it does not seem so strange that success did not attend my efforts.[117]

Burnside's observations ring true. The Army of the Potomac's soul undeniably belonged to George B. McClellan in the winter of 1862–63, and only a decisive victory under a new leader might have altered that fact. But other factors compromised morale more than Little Mac's absence. The paymaster's truancy created significant discontent in the ranks, as did disgust with incompetent regimental and company officers, the perception of a meddling and inefficient Washington administration, and opposition to making emancipation a war aim.

Despite these factors and the devastating defeat on December 13, the evidence does not support a conclusion that grieving for McClellan or any other military malady robbed the army of its potency beyond contributing to a high preexisting desertion rate. The Mud March represented the nadir of the army's self-esteem, but even between January 21 and 24 the troops mustered enough energy and discipline to arrive at their designated destinations and then retrieve their equipment and return to camp under appalling conditions. The army's miraculous rejuvenation within weeks after Hooker's ascension so often described in glowing terms may be partly a function of an exaggerated impression of the depths of its despair in late January.[118]

What Burnside tactfully described as "a lack of confidence on the part of many officers in my ability to handle the army" speaks more directly to an explanation for Burnside's failure. McClellanism in the ranks was essentially benign, but as manifested by officers such as William Franklin and William Smith it did have a chilling effect on army efficiency. Its debilitating symptoms included a natural resistance to action and risk, two tenets of Burnside's military thinking, and a desire to restore Little Mac to command regardless of the effect on current army operations. Such a climate produced in men such as John Newton, John Cochrane, and others the sense that they possessed the right and obligation to intercede at the highest levels of army planning without consequences. Joe Hooker's bombast, while innocent of McClellanesque motivation, added a different but equally unhealthy element to army cohesion.

Burnside should have dispersed this poisonous atmosphere. He failed to do so in part because his superiors declined to provide the context in which the general could confidently purge the army of its disloyal elements. Halleck virtually abdicated any responsibility and failed to champion his beleaguered commander even though he recognized the army's internal malaise. Stanton and Lincoln neither condemned Burnside's leadership after Fredericksburg nor took action to sustain their general. Burnside would sink or swim on his own, paddling about in the shark tank on the Rappahannock. It is always lonely at the top, and Burnside must have felt his isolation every bit as keenly and with as much justification as had McClellan.

Burnside himself contributed to the malignant milieu that permeated his command. His manly acceptance of blame for the outcome at Fredericksburg and his public expressions of personal inadequacy, while attractive on an individual level, undermined trust in his leadership as much as the actions and words of Franklin, Hooker, Smith, and others. The army liked Burnside but did not believe in him.

Only success on the battlefield against Robert E. Lee would rectify the situation, and Burnside continually sought to achieve that success. Might either of Burnside's offensives have brought victory? It is impossible to say. Both his downriver crossing in conjunction with a deep cavalry penetration and his upriver initiative aimed at Lee's left flank had merit. Hooker's much-admired strategy during the Chancellorsville campaign combined elements of maneuver proposed during the winter by Burnside. How Lee would react to an enemy south of the river presented the contingency on which rested triumph or tragedy. The outcome at Chancellorsville is a matter of record, but what would have occurred in January cannot be known.

It is fair to conclude that the Army of the Potomac possessed the strength, spirit, and means to force a crossing of the Rappahannock River in January 1863. Ambrose Burnside had devised reasonable operations designed to bring the war to Spotsylvania County and beyond. But hampered by faithless subordinates, an insipid superior, and meteorological misfortune, Burnside's post-Fredericksburg leadership of the Army of the Potomac resulted in a legacy of defeat and the unfortunate realization of a self-fulfilling prophecy.

Acknowledgments

The author expresses his thanks to several colleagues and friends who provided valuable research assistance during the preparation of this essay. Donald C. Pfanz and Robert K. Krick of the Fredericksburg and Spotsylvania National Military Park made available their extensive manuscript collection and steered me toward some important sources. William D. Matter of Harrisburg, Pennsylvania, generously shared insights and materials gleaned from his exhaustive research on the Fredericksburg campaign. Dr. Richard J. Sommers at the United States Military History Institute in Carlisle, Pennsylvania, provided his usual skillful guidance. The staff at the Manuscript Division of the Library of Congress maintains an astounding level of public service that aided me in finding and using their collections. Finally, I am grateful to my co-contributors William Marvel, Alan T. Nolan, Carol Reardon, and George C. Rable for challenging my assertions in this essay, and to Gary W. Gallagher for bringing our essays together in this book.

Notes

1. Lyman C. Holford Diary, December 15, 1862, Lyman C. Holford Papers, Library of Congress, Washington, D.C. (repository hereafter cited as LC).

2. U.S. War Department, *The War of the Rebellion: A Compilation of the Official Records of the Union and Confederate Armies*, 127 vols., index, and atlas (Washington, D.C.: GPO, 1880–1901), 21:66 (hereafter cited as *OR*; all references are to series 1).

3. *OR* 21:66–68.

4. Charles S. Wainwright, *A Diary of Battle: The Personal Journals of Colonel Charles S. Wainwright, 1861–1865*, ed. Allan Nevins (New York: Harcourt, Brace & World, 1962), 149; *The Dismissal of Major Granville O. Haller of the Regular Army of the United States by order of the Secretary of War in Special Orders No. 331, of July 25th, 1863, also a Brief Memoir of His Military Services, and a Few Observations* (Paterson, N.J.: Daily Guardian Office, 1863), 13; William Orr to his wife, December 21, 1862, William Orr Papers, Indiana University, Bloomington, Ind.; Marsena Rudolph Patrick, *Inside Lincoln's Army: The Diary of Marsena Rudolph Patrick, Provost Marshal General, Army of the Potomac*, ed. David S. Sparks (New York: Thomas Yoseloff, 1964), 195.

5. William Harris to "Dear Brother," December 26, 1862, George Hopper Papers, U.S. Army Military History Institute, Carlisle Barracks, Pa. (repository hereafter cited as USAMHI); Jacob Haas to his brother, January 3, 1863, in Harrisburg Civil War Round Table Collection, USAMHI; *New York Times*, December 19, 1862; U.S. Congress, *Report of the Joint Committee on the Conduct of the War*, Senate Reports, No. 108, 2 vols. (Washington, D.C.: GPO, 1863), 2:57.

6. Samuel S. Partridge to "My dear Ed," December 17, 1862, typescript in bound volume 146, Fredericksburg and Spotsylvania National Military Park Library, Fredericksburg, Va. (repository hereafter cited as FSNMP); Regis de Trobriand, *Four Years with the Army of the Potomac* (1889; reprint, Gaithersburg, Md.: Ron R. Van Sickle Military Books, 1988), 400; diary of unidentified soldier in the 7th Rhode Island Infantry, December 16, 1862, David A. Russell Papers, USAMHI; Robert McAllister, *The Civil War Letters of General Robert McAllister*, ed. James I. Robertson, Jr. (New Brunswick, N.J.: Rutgers University Press, 1965), 242–43.

7. *New York Times*, December 23, 1862. A slightly different version appears in *OR* 21:67, as part of Burnside's December 17, 1862, report to Halleck.

8. Henry W. Raymond, ed., "Extracts from the Journal of Henry J. Raymond," *Scribner's Monthly*, March 1880, 424.

9. Allan Nevins, *The War for the Union*, 4 vols. (New York: Charles Scribner's Sons,

1959–71), 2:365; William Marvel, *Burnside* (Chapel Hill: University of North Carolina Press, 1991), 208. Marvel cited James L. Van Buren's letter of December 23, 1862, to Burnside. As with all aspects of Burnside's military career, Marvel's account of the general's post-Fredericksburg experience is easily the best.

10. T. Harry Williams, *Lincoln and the Radicals* (Madison: University of Wisconsin Press, 1941), 236, 201; Carl Sandburg, *Abraham Lincoln: The War Years*, 4 vols. (New York: Harcourt, Brace, 1939), 2:75.

11. T. Harry Williams, *Lincoln and the Radicals*, 237; William H. Powell, *The Fifth Army Corps (Army of the Potomac): A Record of Operations during the Civil War in the United States of America, 1861–1865* (New York: G. P. Putnam's Sons, 1896), 405.

12. William Child, *A History of the Fifth Regiment New Hampshire Volunteers, in the American Civil War, 1861–1865* (1893; reprint, Gaithersburg, Md.: Ron R. Van Sickle Military Books, 1988), 166; Edmund Halsey Diary, December 20, 1862, Edmund Halsey Papers, USAMHI; Alpheus S. Williams, *From the Cannon's Mouth: The Civil War Letters of General Alpheus S. Williams*, ed. Milo M. Quaife (Detroit: Wayne State University Press, 1959), 154.

13. James M. McPherson, *Battle Cry of Freedom: The Civil War Era* (New York: Oxford University Press, 1988), 574. Maj. Gen. George Gordon Meade and Col. Adrian R. Root led the two penetrations on the Union left.

14. James Carman to "Dear Father," December 17, 1862, photocopy in bound vol. 151, FSNMP; Augustus Woodbury, *Major General Ambrose E. Burnside and the Ninth Army Corps* (Providence, R.I.: Sidney S. Rider & Brother, 1867), 247; McAllister, *Letters*, 253.

15. Rufus R. Dawes, *Service with the Sixth Wisconsin Volunteers* (1890; reprint, Dayton, Ohio: Morningside, 1984), 115; Theodore Dodge Diary, December 20, 1862, Theodore Dodge Papers, LC; William Hamilton to "Dear Boyd," January 3, 1863, William Hamilton Papers, LC.

16. Thomas M. Covert to his wife, December 29, 1862, typescript in bound vol. 153, FSNMP. The officer was Louis P. Di Cesnola of the 4th New York Cavalry.

17. Alex Hamilton to "Dear Sam," December 22, 1862, photocopy in bound vol. 153, FSNMP; William Swinton, *Campaigns of the Army of the Potomac: A Critical History of Operations in Virginia, Maryland, and Pennsylvania from the Commencement to the Close of the War 1861–5* (1866; reprint, Secaucus, N.J.: Blue & Grey Press, 1988), 256; Carl Schurz, *The Autobiography of Carl Schurz*, abridged in one volume by Wayne Andrews (New York: Charles Scribner's Sons, 1961), 228.

18. John Cochrane, "The Army of the Potomac, A Paper read by General John Cochrane, late of U.S.V., at a Meeting of the New York Commandery, Military Order Loyal Legion, December 2, 1885," in *Personal Recollections of the War of the Rebellion, Addresses Delivered before the New York Commandery of the Loyal Legion of the United States, 1883–1891*, ed. James Grant Wilson and Titus Munson Coan, M.D. (1891; reprint, Wilmington, N.C.: Broadfoot, 1992), 57; Wainwright, *Diary of Battle*, 149.

19. Robert Goldthwaite Carter, *Four Brothers in Blue; or, Sunshine and Shadows of*

the War of the Rebellion, a Story of the Great Civil War from Bull Run to Appomattox (1913; reprint, Austin: University of Texas Press, 1978), 212; James R. Coye to "Dear Wife," December 17, 1862, photocopy in bound vol. 147, FSNMP; Joseph B. Osborn to "My dear father," December 24, 1862, typescript in bound vol. 155, FSNMP. Examples of estimates of desertions may be found in T. Harry Williams, *Lincoln and the Radicals*, 237, and Alfred Davenport, *Camp and Field Life of the Fifth New York Volunteer Infantry (Duryee Zouaves)* (1879; reprint, Gaithersburg, Md.: Butternut Press, 1984), 365.

20. Carter, *Four Brothers*, 210–11; William H. Brown to his brother, December 27, 1862, typescript in possession of William D. Matter copied from the original at Brown University, Providence, R.I.; Dexter Macomber letter, December 19, 1862, typescript in possession of William D. Matter copied from the original at USAMHI; Theodore Dodge Diary, December 19, 1862, Theodore Dodge Papers, LC; Rueben W. Shell to "My dear father," December 31, 1862, typescript in bound vol. 151, FSNMP.

21. U.S. Congress, *Report of the Joint Committee on the Conduct of the War in Three Parts* (Washington, D.C.: GPO, 1863), pt. 1, pp. 660, 662, 656 (hereafter cited as *JCCW*; all references are to part 1).

22. McAllister, *Letters*, 249; Carter, *Four Brothers*, 215; *New York Times*, December 23, 1862; Daniel R. Ballou, "The Military Services of Maj.-Gen. Ambrose Everett Burnside in the Civil War, and Their Value as an Asset of His Country and Its History," in *Soldiers and Sailors Historical Society of Rhode Island Personal Narratives, Seventh Series, No. 9* (Providence, R.I.: Published by the Society, 1914), 38–39.

23. Daniel R. Larned to "My dear Henry," December 16, 1862; Daniel R. Larned to "My dear Sister," December 23, 1862; Daniel R. Larned to "My dear Uncle," January 1, 1863, Daniel Reed Larned Papers, LC.

24. William R. Williams to his wife, December 26, 1862, Civil War Miscellaneous Collection, USAMHI.

25. Swinton, *Campaigns of the Army of the Potomac*, 255; Bruce Catton, *Bruce Catton's Civil War* (New York: Fairfax Press, 1984; originally published as *Glory Road* [Garden City, N.Y.: Doubleday, 1952]), 270.

26. Kenneth P. Williams, *Lincoln Finds a General: A Military Study of the Civil War*, 5 vols. (New York: Macmillan, 1949–59), 2:553. In calculating the army's absentee rate, Williams included the soldiers in the Washington defenses. Absentees may have been soldiers on leave or away in hospitals, not merely those absent without leave. Nevertheless, when used as relative numbers between November and January, Williams's comparison is valid. See ibid., 2:830–31 n.23.

27. *New York Times*, December 25, 1862; *OR* 21:868–70.

28. For ratification of Franklin and Smith's thinking, see George Gordon Meade, *The Life and Letters of George Gordon Meade*, ed. George G. Meade, 2 vols. (New York: Charles Scribner's Sons, 1913), 1:340–41, and Emerson Gifford Taylor, *Gouverneur Kemble Warren: The Life and Letters of an American Soldier, 1830–1882* (1932; reprint, Gaithersburg, Md.: Ron R. Van Sickle Military Books, 1988), 96. Lincoln's letter to

Franklin and Smith is in Abraham Lincoln, *The Collected Works of Abraham Lincoln*, ed. Roy P. Basler, 8 vols. and index (New Brunswick, N.J.: Rutgers University Press, 1953–55), 6:15.

29. *JCCW*, 716–17. Burnside spells the local landmark *Sedden*.

30. *JCCW*, 747–49; William Howard Mills, "From Burnside to Hooker," *Magazine of American History* 15 (January–June 1886): 44. Averell provided a detailed outline of his plan in a December 28, 1862, message to Burnside in *OR* 21:895–96.

31. *OR* 21:895, 899.

32. *OR* 21:742–43.

33. *OR* 21:900, 902, 923.

34. *JCCW*, 726–28; Meade, *Life and Letters of Meade*, 1:343; Catton, *Bruce Catton's Civil War*, 265; Kenneth P. Williams, *Lincoln Finds a General*, 2:553.

35. Douglas Southall Freeman, *Lee's Lieutenants: A Study in Command*, 3 vols. (New York: Charles Scribner's Sons, 1942–44), 2:413, 429.

36. *JCCW*, 738; John Cochrane, *The War for the Union: Memoir of Gen. John Cochrane* (New York: n.p., 1885), 47–48.

37. Ezra J. Warner, *Generals in Blue: Lives of the Union Commanders* (Baton Rouge: Louisiana State University Press, 1964), 344, 86; Lawrence F. Kennedy, chief comp., *Biographical Directory of the American Congress, 1774–1971* (Washington, D.C.: GPO, 1971), 759.

38. *JCCW*, 730–36, 741.

39. *JCCW*, 742.

40. *JCCW*, 731, 742, 745–46; Cochrane, *Memoir*, 48–51.

41. Cochrane, *Memoir*, 50–51; *JCCW*, 731, 737, 742.

42. Cochrane, *Memoir*, 52; *JCCW*, 743, 732, 717.

43. *JCCW*, 717–18.

44. *JCCW*, 718; Marvel, *Burnside*, 209.

45. *OR* 21:941; *JCCW*, 718–19; Marvel, *Burnside*, 210. A bitter controversy raged later in the year regarding whether Burnside had called for Stanton's and Halleck's removal in those men's presence. He had not. See Marvel, *Burnside*, 210–11, 456–57 n. 22.

46. *OR* 21:940.

47. *OR* 21:940–941; Lincoln, *Collected Works*, 6:31. Lincoln noted that he withdrew his letter to Halleck because the general considered it "harsh."

48. *JCCW*, 718.

49. *JCCW*, 711–12.

50. Cochrane, *Memoir*, 56; Stewart Sifakis, *Who Was Who in the Civil War* (New York: Facts on File, 1988), 131; Marvel, *Burnside*, 458 n. 2.

51. Thomas Francis Galwey Journal, December 18, 1862, January 1, 1863, Thomas Francis Galwey Papers, LC; James P. Coburn Diary, January 24, 1863, Coburn Collection, USAMHI; Carter, *Four Brothers*, 211.

52. Louis R. Fortescue to "Friend Sam," January 9, 1863, photocopy in bound vol. 153, FSNMP.

53. Frederick Pettit to "Dear Brother Evan," n.d. (ca. January 13, 1863), typescript in bound vol. 185, FSNMP.

54. Samuel S. Partridge to "My Dear Ed," January 6, 1863, typescript in bound vol. 146, FSNMP.

55. William Franklin Draper to "My dear father," January 9, 1863, typescript in the William Franklin Draper Papers, LC; Allen Landis to "Dear Parents," January 1, 1863, Allen Landis Papers, LC; Cleveland *Plain Dealer*, January 10, 1863; Daniel R. Larned to "My dear Sister," January 11, 1863, Daniel Reed Larned Papers, LC.

56. John Morton to "Dear Mother," January 13, 1863, typescript in the possession of William D. Matter copied from the original at USAMHI; John T. Boyle to Peter Filbert, January 13, 1863, typescript in bound vol. 155, FSNMP; Edwin O. Wentworth to "My dear Carrie," January 5, 1863, typescript in the Pvt. Edwin O. Wentworth Papers, LC; Charles Gibson to "My Dear Sister Laura," January 6, 1863, photocopy in bound vol. 182, FSNMP.

57. William Hamilton to "My dear Mother," January 6, 1863, William Hamilton Papers, LC; Warren quoted in Taylor, *Gouverneur Kemble Warren*, 97.

58. McAllister, *Letters*, 256; Washington *Daily Intelligencer*, January 12, 1863. The observers, both Republicans, were Lyman A. Coe of the Connecticut state senate and S. P. Allen, former editor of the Rochester *Democrat*.

59. Alexander W. Acheson letter, January 11, 1863, typescript in the possession of William D. Matter copied from the original in the Save the Flag Collection, USAMHI; Gideon Welles, *Diary of Gideon Welles*, ed. John T. Morse, Jr., 3 vols. (Boston: Houghton Mifflin, 1911), 1:226.

60. James Kelaher to "Dear Cousin," January 21, 1863, James Kelaher Papers, LC; Jacob W. Haas to his brother, January 3, 1863, typescript in bound vol. 155, FSNMP; Theodore Dodge Diary, January 2, 1863, Theodore Dodge Papers, LC; Jonathan Hutchison to "Dear Cousin," January 7, 1863, Norwich Civil War Round Table Collection, USAMHI. For a discussion of McClellan's views on emancipation, see Stephen W. Sears, *George B. McClellan, the Young Napoleon* (New York: Ticknor and Fields, 1988), 324–27.

61. T. Harry Williams, *Lincoln and the Radicals*, 262; John G. Nicolay and John Hay, *Abraham Lincoln: A History*, 10 vols. (New York: Century, 1890), 6:213; Patrick, *Inside Lincoln's Army*, 199. Brooks commanded the first division of the Sixth Corps, an organization rife with anti-Burnside officers.

62. *OR* 21:916–18; *New York Times*, January 13, 1863.

63. Lincoln, *Collected Works*, 6:46–47.

64. *OR* 21:945.

65. *OR* 21:953–54.

66. Ambrose E. Burnside to William W. Averell, January 6, 1863, Telegrams Collected by the Office of the Secretary of War, 1860–1870, RG 107, microcopy 504, National Archives, Washington, D.C. (repository hereafter cited as NA); Patrick, *Inside Lincoln's Army*, 203; *OR* 21:965, 976; Raymond, "Extracts from the Journal of

Henry J. Raymond," 420; Daniel R. Larned to "My Dear Henry," January 16, 1863, Daniel Reed Larned Papers, LC; Russell C. White, *The Civil War Diary of Wyman S. White* (Baltimore: Butternut and Blue, 1991), 120.

67. Henry J. Hunt to "Col. Richmond," January 25, 1863, Henry J. Hunt Papers, LC; *JCCW*, 719; *OR* 21:977.

68. George W. Redway, *Fredericksburg: A Study in War* (New York: Macmillan, 1906), 242–43; *OR* 21:77–81, 752–53, 127.

69. Henry Ropes to "Dear John," January 21, 1863, typescript in the possession of William D. Matter copied from original at the Boston Public Library, Boston, Mass.; *New York Times*, January 24, 1863; Zerah C. Monks to "Hattie," January 25, 1863, typescript in the possession of William D. Matter.

70. Samuel R. Beardsley to "Did," January 17, 1863, Samuel R. Beardsley Papers, USAMHI; Wainwright, *Diary of Battle*, 158.

71. Meade, *Life and Letters of Meade*, 1:345, 348; John H. Pardington to "My dear wife," January 18, 1863, in bound vol. 153, FSNMP; James Carman to "Dear Uncle," January 19, 1863, in bound vol. 151, FSNMP.

72. Douglas Southall Freeman, *R. E. Lee: A Biography*, 4 vols. (New York: Charles Scribner's Sons, 1934–35), 2:473; *OR* 21:1064; Redway, *Fredericksburg*, 235, 237; *New York Times*, December 18, 1862; Peggy Vogtsberger, "The Dumfries Raid," *Cannoneer* 11 (May 1993): 4–9.

73. Redway, *Fredericksburg*, 242, 244–45; *OR* 21:968, 1091, 1096; Freeman, *Lee's Lieutenants*, 2:421.

74. *OR* 21:977, 755; Robert E. Lee, *The Wartime Papers of R. E. Lee*, ed. Clifford Dowdey and Louis H. Manarin (Boston: Little, Brown, 1961), 393; Redway, *Fredericksburg*, 247; John J. Pullen, *The Twentieth Maine: A Volunteer Regiment in the Civil War* (1957; reprint, Dayton, Ohio: Morningside, 1984), 69.

75. Davenport, *Fifth New York*, 365; Raymond, "Extracts from the Journal of Henry J. Raymond," 421; Cleveland *Plain Dealer*, January 24, 1863; Captain Eugene Arus Nash, *A History of the Forty-Fourth Regiment New York Volunteer Infantry in the Civil War, 1861–1865* (1911; reprint, Dayton, Ohio: Morningside, 1988), 123; Charles Bryant Fairchild, *History of the 27th Regiment New York Volunteers, Being a Record of Its More Than Two Years of Service in the War for the Union, From May 21st, 1861, to May 31st, 1863* (Binghamton, N.Y.: Carl & Matthews, 1888), 134–35.

76. De Trobriand, *Four Years*, 407; Fairchild, *History of the 27th New York*, 134–35.

77. *OR* 21:78–79, 991; Ambrose E. Burnside to Edwin V. Sumner, January 21, 1863, and Ambrose E. Burnside to Joseph Hooker, January 21, 1863, Telegrams Collected by the Office of the Secretary of War, 1860–1870, RG 107, microcopy 504, NA; Daniel R. Larned to Mrs. A. E. Burnside, January 28, 1863, and Daniel R. Larned to "Dear Henry," January 21, 1863, Daniel Reed Larned Papers, LC.

78. Daniel R. Larned to "Dear Henry," January 21, 1863, Daniel Reed Larned Papers, LC; Pullen, *Twentieth Maine*, 61.

79. Powell, *Fifth Army Corps*, 408; James W. Latta Diary, January 23, 1863, James W.

Latta Papers, LC; William Hamilton to "My dear Mother," January 27, 1863, William Hamilton Papers, LC; Swinton, *Campaigns of the Army of the Potomac*, 260; Charles A. Stevens, *Berdan's United States Sharpshooters in the Army of the Potomac, 1861–65* (St. Paul, Minn.: Price-McGill, 1892), 231; George H. Mellish to his mother, January 24, 1863, typescript in the possession of William D. Matter copied from original at the Huntington Library, San Marino, Calif.; Alpheus S. Williams, *From the Cannon's Mouth*, 159.

80. *OR* 21:989–90; Raymond, "Extracts from the Journal of Henry J. Raymond," 421; George T. Stevens, *Three Years in the Sixth Corps. A Concise Narrative of Events in the Army of the Potomac, from 1861 to the Close of the Rebellion, April 1865* (Albany, N.Y.: S. R. Gray, 1866), 176.

81. Carter, *Four Brothers*, 227; White, *Diary of Wyman S. White*, 122; Alfred Bellard, *Gone for a Soldier: The Civil War Memoirs of Private Alfred Bellard*, ed. David Herbert Donald (Boston: Little, Brown, 1975), 198; Dayton E. Flint to his father, January 27, 1863, Civil War Miscellaneous Collection, USAMHI. Robert Carter describes the fight as the "unfortunate whiskey riot" and reports that the 2nd Maine and the 1st Michigan also became embroiled. See Carter, *Four Brothers*, 226.

82. Mills, "From Burnside to Hooker," 50; David A. Ward, "Amidst a Tempest of Shot and Shell: A History of the Ninety-Sixth Pennsylvania Volunteers" (M.A. thesis, Southern Connecticut State University, New Haven, Conn., 1988; copy at FSNMP), 253; Theodore Dodge Diary, January 24, 1863, Theodore Dodge Papers, LC; Thomas Frances Galwey Journal, January 21, 1863, Thomas Frances Galwey Papers, LC; Raymond, "Extracts from the Journal of Henry J. Raymond," 422; *JCCW*, 719.

83. *OR* 21:995, 82, 993.

84. White, *Diary of Wyman S. White*, 123; Meade, *Life and Letters of Meade*, 1:348; Mills, "From Burnside to Hooker," 50–51; George T. Stevens, *Three Years in the Sixth Corps*, 177.

85. "Reminiscences of Zenas R. Bliss," 4:46, Zenas R. Bliss Papers, USAMHI. Colonel Bliss commanded the 7th Rhode Island in the Ninth Corps.

86. Edmund Halsey Diary, January 25, 1863, Edmund Halsey Papers, USAMHI; DeWitt C. Kitchen, "Burnside's Mud March. Days During Which the Army of the Potomac Suffered Terribly," Philadelphia *Weekly Times*, March 4, 1882; James P. Coburn to "Dear Father," January 28, 1863, James P. Coburn Papers, USAMHI.

87. Lyman Holford Diary, January 25, 1863, Lyman Holford Papers, LC; *OR* 21:1010; Darius N. Couch, "Sumner's 'Right Grand Division,'" in *Battles and Leaders of the Civil War*, ed. Robert Underwood Johnson and Clarence Clough Buel, 4 vols. (New York: Century, 1887–88), 3:118–19 (hereafter cited as *B&L*); Catton, *Bruce Catton's Civil War*, 271.

88. Henry H. Humphreys, *Andrew Atkinson Humphreys: A Biography* (1914; reprint, Gaithersburg, Md.: Ron R. Van Sickle Military Books, 1988), 182; Wainwright, *Diary of Battle*, 160–61; Cleveland *Plain Dealer*, January 28, 1863; Isaac Newton Durboraw to "Capt. McPherson," January 25, 1863, Isaac Newton Durboraw Papers, Harrisburg Civil War Round Table Collection, USAMHI.

89. Meade, *Life and Letters of Meade*, 1:349; *JCCW*, 729; *OR* 21:1103, 1111.

90. Burnside reported, "Could we have had the pontoons there, ready to have crossed early on the 21st . . . there is scarcely a doubt but that the crossing could have been effected, and the objects of the movement attained." This assessment may be dismissed as self-serving; however, other officers confirmed it, while admitting that events on the south bank would have been less certain. William Marvel reminds readers that had Burnside been permitted to advance earlier, he would have experienced good campaigning weather. See *OR* 21:69; "Reminiscences of Zenas R. Bliss," 4:47, Zenas R. Bliss Papers, USAMHI; Marvel, *Burnside*, 213.

91. George T. Stevens, *Three Years in the Sixth Corps*, 17; William Franklin Draper letter, January 23, 1863, William Franklin Draper Papers, LC; Patrick, *Inside Lincoln's Army*, 207.

92. Samuel S. Partridge to "My dear Ed," January 25, 1863, typescript in bound vol. 146, FSNMP; Joseph H. Law to "Mary," January 26, 1863, Law Family Collection, USAMHI; Alpheus S. Williams, *From the Cannon's Mouth*, 159–60.

93. G. D. Mace to "Dear Uncle," January 28, 1863, in bound vol. 183, FSNMP; Joseph B. Osborn to "Dear Sister Mary and folks at home," January 25, 1863, Joseph B. Osborn Papers, LC; Harry W. Roose to "Dear Cousin," February 5, 1863, Hannah Delp Papers, Harrisburg Civil War Round Table Collection, USAMHI; William Hamilton to "Dear Boyd," January 31, 1863, William Hamilton Papers, LC; Dayton E. Flint to his father, January 27, 1863, published in the Washington *Star*, January 26, 1911, typescript in the Civil War Miscellaneous Collection, USAMHI.

94. *New York Times*, January 27, 1863.

95. *JCCW*, 723. The storm would render the wisdom of Burnside's gamble moot.

96. Raymond, "Extracts from the Journal of Henry J. Raymond," 423. Kenneth P. Williams, in *Lincoln Finds a General*, 2:545–46, addresses Halleck's role in the genesis of General Orders No. 8 and speculates about how the general in chief would have reacted to Burnside's dilemma.

97. William F. Smith, *Autobiography of Major General William F. Smith, 1861–1864*, ed. Herbert M. Schiller (Dayton, Ohio: Morningside, 1990), 65–66; *OR* 21:998–99. The other officers Burnside designated for reassignment included Brig. Gen. Samuel D. Sturgis, Brig. Gen. Edward Ferrero, and Lt. Col. Joseph H. Taylor. Raymond testified that Burnside intended to relieve Woodbury as well, but the engineer's name did not appear in General Orders No. 8. See Raymond, "Extracts from the Journal of Henry J. Raymond," 704.

98. Raymond, "Extracts from the Journal of Henry J. Raymond," 703–4; Mills, "From Burnside to Hooker," 52.

99. *JCCW*, 720. Raymond, "Extracts from the Journal of Henry J. Raymond," 702, mentions Dr. Church's presence during these discussions but does not explicitly identify him as the contributor to Burnside's decision. Burnside recognized that he had no authority to remove an officer without a trial but that the president did. Lincoln exercised that power no fewer than 131 times in 1862. See Kenneth P. Williams, *Lincoln Finds a General*, 2:544–45.

100. *OR* 21:998; Daniel R. Larned to Mrs. A. E. Burnside, January 28, 1863, Daniel Reed Larned Papers, LC; Raymond, "Extracts from the Journal of Henry J. Raymond," 704. Raymond identifies the telegrapher's station as being at Stoneman's Switch, while Larned says the Falmouth Depot. I have chosen to follow Larned because he wrote closer to the events. For details about Burnside's misadventures on the night of January 23, see Marvel, *Burnside*, 214–15.

101. *JCCW*, 720–21; Daniel R. Larned to Mrs. A. E. Burnside, January 28, 1863, Daniel Reed Larned Papers, LC; Raymond, "Extracts from the Journal of Henry J. Raymond," 706–7; *OR* 21:1004, 1009.

102. *JCCW*, 721–22; *OR* 21:1004–5. Raymond, "Extracts from the Journal of Henry J. Raymond," 706–7, provides more details of Burnside's conversation with Lincoln, including the general's agreement that Sumner and Franklin also should be relieved.

103. Hooker quoted in Walter H. Hebert, *Fighting Joe Hooker* (1944; reprint, Gaithersburg, Md.: Butternut Press, 1987), 167, and in Mills, "From Burnside to Hooker," 55. On Hooker's relationship with Chase, see Smith, *Autobiography*, 66 n. 30, and Hebert, *Fighting Joe Hooker*, 164.

104. Charles F. Benjamin, "Hooker's Appointment and Removal," in *B&L*, 3:239–40. McClellan and John Pope provided negative models of western theater commanders transferred to the eastern armies.

105. *OR* 21:1009; Benjamin, "Hooker's Appointment and Removal," 240.

106. Raymond, "Extracts from the Journal of Henry J. Raymond," 705.

107. For Lincoln's letter to Hooker, one of the classic communications of the Civil War, see Lincoln, *Collected Works*, 6:78–79.

108. Hebert, *Fighting Joe Hooker*, 167; Lyman C. Holford Diary, January 27, 1863, Lyman C. Holford Papers, LC; Theodore Dodge Diary, January 28, 1863, Theodore Dodge Papers, LC; William Hamilton to "Dear Boyd," January 31, 1863, William Hamilton Papers, LC.

109. Meade, *Life and Letters of Meade*, 1:351.

110. Hebert, *Fighting Joe Hooker*, 167–69; William Henry Chase Whiting in *OR* 27(3):966.

111. Aida Craig Truxall, ed., *"Respects to All": Letters of Two Pennsylvania Boys in the War of the Rebellion* (Pittsburgh: University of Pittsburgh Press, 1962), 38; photocopy of letter to "Dear Uncle," January 27, 1863, in bound vol. 150, FSNMP; White, *Diary of Wyman S. White*, 125; *New York Times*, January 29, 1863; James P. Coburn Diary, January 26, 1863, Coburn Collection, USAMHI.

112. A. S. West to "Dear Father," n.d., photocopy in bound vol. 74, FSNMP; Frederick Pettit to "Dear Sister Margaret," January 28, 1863, typescript in bound vol. 185, FSNMP; Carter, *Four Brothers*, 231.

113. Daniel R. Larned to Mrs. A. E. Burnside, January 28, 1863, Daniel Reed Larned Papers, LC; *OR* 21:1005.

114. Daniel R. Larned to Mrs. A. E. Burnside, January 28, 1863, Daniel Reed Larned Papers, LC; *OR* 25(2):5.

115. Daniel R. Larned to Mrs. A. E. Burnside, January 28, 1863, Daniel Reed Larned Papers, LC; "Reminiscences of Zenas R. Bliss," 4:48–49, Zenas R. Bliss Papers, USAMHI.

116. Patrick, *Inside Lincoln's Army*, 208; Louis R. Fortescue to [?], photocopy of undated letter (probably January 26, 1863) in bound vol. 153, FSNMP; Daniel R. Larned to Mrs. A. E. Burnside, January 28, 1863, Daniel Reed Larned Papers, LC. For an excellent summary of Burnside's last days with the army, see Marvel, *Burnside*, 216.

117. *OR* 21:96.

118. See, for example, McPherson, *Battle Cry of Freedom*, 585; Edward J. Stackpole, *Chancellorsville: Lee's Greatest Battle* (Harrisburg, Pa.: Stackpole, 1958), chap. 2; Ernest B. Furgurson, *Chancellorsville 1863: The Souls of the Brave* (New York: Knopf, 1992), 31. These accounts document improvements in army organization but imply that Hooker rebuilt his command from the bottom up. George Meade told the Joint Committee on the Conduct of the War on March 16 that "the measures initiated since General Hooker has taken command . . . have had the effect of very much improving the condition of [the] army. I never did think the army in as bad condition as many persons away from the army have seemed to think." K. P. Williams concluded that the army's performance during the Mud March "proved both its great efficiency and its reliability under great difficulties, in spite of disaffection and many recent desertions." See *JCCW*, 693; Kenneth P. Williams, *Lincoln Finds a General*, 2:543.

BIBLIOGRAPHIC ESSAY

Readers seeking the sources on which the essays are based should consult the notes. Those who pursue a more general understanding of Fredericksburg will discover that the campaign has inspired a far more modest literature than such intensively studied operations as Gettysburg, Vicksburg, and Atlanta, and they will learn as well that virtually all the specialized writings on Fredericksburg concentrate on military elements of the campaign. Full-scale explorations of some of the topics addressed by the contributors to this volume remain to be written.

The starting point for any serious investigation of Fredericksburg is U.S. War Department, *The War of the Rebellion: A Compilation of the Official Records of the Union and Confederate Armies*, 127 vols., index, and atlas (Washington, D.C.: GPO, 1880–1901). Series 1, vol. 21, of the *Official Records* (or *OR*, as this set is popularly known) contains more than 1,100 pages of official reports, correspondence, and orders relating to Fredericksburg, while series 1, vol. 19, pts. 1–2, include material on the opening phase of the campaign. For northern recriminations after the battle, testimony given before the Joint Committee on the Conduct of the War, which the Government Printing Office published in various editions during the war, is essential. James Longstreet, Darius N. Couch, William Farrar "Baldy" Smith, and other participants contributed pieces on Fredericksburg to the frequently cited *Battles and Leaders of the Civil War*, ed. Robert Underwood Johnson and Clarence Clough Buel, 4 vols. (New York: Century, 1887). As with all postwar accounts, these sketches must be used with care. Other Confederate testimony may be found in *The Southern Historical Society Papers*, ed. J. William Jones and others, 52 vols. (1877–1959; reprint, with 3-vol. index, Wilmington, N.C.: Broadfoot, 1990–92), while on the Union side, papers read before the state commanderies of the Military Order of the Loyal Legion of the United States (usually abbreviated to MOLLUS) offer much of value on Fredericksburg (a comprehensive edition of the MOLLUS papers projected at 75 volumes is in production at Wilmington, N.C.: Broadfoot, 1991–).

The battle of Fredericksburg awaits full scholarly treatment. The best study to date is Vorin E. Whan, Jr., *Fiasco at Fredericksburg* ([University Park]: Pennsylvania State University Press, 1961), a brief but balanced discussion of the campaign through Burnside's withdrawal across the Rappahannock on December 15. Far less satisfactory, though more widely read, Edward J. Stackpole's *Drama on the Rappahannock: The Fredericksburg Campaign* (Harrisburg, Pa.: Military Service Publishing, 1957) draws on only a handful of sources and sacrifices accuracy for color. G. F. R. Henderson's *The Campaign of Fredericksburg, Nov.–Dec., 1862, A Tactical Study for Officers* (1886; reprinted in Jay Luvaas, ed., *The Civil War: A Soldier's View, A Collection of Civil*

War Writings by Col. G. F. R. Henderson [Chicago: University of Chicago Press, 1958])
presents a careful analysis by an important British student of the Civil War. Another
venerable but still useful treatment is former Union general Francis W. Palfrey's *The
Antietam and Fredericksburg* (1882; reprint, Wilmington, N.C.: Broadfoot, 1989),
which focuses on Union activities, criticizes Burnside heavily, and defends the performance of William B. Franklin. In *"Stonewall" Jackson at Fredericksburg: The Battle for
Prospect Hill, December 13, 1862* (Lynchburg, Va.: H. E. Howard, 1993), Frank A.
O'Reilly examines a wealth of unpublished material to fashion the best discussion of
any one phase of the battle.

A trio of titles aimed at a popular audience is Richard Wheeler, *Lee's Terrible Swift
Sword: From Antietam to Chancellorsville, an Eyewitness History* (New York: Harper/
Collins, 1992), which conveniently gathers well-known accounts by Federals and
Confederates; William Marvel, *The Battle of Fredericksburg* ([Conshohocken, Pa.]:
Eastern National Park and Monument Association, 1993), a volume in the National
Park Service's Civil War Series that offers the best brief introduction to the campaign;
and William K. Goolrick and the editors of Time-Life Books, *Rebels Resurgent: Fred-
ericksburg to Chancellorsville* (Alexandria, Va.: Time-Life Books, 1985), which includes
a wealth of pictorial material. Another pictorial volume, *The Embattled Confederacy*,
ed. William C. Davis (vol. 3 of William C. Davis, ed., *The Image of War: 1861–1865*
[Garden City, N.Y.: Doubleday, 1981–84]), contains a chapter on Fredericksburg that
combines a series of excellent photographs and a thoughtful text by Peter J. Parrish.

Visitors to the Fredericksburg battlefield would do well to carry a copy of Jay
Luvaas and Harold W. Nelson, eds., *The U.S. Army War College Guide to the Battles of
Chancellorsville and Fredericksburg* (Carlisle, Pa.: South Mountain Press, 1988). This
work, using maps and excerpts from wartime accounts, conveys through the words of
participants a sense of how the battle unfolded.

The important role of artillery at Fredericksburg is covered in two standard volumes. Jennings C. Wise, *The Long Arm of Lee, or The History of the Artillery of the
Army of Northern Virginia, with a Brief Account of Confederate Ordnance*, 2 vols.
(Lynchburg, Va.: J. P. Bell, 1915), argues that Lee's artillery was crucial to Confederate
victory. L. Van Loan Naisawald similarly lauds the Union artillery for its support of
assaults against Jackson's front on December 13 and for covering the army's subsequent retreat in *Grape and Canister: The Story of the Field Artillery in the Army of the
Potomac* (New York: Oxford University Press, 1960).

Several biographies belong on any shelf of books devoted to Fredericksburg. In *R.
E. Lee: A Biography*, 4 vols. (New York: Charles Scribner's Sons, 1934–35), Douglas
Southall Freeman takes his subject's view that the battle was an empty victory. For
Lee's two principal lieutenants, see Jeffry D. Wert, *General James Longstreet: The
Confederacy's Most Controversial Soldier, a Biography* (New York: Simon and Schuster,
1993), which highlights Longstreet's cheerful satisfaction at winning a defensive vic-
tory, and Frank E. Vandiver, *Mighty Stonewall* (New York: McGraw-Hill, 1957), a
sound and well-written telling of Jackson's difficult morning on the Confederate

right. For the Federals, William Marvel's *Burnside* (Chapel Hill: University of North Carolina Press, 1991) mounts a deeply researched challenge to the caricature of Burnside as a military fool. A concise statement of the negative view of the Federal commander is in Warren W. Hassler, Jr., *Commanders of the Army of the Potomac* (Baton Rouge: Louisiana State University Press, 1957). Walter H. Herbert's generally sympathetic *Fighting Joe Hooker* (Indianapolis: Bobbs-Merrill, 1944) also dismisses Burnside as a bumbler.

A few titles stand out among the many sets of recollections, letters, and diaries pertinent to Fredericksburg. Confederate artillerist Edward Porter Alexander wrote a pair of books unique in their combination of rigorous analysis and telling personal anecdotes: *Military Memoirs of a Confederate: A Critical Narrative* (New York: Charles Scribner's Sons, 1907) is the more scholarly; *Fighting for the Confederacy: The Personal Recollections of General Edward Porter Alexander*, ed. Gary W. Gallagher (Chapel Hill: University of North Carolina Press, 1989), the more lively and personal. James Longstreet's gruff pride in the way he fought the battle shines through his *From Manassas to Appomattox: A Memoir of the Civil War in America* (Philadelphia: J. B. Lippincott, 1896). *Inside Lincoln's Army: The Diary of Marsena Rudolph Patrick, Provost Marshal General, Army of the Potomac*, ed. David S. Sparks (New York: Thomas Yoseloff, 1964), includes valuable material on the occupations of Fredericksburg and problems of discipline in the Army of the Potomac, and William F. Smith's *Autobiography of Major General William F. Smith, 1861–1864*, ed. Herbert M. Schiller (Dayton, Ohio: Morningside, 1990), devotes considerable attention to the campaign from the perspective of a man who saw Hooker as a greater threat than Burnside to the army's success.

Four multivolume works merit the attention of anyone interested in Fredericksburg. Douglas Southall Freeman examined the battle within the framework of Confederate leadership in volume 2 of *Lee's Lieutenants: A Study in Command*, 3 vols. (New York: Charles Scribner's Sons, 1942–44); Kenneth P. Williams did the same from a Union perspective in volume 2 of *Lincoln Finds a General: A Military Study of the Civil War*, 5 vols. (New York: Macmillan, 1949–59). Williams followed a far less censorious script than most authors regarding Burnside. In *Glory Road*, volume 2 of his trilogy on the Army of the Potomac (Garden City, N.Y.: Doubleday, 1952), Bruce Catton applied his formidable stylistic gifts to the Federal prosecution of the campaign. Shelby Foote's *The Civil War: A Narrative, Fredericksburg to Meridian* (New York: Random House, 1963), the second of his three volumes on the conflict, matched Catton's writing ability and covered both the Union and Confederate efforts.

These titles, together with those cited in the various essays, should afford readers a good sampling of the printed materials on the Fredericksburg campaign.

CONTRIBUTORS

WILLIAM A. BLAIR received his doctoral training in American history at Pennsylvania State University. His publications include *A Politician Goes to War: The Civil War Letters of John White Geary*, and he presently is completing a book on the Virginia home front during the Civil War.

GARY W. GALLAGHER is John L. Nau III Professor of History at The University of Virginia. He is the author of *Stephen Dodson Ramseur: Lee's Gallant General*, editor of *Fighting for the Confederacy: The Personal Recollections of General Edward Porter Alexander*, and editor and coauthor of *The Third Day at Gettysburg and Beyond*.

A. WILSON GREENE holds degrees in American history from Florida State University and Louisiana State University. He is the author of *Whatever You Resolve to Be: Essays on Stonewall Jackson* and *J. Horace Lacy: The Most Dangerous Rebel of the County* and coauthor of *National Geographic Guide to the National Civil War Battlefields*.

WILLIAM MARVEL has published widely on the Civil War. He is the author of *Race of the Soil: The Ninth New Hampshire Regiment in the Civil War*, *Burnside*, and *Andersonville: The Last Depot* and coauthor of *The Battle of the Crater: "The Horrid Pit," June 25–August 6, 1864*. His current project is a study of the naval duel between the *Alabama* and the *Kearsarge*.

ALAN T. NOLAN, an Indianapolis lawyer, is a graduate of Indiana University and the Harvard Law School. He is chairman of the board of trustees of the Indiana Historical Society and a member of the Indianapolis Civil War Round Table. His books include *The Iron Brigade: A Military History* and *Lee Considered: General Robert E. Lee and Civil War History*.

GEORGE C. RABLE is professor of history at Anderson University and a specialist in nineteenth-century American history. Among his many publications are *But There Was No Peace: The Role of Violence in the Politics of Reconstruction*, *Civil Wars: Women and the Crisis of Southern Nationalism*, and *The Confederate Republic: A Revolution against Politics*.

CAROL REARDON is the military historian at Pennsylvania State University and author of *Soldiers and Scholars: The U.S. Army and the Uses of Military History, 1865–1920*. Her current projects include a book-length study of the image of "Pickett's Charge" in American history.

INDEX

189,500

$ 151,000   Kyle Hobin
             214-221-1922
             Julie # Caywood
             214 355 9018

64,000
38,000
       _____
                      2,100
6) 26,000   = 500⁰⁰
   12) 6 000
      17) 4600   4,000⁰⁰
                     _____
                     $ 1,200
                        200
                     _____
                     ~~2000~~
                     $ 400